Autumn was ten when her father abandoned her family. Since then she's been helping her mother raise her two little brothers and earning a living while keeping her grades up so she can go to college. Her faith in God gives Autumn strength, but who will give her the money she needs when she's offered the opportunity of a lifetime?

From the outside, **Jordan**'s life looks perfect. He hangs out with the "rich white kids," rows on the crew team, built his own darkroom, and applied early to an East Coast college. But Jordan's father died last year, leaving Jordan reeling with emotions that make his life feel anything but perfect and his future seem less than certain.

A third-generation Berkeley High student, **Keith** is bright and popular, a talented football player who hopes to play college ball and one day go pro. But Keith has a reading problem that threatens his NFL dream. And the Berkeley police have a problem with Keith that threatens his very freedom.

"Revealing and realistic . . . The poetry is fist-in-the-face powerful; it truly reveals the students' lives. This is the reason to read *Class Dismissed*." —*USA Today*

"An altogether engrossing and often humbling account of the stark realities of public education." —*Publishers Weekly* (starred review)

"From any angle Berkeley High is a fascinating place. . . . Maran [shows] that Berkeley High is a little society as complicatedly and irremediably confused about its achievements and problems as America." —*San Francisco Chronicle Book Review*

"A lively, dramatic, and provocative story . . . a passionate and intelligent account." —*Kirkus Reviews*

"Compelling. Maran effectively captures the bureaucratic ineptitude of a large public high school on the verge of collapse." —*Teacher Magazine*

"The supporting cast of this riveting story includes teachers, students, parents, and community members, but the real star is the school itself. Everyone who cares about young people should read this revealing book." —*Library Journal*

"Maran illustrates some of today's most serious societal problems through the three teenagers she shadows. Maran examines academic tracking, school safety in the wake of Columbine, teen sex, suicide, school system politics, decaying campuses, and the everyday trials of being a teenager—and a teacher—in today's high school." —Amazon.com

"Maran guides us through [the teenagers'] lives, to class, football games, true love, jail, and emotional breakdowns. She does it so easily that the reader doesn't notice she is also showing us the machinations behind their lives, from teachers' meetings to national trends." —*Biloxi Sun Herald*

"A rich tale . . . compelling because everyone's story is complicated and full of life's odd twists . . . inspiring." —*San Jose Mercury-News Book Review* (cover review)

ALSO BY MEREDITH MARAN

What It's Like to Live Now

Notes from an Incomplete Revolution:
Real Life Since Feminism

Ben & Jerry's Double-Dip

CLASS DISMISSED

A YEAR IN THE LIFE OF AN AMERICAN HIGH SCHOOL,

A GLIMPSE INTO THE HEART OF A NATION

MEREDITH MARAN

ST. MARTIN'S GRIFFIN

NEW YORK

www.stmartins.com

All photos except as noted © Meredith Maran

Berkeley High map © Jesse Drew Graham (Meredith's son)

Library of Congress Cataloging-in-Publication Data

Maran, Meredith.
    Class dismissed : a year in the life of an American high school, a glimpse into the heart of a nation / Meredith Maran.
      p. cm.
    ISBN 0-312-26568-9 (hc)
    ISBN 0-312-28309-1 (pbk)
    1. Berkeley High School (Berkeley, Calif.)   I. Title: a year in the life of an American high school.   II. Title.

LD7501.B5 M27 2000
373.794'67—dc21

00-040517

10 9 8 7 6 5 4 3

Contents

BERKELEY HIGH

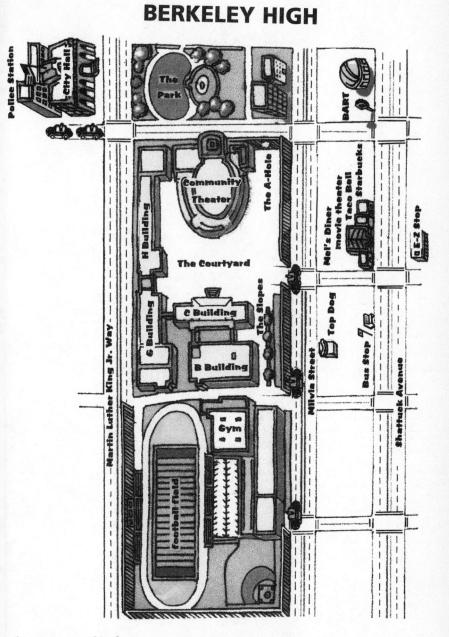

Map by Jesse Drew Graham, Berkeley High Class of '98

Introduction

All I Really Needed to Know I Learned in High School

We're all worried about our teenagers these days. And we have reason to worry—yes, even more than our parents did. They're shooting at each other, at their teachers, at us. They're doing scary drugs, having scary sex. They're scarring their bodies with piercings and tattoos. They wear pants that sag to their crotches, tank tops that cling to their cleavage, headphones everywhere they go. They cut class, they disrupt class, they sleep through class. They aren't learning; at least, not what we think they should learn in the ways we think they should learn it. Worst of all, they won't tell us what they're doing. And when we find out, they won't tell us *why*.

Even before Littleton we knew: the stakes are terrifyingly high. From Compton to Columbine, death lurks in every sexual encounter, on every crack dealer's corner, on every freeway, and now, it seems, in every classroom. On lush suburban campuses and in hardscrabble ghetto hallways, learning is undermined by the ominous pulse of anger, the palpable pulse of fear. Who among us, students and teachers eye each other and wonder, might be the next to blow? Talk of academic standards and accountability, of education, even, seems pie-in-the-sky, when our high schools and our teenagers seem so volatile, so unfathomable, so desperately in need of—what? We don't know.

High school is a slow-motion milestone moment: we enter as children, leave as adults. When I went to high school, my parents didn't worry about school shootings or HIV—but I gave them plenty to worry about nonetheless. They'd found a diaphragm in my underwear drawer and a hash pipe in my purse. I think I broke the world's record for lowest-ever SAT math scores. I showed absolutely no interest in high school, let alone college; the only class I attended regularly was my weekly folk guitar lesson. Three decades later, I realize that although I was an awful student, although I hated being there, the four years I spent in high school made me the person I am. I didn't learn to calculate logarithms or speak Latin; I failed to memorize Shakespeare's sonnets or the periodic table of the elements. Still, I realize now, in high school I learned all I ever needed to know.

I learned how the world works: what happens when you accept things as they are, and what happens when you try to change them. I learned what I was good at, and what I wasn't, and which of those things mattered to me. I learned about friendships: why I need them; how to keep them. I learned about love, trying to find a place to make it; trying to find a place to get birth control; trying to ignore the adults who reduced my four-year relationship to a case of "raging teenage hormones."

I learned about racism. My newly built, extravagantly equipped, admission-by-exam-only public school was 97 percent white; the crumbling, ancient neighborhood school a block away was nearly all black, and I didn't buy the explanation I was given for the discrepancy—that "we" deserved more because we'd taken a test to get in; that "we" would "do more with our education" than "they" would.

I learned how to write, because my friends and I published an underground newspaper and its pages needed to be filled. I learned *why* to write, because when our classmates bought our paper for a nickel (clandestinely, in the bathrooms; it was banned on school property) they *did* things inspired by what we wrote: honored our striking teachers' picket line, smoked banana peels, refused to fight in Vietnam. I learned who the good guys were, and the bad guys—in our school, in society, in the world—and I daresay, I got it right.

Although I swore I'd never be as "paranoid" as my parents were, I cannot deny that my sons' high school years, just ended, were the most worrisome of my life. I said *my* life, mind you, not theirs. For although they had their share of teenage troubles—they got some crummy grades, got fired from some crummy jobs, lost friends to drive-bys and car accidents, had problems with their parents, got ditched at the Prom, got arrested, got depressed—my sons had a pretty great time in high school. A pretty *educational* time.

For better or for worse, I wanted my sons to have the same kind of high school education I had. And they did, only more so. Jesse and Peter were six and seven when I decided that, even though we lived in Oakland, somehow they were going to go to Berkeley High. I'd recently spent three months on assignment for the Sunday magazine of the *San Francisco Chronicle/Examiner*, writing about four Berkeley High seniors of the Class of 1986: a rich white water polo star, a biracial teen mom, an out white lesbian who'd grown up on communes, and an African-American girl who worked full-time at Carl's Junior's. I couldn't believe that such different kids all went to one high school. I couldn't believe that they all went to one high school and none of them knew each other. I couldn't believe how *alive* the school was, with its African-American Studies and Women's Studies Departments, its world-renowned jazz band, the twenty-some National Merit scholars it cranked out each year; its free, student-staffed child-care center; its long list of well-attended advanced placement classes; its extraordinarily energetic, extraordinarily socially aware teachers.

Unlike my high school, Berkeley High wasn't all-white (although it was, and is, somewhat segregated socially and academically). Unlike my school, Berkeley High wasn't open to the academic elite only (although there *is* an exclusive, elite school operating within its walls). At Berkeley High my kids and their friends didn't get sent home, as I did, for wearing their skirts too short or their pants too big. They didn't have to sneak into the bathroom to get the *real* news from a mimeographed underground newspaper; the award-winning, school-sanctioned *Berkeley High Jacket* gave them "the 411" on the hottest controversies at school, in the nation, in the world—and detailed reports on Berkeley High's sixty sports teams.

As I did, my sons cut classes and slept through classes and loved and excelled in a few classes in high school, and acquired a small store of book knowledge, and got into some trouble, and caused their parents great anxiety. They also acquired deep, intimate knowledge of the most critical issues facing our nation and our world, thanks to Berkeley High—which the *New York Times* labeled "the most integrated high school in America." Engaging in fiery classroom discussions, partying on Friday nights and playing on basketball teams with Berkeley's richest kids and its poorest—kids bound for Yale and kids bound for jail—my sons experienced firsthand the vast disparities in the economic, emotional, and academic resources allocated to different people and different groups of people in America. Questions of inequity and opportunity are very real to them as a result. As I did, my sons left high school with a feeble grasp of history, math, and how to diagram a sentence, and a profound understanding of themselves and of society. Their passion for justice, their abhorrence of injustice, is what guides their lives and their continued learning to this day. For their sakes and our country's, I hope this is what will guide them always.

From the day I first entered its funky halls as a journalist in 1986, I was fascinated by Berkeley High. My fascination deepened through my years as a parent and parent volunteer. Berkeley High seemed to me both a microcosm of, and a model for, America. So, thirteen years after I first wrote about the school and two years after my younger son left it, I went back to have another, deeper look.

In July of 1999 I conceived the idea of spending the next year at Berkeley High, following a diverse group of seniors from their first day of school through graduation: getting to know their friends, families, and teachers, shadowing them at their jobs, at church, on the football field as well. The idea seemed thrilling but impossible. It was the middle of summer, five weeks before the first day of school. How would I get the necessary approvals in time from the district, the school administration, the teachers? How would I find the right students? The teachers—my path into the story, to the students—would be away on vacation. That's why teachers' low salaries aren't *really* low, I'd always heard: they don't work during the summer. And even if I managed to find a few teachers in town, what were the odds that they'd agree to let me sit in their classrooms all year, observing, analyzing, possibly criticizing their life's work?

Realization number one: teachers—good teachers—*do* work during the summer. And not just those who teach summer school, as many do, to try and make ends meet. As I started calling teachers I'd known during my sons' Berkeley High years, I began to get a truer picture of their lives. They weren't exactly lolling around on sun-kissed beaches. They were preparing lesson plans. Bailing students out of Juvenile Hall. Meeting with their teaching partners. Attending union negotiation sessions. Hanging out with students who were in emotional, financial, or family crises—or hanging out with students just for fun. Cleaning out their closets, painting their bathrooms, getting their cars tuned up because they wouldn't have time to do that again until July.

Realization number two: teachers—good teachers—want the world to know what happens in their classrooms. Every single teacher I spoke with invited me to sit in as often as I liked, asked provocative questions about the kinds of students I was looking for, critiqued my criteria, then gave me names of several students along with insightful, loving profiles of each.

During the summer of 1999 I met with about twenty Berkeley High seniors. By August I'd honed the list to eight whom I thought would provide a representative picture of Berkeley High, of the new world order that Berkeley High foretells. It was a one-from-column-A, two-from-column-B mix of ethnicities, genders, sexual orientations, academic levels, life circumstances, and personalities. I'd also recruited a volunteer research assistant—Sara Momii Roberts, a junior high girlfriend of my son's and 1996 Berkeley High graduate, now an American Studies major at UC Berkeley—to help with what I was starting to realize was an exceedingly ambitious project.

The next step was to ask Berkeley High's principal, Theresa Saunders, and the Berkeley Unified School District—then locked in charged contract negotiations with the Berkeley Federation of Teachers—to grant me unrestricted access to the school. I was asking a lot and I knew it. A few years earlier, a PBS crew had spent a school year filming a documentary about Berkeley High's racial tensions and divisions. When *School Colors* aired in 1994, many in the school community felt misrepresented and exploited, burned and betrayed—feelings that remain inflamed to this day.

Much to my surprise, the district said yes. And the principal said yes, adding in her E-mail, "I will gladly work with you regarding issues at BHS. . . . I am hopeful that this information will be useful to us as we plan for years to come." The project was on!

Two months in, I realized that if I was going to get to know the students, the teachers, and the school as deeply as I wanted to (and still allow for a few hours' sleep each night), eight students was five too many. By then one of the eight had dropped out of school and disappeared. I'd already grown attached to the remaining seven. It felt like Sophie's Choice to choose three; it was difficult letting go of the illusory "representative sample." But as I began focusing on Autumn, Jordan, and Keith, the benefits of the trade-off became clear. I could go to more of their classes, hang out with them more on weekends, and interview them and their teachers, friends, and families more often to check my recollections and perceptions against theirs.

This, then, is what I did. From September 1, 1999, through June 15, 2000, I followed Autumn, Jordan, and Keith through their classes and their lives. I saw them bored to tears in some classes, challenged beyond their limits in others, fully engaged and achieving to the peak of their abilities in a few. I watched Autumn audition for an amateur production of *The Wiz*. I watched Keith watch himself make a touchdown on TV. I watched Jordan cook dinner for himself and his "baby-sitter" when his mom was out of town. Committed to this project, to helping bring forth a fair portrayal of teenagers' lives, these young people and their families made huge sacrifices of privacy and time. They invited me into their kitchens, their court hearings, their church services, their most tender and most difficult family moments.

Berkeley High School itself is more than a backdrop in this book. It's a character, too—an eccentric, complex, formidable one, also demanding great amounts of attention and examination. So, after school I followed the teachers to staff meetings and protest rallies; the parents to PTSA meetings and community forums; the students to poetry slams and walkouts. With very few exceptions, I and my frantically scribbling pen and fast-filling spiral notebooks were welcomed without restriction. The staff, the students, and the members of the Berkeley High community gave me everything I asked for, and more.

Whether I had followed three students or three thousand, it would have been impossible for me to experience, let alone report on, the 3,200 students, 185 teachers, and hundreds of programs, activities, clubs, and teams of Berkeley High. I didn't see everything, and what I did see I reported through the filter of my own experiences, prejudices, and intentions. I recommend that whether you live in the Bay Area or elsewhere, whether you've got children enrolled in your local high school or not, you visit the school and gather your own impressions. There's more to learn there about your children, your community, and your country than you might suspect.

A few words of clarification: every character and event in this book is real. In some cases, two or more discussions or events have been conflated into one. Some poems and other writings have been excerpted; a few names and descriptions have been changed. Events described from the points of view of Autumn, Jordan, Keith, and others are repeated as they were told to me. I personally witnessed and recorded most of what I have reported in these pages; when anecdotes were recounted to me, I did my best to verify them with the person or people involved.

So this is the story, yes, of three teenagers and their school, during a year that proved to be Berkeley High's most tumultuous ever. But my hope is that you take from this story, and make from this story, a bigger one. My hope is that in coming to know Autumn, Jordan, and Keith you also come to better understand your own beliefs, ideals, and decisions—as I did in the course of spending their senior year of high school with them.

I hope that reading this book will cause you to consider the impact of what you think and say and do—not only on the children in your life today, but on our country and our world tomorrow. Where our children are concerned, we get only as good as we give. As a nation we have been giving our young far less than our best, with entirely predictable results. Giving more, giving better to our public schools is an excellent place to start.

Meredith Maran
Oakland, California
June 2000

Prologue—April 2000
FIRE!

"All students must leave the campus! Evacuate the campus *now!*" The burly school safety officer yells into the bullhorn. "Move it, young people! Everyone off campus! *Go!*"

For the second time in twenty-four hours, every fire truck in Berkeley and a dozen of its police cars scream through the streets, converging on the town's only high school. Firemen frantically uncoil hoses, gallop into classrooms lugging axes and power saws. Police officers block Milvia Street with their cars, diverting morning rush-hour traffic; others rope off the B building, the C building, the teachers' parking lot, Memorial Grove, with flapping lengths of yellow tape. "Police Lines. Do Not Cross."

For the second time in twenty-four hours, smoke billows from the B building, finishing off the damage that yesterday's fire inflicted on this, the nerve center of the school. It's all gone now: the administrative, counseling, and security offices; the health center with its counseling rooms, HIV testing kits, and boxes of free condoms; the classrooms specially equipped for English language learners and wheelchair-bound students; the library with its hard-won, brand-new banks of G3 computers. They're all submerged, now, in water and debris.

For the second time in twenty-four hours, Berkeley High's thirty-two hundred students, chased from their classrooms by grim-faced safety officers with walkie-talkies in one hand and cell phones in the other, mill around the school's central courtyard in the tentative morning sunshine. Some are laughing, some are crying, many are doing first one, then the other. This is Berkeley High's third arson fire in two weeks, its tenth this school year. Last year there were eighteen. Recently the school conducted an emergency evacuation drill, but no Berkeley High student needs practice anymore. They hear the alarms, smell the smoke, grab their backpacks, get out—*quick*.

But even to these crisis veterans, this fire feels different. Serious. "This isn't some kid pulling a prank, a trash can fire like the others," a Berkeley Fire Department official tells a reporter from the *Jacket,* Berkeley High's school paper. "This is a person who is trying to burn down the school."

"Do not return to school today or tomorrow! Do not return to school until after Spring Break!" The safety officer's amplified voice booms across the courtyard, barely audible above the wail of sirens, the rhythmic, regurgitating groan of fire trucks pumping water into the principal's office, the parent-staffed information booth, the records center, where every student's transcript—much in demand now, at the height of college admissions season—is stored. Or was.

"I said *go!* Move it, people!"

Teachers cluster on the steps of the C building, watching as the principal and two vice principals, the assistant superintendent of schools, and the district security supervisor wade through the crowd of agitated students, sweeping them out the school gates and onto an eerily empty Milvia Street. "Can we go inside to get our stuff?" an English teacher asks the security supervisor. "We can't get home without our keys."

The supervisor frowns, barks a few words into his walkie-talkie. He turns back to the teachers, his face impassive behind black wraparound sunglasses. "I'll take you in, one at a time, at your own risk. Who's first?"

It's 9:10 a.m. on April 13, 2000—seven days before the one-year anniversary of the Columbine High School shooting. In Littleton and across the country, commemorations are being planned. All this week the media have been replaying the awful videotapes, retelling the grisly story, rehashing the unanswerable questions. Last year, Berkeley High sent a delegation of students to Littleton for the memorial services. "I've always thought this nation needs to pay more attention to our children," one of those students wrote in the *Jacket* upon her return. "After witnessing the outpouring of care and grief in Littleton and across the nation, I am optimistic. I believe that we can take a new path with education and the well-being of our children." That issue of the *Jacket*, dated April 30, 1999, bore the headline, "Arson Plagues BHS."

Spring Break was supposed to start on Monday. Yesterday's fire broke out just after lunch, so afternoon classes were cancelled; today's fire ended the school day before it had quite begun. Now school will be closed tomorrow, too. Some kids appear jubilant about their extended vacation, giving each other high fives, shouting "Spring Break starts *now!*" Others are sober. Scared. "What if whoever it is plants a bomb next time?" one bell-bottomed, bare-bellied girl asks another. The two of them wrap their arms around each other's narrow waists, bob along in the tide of students rolling across the courtyard and out the Milvia gate. "Some dude be *trippin',*" a boy mutters, his eyes agape as he stares at the smoldering B building. "Some dude be *crazy.*"

"Women, children, and doughnuts out first!" The teachers on the steps laugh as a long-time history teacher, known for the trays of pastries he always keeps in his classroom, emerges from the sealed-off C building bearing one of those trays above his head. The teachers, many of them health food devotees, encircle the sweets like lions at the kill, devouring the fried dough as if it offered salvation itself.

"Staff meeting in the community theater—now," Principal Saunders announces into a bullhorn. The teachers follow her across the courtyard and into the theater. Although the hundred and fifty of them fill just the first few rows of the 3,000-person auditorium, Saunders takes the stage, her dark skin gleaming in the footlights.

"There was no bomb," Saunders begins. "That's a good thing."

"Were they looking for a bomb?" one teacher whispers to another.

"But the smoke from the B building is quite pervasive in the C building," Saunders continues. "If you need to go in there to get your things, please know you do so at your own risk."

Theresa Saunders—Berkeley High's fourth principal in ten years—is characteristically composed, delivering distressing information crisply and efficiently, as she has had to do so many times in her less than two years on the job. "The police and fire departments are conducting an investigation. They've contacted the Alameda County Crisis Unit. If the investigation is finished by the end of the day on Friday, we'll start clean-up on Monday. If not . . ."

For the first time during these adrenaline-drenched days, the teachers are invited to consider how they might survive the last eight weeks of the school year—the culmination of the all-important college admissions process, two Proms (Junior and Senior), six graduations (Black Graduation, Chicano/Latino Graduation, Asian/Pacific Islander Graduation, one for each of Berkeley High's two schools-within-a-school, and one for all seven hundred graduating seniors)—without the essential support services that emanated, until yesterday, from the B building.

"We cannot continue like this," Saunders says, her normally steady voice rising. "We can't live like this! Officer Rosie Brown *ran for his life* this morning. He's a trained police officer. He's been stationed at Berkeley High for many years. If Rosie is running for his life on our campus, my God"—the unflappable Saunders looks wild-eyed at the teachers— "what we going to do?"

A gaggle of TV and newspaper reporters, ejected from the staff-only meeting in the theater, have cornered Berkeley's fire chief and assistant school superintendent beneath the canopy of one of Berkeley High's few trees. With news helicopters buzzing overhead, filming from above as firemen cut gaping holes through the B building roof, the impromptu press conference begins.

"What are you going to do to keep this from getting worse?" a TV reporter asks.

"We're putting in cell phones, walkie-talkies, trying to improve the communications system," the assistant superintendent answers. "And we're meeting with the City today—the fire department, police department, the principal, myself—to discuss other measures."

"Do you think the arsonist could be a disgruntled teacher?" a local newspaper writer asks. With good reason: that same reporter was here two weeks ago, covering the boisterous rally the teachers held to protest their low pay and poor working conditions. It's no secret that after Spring Break, the teachers are scheduled to begin a slow-down, refusing to work more than the six-and-a-half hours per day for which they are paid starting salaries of $29,000.

"Or an angry student?" another reporter asks. Berkeley High students have had plenty of media coverage this year, too. They've been walking out of classes to demand better pay for their teachers, more funding for programs aimed at closing the yawning achievement gap between white students and students of color, an end to the "paddy wagon sweeps" of downtown Berkeley during which tardy students—and several young people who were neither tardy nor Berkeley High students—were loaded into police vans and hauled back to the school.

"No, no, no," the school official shakes her head.

Suddenly the press conference is interrupted by a burst of activity around the theater. Firemen are summoned from the B building; police and school safety officers run to the scene. A teacher, it turns out, has gone to the women's bathroom, smelled smoke, discovered a freshly lit fire burning in a trash can there.

"To go into the bathroom after we've just had this big meeting about what our next steps are," that teacher says on the five o'clock news that night, "and to smell smoke *again* in a completely different building is unnerving. It makes me not want to be here."

"The students don't feel safe here," a history teacher says into the camera. "And I think they have good reason not to feel safe."

"There was a fire just last week in another building," a mother in dreadlocks adds, the ravaged B building, flooded school grounds, and a snake pit of fire hoses visible behind her. "So do I keep my kids here and wait for someone to get hurt, knowing it could be one of my kids? Or do I find some alternative? And what is the alternative?"

What is the alternative, indeed?

August 1999: Same Old Same Old

JORDAN ETRA

"Yo! Jordan! What's up!" As he's making his way across the pile of dirt and rubble that used to be the teachers' parking lot, Jordan stops to wait for his friend Ari. The two boys hug awkwardly, pat each other on the back a few times, then pull apart.

"Same old same old," Jordan replies, looking around at the campus. In the gauzy August morning light Berkeley High looks even worse than it did the last time he saw it in June. Classes start next week, but the promised renovation seems to be stuck in the demolition phase. Abandoned bulldozers and overflowing dumpsters are parked where the foreign-language portables used to be. The B building, encased in construction plastic, looks as if it's wearing a giant condom. From here Jordan can see the tall red letters that were stenciled onto the C, G, and H buildings last year, when kids set so many fires that the fire department insisted the school make its buildings easier to identify.

"Same old funky B-High," Ari sighs, and he and Jordan set off together, negotiating the obstacle course of sagging cyclone fences that bifurcate the campus. Jordan nods, but secretly he's glad to be back. Even with all its problems, Berkeley High is still a whole lot better than the other schools he's gone to—not to mention the schools he *could* have gone to. Drinking his smoothie this morning, he watched the TV

6

news coverage of the Littleton students going back to class for the first time since the massacre last April. It reminded him of the group counseling sessions that were held at Berkeley High the day after Littleton happened: girls crying, boys acting macho, therapists spouting New Age jargon—and everyone wondering how the parents could have missed the signs. That was no mystery to Jordan. He'd found out the hard way that as long as a kid's doing okay in school, adults will think the kid has no problems.

"Hey, how was your summer, dude?" Ari asks as they walk. Anyone who knows Jordan—and a lot of people do—knows he'd been dreading the summer, the first anniversary of his father's death.

"Tough," Jordan answers. "On Father's Day I went camping by myself in Yosemite. Weird, huh? My dad falls off a cliff and dies, and a year later I decide to spend my first Father's Day without him on a mountain. It seemed like a good idea at the time, but I ended up in the hospital with mono. Plus, I missed my summer internship at Skidmore."

"Bummer."

"*Major* bummer." Jordan kicks at a Doritos wrapper that's stuck itself to his shoe. "When I got better, I went to see my dad's family in New Jersey," he goes on. "They haven't dealt with their emotions at all. So I couldn't even talk to them about my dad. They still don't know if he jumped or got pushed or what. Not that it matters, really." Jordan shrugs. "My mom came out in August. We took the East Coast college tour. Eight schools in seven days. The colleges were cool. I fell in *love* with Bard. But a week on the road with my mom—that was hard on both of us. She's so damn intense."

"I feel you, dude," Ari says. "My parents always look a whole lot better to me from a few thousand miles away."

Jordan and Ari fall into the surging stream of students all headed for the same destination: the Berkeley Community Theater. Bordering the north end of the seventeen-acre Berkeley High campus, embellished with carvings of ancient Greek philosophers, the round white stucco building doubles as the school's auditorium and the town's only concert hall.

By night the theater throngs with Ani de Franco fans, Thich Nhat

Hanh devotees, supporters of benefits for Earth First, affirmative action, Mumia Abu-Jamal. By day it plays a different role. Each weekday its wide brick steps, overlooking the central courtyard of the only public high school in America's most famously politically correct town, become a citadel of segregation. Before school, after school, and at lunchtime the steps are home to several of the myriad cliques into which Berkeley High students divide themselves—during the hours, that is, when those divisions are not imposed by the school itself.

But just for today, all seven hundred seniors of the Class of 00 will spend a few hours together at the theater, riding the merry-go-round of Berkeley High bureaucracy. Those who are lucky and persistent enough will catch the brass ring: the school ID cards and class schedules they need to register for next semester. Some of the others will be back tomorrow to try again. Many more will show up on the first day of school without proof of enrollment or any clue as to where they're supposed to be. A few won't be back at all.

"Shit," Jordan groans when he sees the line, ten students thick, that snakes around the theater. "Nine o'clock in the morning, man. I thought we'd beat the mob."

"At this place?" Ari answers. "Never." Before they transferred to Berkeley High, Jordan, Ari, and most of the kids in their crowd were classmates at Head Royce or one of the other small, exclusive private schools in the Berkeley-Oakland area. Years later, they still make many of these shorthand comparisons.

"Hey Jordan! Ari!" Two girls, both wearing tank tops, cut-offs, and platform flip-flops, their long hair coiled into matching buns held in place with chopsticks, run up and give each boy a hug. "Can we cut?" one of the girls asks teasingly. Jordan glances over his shoulder, catches the scowl of the boy behind him, and shrugs. "Guess not." "Okay then. Later," the girls trill, and bounce off to join the end of the line.

By ten o'clock Jordan and Ari are only a few yards closer to the theater. The morning fog has burned off; the heat of the day is rising. Jordan's shirt is stuck to his back. He's glad he buzzed most of his hair off yesterday.

"Hey! Y'all think we got nothin' better to do wit' our time than *this?*" a black girl in front of them starts yelling. "I ain't gon' wait on this goddamn line all day!" Her friends laugh, egging her on. "Who be runnin' this shit 'round here anyways?" she shouts.

The girl stomps off the line and up to the parent volunteer who's sitting behind a table handing out the red-and-gold student organizers that the Parent-Teacher-Student-Association (PTSA) donates to all students every September. The woman, one of the many white moms who are volunteering here today, recoils as the girl approaches.

"Y'all need to *go* to school to learn how to *run* this school," the girl says loudly. The mom's eyes dart around wildly. "You people can't do nothin' right!"

Why can't white people ever stand up for themselves? Jordan thinks, watching. He hates feeling embarrassed by white people acting weak. And it happens all the time at Berkeley High.

"That's enough, young lady." A stocky, middle-aged African-American man grabs the girl by the arm.

"Ooh! Check it OUT! Wiggins got a toupee!" her friends hoot at the school's detested security supervisor, who was bald last time they saw him in June. "Wiggins got a Gheri Curl!"

"You're out of here! Now!" Barry Wiggan barks, and escorts the girl away.

Jordan glances at Ari, who rolls his eyes in disgust—at Wiggins (as the kids all call him), or at the black girl? Jordan wonders. With his white friends, Jordan often feels like Mister P.C., pointing out their privileges and prejudices. Last year he and one of his closest friends stopped speaking because they couldn't stop arguing about whose fault it is that African-American and Latino kids don't do well at Berkeley High; and why it is that rich white "hills" parents like hers—Harvard grads, Rhodes scholars, friends of the Clintons—have the time and power to rule the school in their own self-interest and nobody else's. Jordan wonders sometimes whether he feels different from kids like her because his mom is an ex-hippie, now a staunch liberal; or because his dad was Jewish and he taught Jordan to be conscious of discrimination, or because Jordan and his mom live in a middle-class North Oakland neighborhood, not the Berkeley hills. *Whatever the reason,* he thinks, *I'm not going to have that argument now. Not before school even starts.*

An hour later Jordan reaches the top of the steps. A student he doesn't recognize hands him his ID card and asks him for a dollar. "Isn't that illegal?" Jordan asks. "To make us pay for our ID cards? And what about the kids who don't have a dollar?" Without waiting for an answer he nods good-bye to Ari, hands over the money, and goes inside to have his picture taken. Laminated photo in hand, he finds the "A–E" table and shows it to the mother of a kid he knows from Head Royce. She greets him by name and hands him his schedule.

"Thanks, Jean," Jordan says politely. He steps aside, glances at the printout in his hand, and curses silently. Unlike most of his classmates, he turned in his schedule request form on time last June. He even by-passed the envelope taped to his counselor's door and waited on line all through lunch to hand it to her in person instead. Now Jordan sees that of the seven classes he needs, he's only been assigned to two—one of them during the wrong period. So he trudges over to the B building, stepping over the red-and-gold-lettered "Welcome Back Seniors!" signs he'd seen taped to the buildings earlier today. Jordan realizes that the parent volunteers must have put them up to cover the spray-painted graffiti messages visible beneath them, now that they've been thrown on the ground. "00 Rules. Fuck 01."

Jordan pushes through the plastic-covered doors to the B building and joins the long line that's spilling out of the counseling department. The scribbled names taped to the wall beside each office are unfamiliar to him. *They fired all the counselors—again,* he realizes. Two hours later Jordan meets his new counselor, Guillermo—a cool guy, Jordan quickly decides. Not that it matters. With Berkeley High's six counselors serving more than five hundred students apiece, Jordan knows that this fifteen-minute meeting is likely to be the longest one he and Guillermo will ever have.

Four hours after arriving, Jordan leaves Berkeley High with the two items he came for: the ID card all students are required to present on demand (the black kids, Jordan often reminds his friends, get carded and suspended regularly, while the white kids are never even asked to show their IDs) and the same schedule he'd requested last June.

Jordan is taking two advanced placement classes this semester: Statistics and Biology. The truth is, he couldn't care less about either subject and wouldn't bother making the extra effort that the college-level classes demand, except that he sees them as "Bard insurance": extra points on his transcript to make him more appealing to college admissions officers.

The worst part about AP classes is that most of the people in them are Ivy League–bound Hills kids—*hella* boring. Diversity is the main reason Jordan transferred to Berkeley High, but it's not easy to come by. Because of tracking, a truly mixed group is even rarer in a classroom than it is at lunchtime. That's why as soon as Jordan signed up for Berkeley High, he signed up for the racially, economically, and academically diverse school-within-a-school called CAS—Communication Arts and Sciences.

"Since money influences people's thinking more than anything," Jordan says, "in order to get an objective view of life you need to hear the perspectives of people who don't have much of it." The two CAS classes he takes every day are full of all kinds of kids from all kinds of backgrounds, so the often-heated discussions are always thought provoking, never boring. Plus, CAS gives him lots of "warm and fuzzies," as his mom says, like the overnight retreats that always manage to bond the group, despite all the differences between its members. "There isn't enough of that kind of bonding in the adult world," Jordan says—his mom's friends are cool, but they're almost all white—and he's determined to take advantage of it while he can.

Last year CAS provided Jordan with an unexpected benefit. After his dad died, CAS founder and director Rick Ayers became a second father to him, calling Jordan at home at night to make sure he was okay, hanging out with him on the weekends when Jordan needed someone to talk to. Mr. Ayers doesn't teach seniors, so Jordan won't see him every day this year. But as long as Jordan's part of the CAS family, he knows that Mr. Ayers and the other CAS teachers will be there for him.

Looking over his schedule now, Jordan feels that he's struck a good balance: CAS in the morning, AP in the afternoon. Two AP classes is enough, he tells himself. Jordan's not like his Head Royce friends, living their whole lives to get into Harvard. Bard will be just fine. Better than fine. Bard will be *tight*.

On his way back to the 1990 Blazer his mom bought him for six thousand dollars, Jordan passes a bunch of guys in front of Taco Bell on Shattuck. "What's up, Darnell," Jordan calls to a guy he knows from CAS.

" 'S'up, Jordan."

"Got your schedule?" Jordan asks.

Darnell shrugs. "That line's too long. And life's too short."

The two boys' eyes meet briefly. "Awwight, man. See you next week," Darnell says, and turns back to his friends.

"Next week," Jordan repeats. He can't believe the summer's almost over. Can't believe he's a senior already. *A year ago this week I was at Dad's funeral,* he thinks. *Next year at this time I'll be in college.*

Jordan decides to treat himself to a frappacino before he heads home. He walks past Taco Bell and into the cool, dim light of the Starbucks next door.

MS. CRAWFORD

As usual, in June Amy Crawford promised herself a summer vacation. And as usual, she reflects as she finishes up her lesson plans a week before school begins, she hasn't really had one.

Amy hasn't spent a summer not working since she started teaching five years ago, right out of Mills College. She reads only books she assigns to her classes, makes and takes parent phone calls on weekends, hires her students to pull ivy from her garden, feeds them peanut-butter-on-whole-wheat sandwiches at her kitchen table. Her husband comes home from his graphics job at six every night ready to kick back and relax. Amy comes home at five with a stack of papers to grade. Philosophically, she resents the unremitting unpaid labor her job demands, but secretly she pities her husband his office job, his days spent with adults and computers, deprived of the joy that she knows on the best of days, watching teenagers grow.

It's not like I didn't have fun this summer, she tells herself, packing file folders into her well-worn orange backpack. One of the delights of teaching in CAS, the two-year-old alternative program within Berkeley High, is that she and her team-teaching partner, Dana Richards, truly delight in each other—although not in the way their students suspect. (At last year's CAS retreat, in answer to the kids' giggling Truth or Dare question, Dana held up his hands in mock surrender and announced with characteristic sarcasm, "Okay, you guys. It's true. I've just notified my wife that Ms. Crawford is actually the mother of our two children.")

It's damn lucky we do get along so well, Amy thinks, because she and Dana have once again spent not only every day of the school year together but also most of the summer, picnicking at Lake Anza, going to the movies, hanging out in the backyard of Amy and her husband's new house in Oakland, trying to make sure that next year goes a whole lot better than last year did.

There are good years and hard years in a teacher's life; classes in which, magically, almost nothing goes wrong and classes in which, mysteriously, almost everything does. Last year's CAS class was Amy's hardest ever. The first crop of CAS kids, recruited as sophomores in 1997— Amy's first year at Berkeley High—became, as juniors, not only academically apathetic but also stubbornly cynical. "The majority of the kids were just not interested in an academic challenge," she says. "It was always, 'What's the least amount of work I can do to get an A?' The prevailing attitude was that the world is harsh, society sucks, there's nothing you can do about it. Well, we *know* society sucks. That's why CAS exists—to change that."

About to begin its third year and graduate its first class of seniors, CAS is a work in progress, its paradoxes as glaringly evident as its potential. "You set up a small school in a big school, you recruit kids who want intimacy, diversity; a respite from the impersonal, indifferent, big-school environment. And what do you get? Students who are alienated from the mainstream, wanting lots of personal attention, discontent with the status quo. There's an up side to a group like that, but there's also a down side."

Founded by English teacher Rick Ayers, an unapologetic radical (whose brother and sister-in-law are the infamous Weathermen fugitives turned inner-city educators Bill Ayers and Bernadine Dohrn), CAS is admired by some Berkeley High teachers, denounced by others. "The reason public schools were set up," Ayers wrote in defense of his beloved program in the pages of the *East Bay Express,* "was not to re-create social inequities, but to actually interrupt them and work on the problem."

If the CAS program is to survive the criticism of those who threaten its existence; if Amy and Dana are to maintain the enthusiasm and creativity their jobs require; if the sixty seniors of the CAS Class of 2000 are to emerge into the world ready, willing, and able to change it for the better, Amy and Dana can't let the problems of the last year follow them into the next. So, as soon as school ended in June, they started working on a program for the seniors that would "give the kids a different lens, a way to go out and improve their communities, to realize they can make things better."

Amy and Dana have some things going for them that most teachers preparing for the next school year don't. "We know the kids, their strengths and weaknesses, so we know which pieces of education will have the biggest effect. We know the parents: how much support we can expect, what kind, from which ones. And we know the class dynamic: what it takes to teach A students and D students, rich white kids and poor black kids, shy kids and confident kids in the same room."

"I'm not going to spend another year telling them what they have to do to get an A," Amy told Dana last June. "We need to present them with a program they actually want to do because it has some intrinsic value." So they threw out the planned curriculum and invented a new one. They agreed to divide the class into three twenty-student seminars (one led by a student teacher they'd recruited from Mills College) and require each student to spend three mornings a week—the two hours they would normally spend in the double-period CAS class—interning at the nonprofit organization of their choice. On Mondays and Fridays the seminars will meet to discuss their internships, the books and essays they've been assigned to read, the group journals they've been assigned to write. *There will be no shortage of experiential learning for these seniors this year,* Amy thinks. *And no shortage of homework, either.*

What the kids will do with what they're offered, Amy muses as she starts a load of laundry, *now, that is the great unknown.*

AUTUMN MORRIS

Autumn is awakened, as she is every morning, by the alarm clock she never has to set: her five-year-old brother begging for his breakfast. "All right, RaShawn," she says, sitting up in her bed, looking over at his. "But you don't get your Cap'n Crunch till that bed of yours is made. And do it nicely, please, the way I showed you."

Twelve-year-old Michael is already eating at the dining-room table that's squeezed between the tiny kitchen and the living room. "I need you to stay home with him today," Autumn tells Michael as she pours a bowl of cereal for RaShawn. "I'm going to Berkeley High. Then Youth Radio. Then I'll be at work till eleven."

Michael continues reading the back of the Cap'n Crunch box. "I ain't got nowhere to be."

"You don't have anywhere to be," Autumn corrects him automatically. "Maybe you can get him to take a nap," she adds. "Then you can get your reading done." She waits. "Michael. You promised me you'd finish two books before school starts. And you haven't even started one yet."

"Get off my case," Michael says. "I'm too grown for this."

Autumn grabs the cereal box. "You so grown you got all Ds on your last report card. Who gon' git on your case if not me?" She rattles the box in Michael's face. "Just don't think you gon' stay at *my* house when you grown for real and you homeless like our daddy!"

She stomps into the bedroom she shares with her brothers and finds RaShawn tugging at his blankets. "That's good enough," Autumn tells him. She starts pulling clothes from her half of the closet. "Go eat your breakfast now. Let me get dressed in peace." Autumn wasn't really expecting Michael to do his reading, but he might as well get used to her bugging him. She's planning to do a lot of that. If she's going to go away to college next year—which she is *definitely* going to do—she's got to make sure these boys get some decent study habits before she goes.

A few minutes later, her curly black hair smoothed back into a bun, Autumn emerges from the bedroom dressed in a clinging, ankle-length skirt that makes her look even more statuesque than her five feet eight inches. She dabs the milk off RaShawn's face, wipes down the table, washes the breakfast dishes, and scribbles a note—"Home late. Love, Autumn"—that her mother will read when she gets home from her job at the San Francisco Hyatt. Then Autumn slings her backpack over her shoulder and heads out the door, locking it from the outside. If she's lucky, the bus and the BART train will come on time and the trip from Alameda to Berkeley—soon to be her daily commute again, as it's been for the past three school years—will only take an hour. If she's unlucky, it might take two.

On BART, Autumn reads the newspaper she finds on the seat. The headlines are all about the kids going back to school this week at Columbine High. Two of the students are still in wheelchairs. *Nothing that wack could happen at Berkeley High*, Autumn tells herself now, as she kept saying right after the shooting, when it seemed that no one could talk about anything else. *You couldn't grow up in Berkeley and be that racist, hunting down a black kid like a dog.* Then she has a chilling thought. *Unless you got so tired of hearing about race that it* made *you racist, like those trench coat Mafia dudes.*

It takes Autumn a half hour to walk the three blocks to Berkeley High from the downtown Berkeley BART station; she keeps running into people she knows. "How you doin'," calls Darnell, a guy who's in CAS with her, as she passes Taco Bell. "Hey girl!" Jamilah greets her with a hug as she walks down Milvia Street. "What's up, Autumn," says Jordan, another CAS kid, as they approach the Milvia gate from opposite directions.

When she sees the line around the theater, the sun beating down on all those sweating kids, Autumn sighs, wishing she lived closer so she could have gotten here earlier. *Just be glad you get to go here at all*, she reminds herself, as she does on the many occasions when Berkeley High craziness starts to make *her* crazy.

Autumn's first request for an intra-district transfer from Richmond, where her family lived during her freshman year, was turned down. Before Berkeley High finally let her in, she had to write a second letter explaining that she'd been attacked by girls at her neighborhood school who hated "mixed" girls like her with light skin and long hair. When Autumn's mom, a dark-complected black woman, came to pick Autumn up at school one day, the Richmond girls had taunted her, saying, "That can't be *your* mother!" Except for the one bad semester she had last year—distracted by a new boyfriend and problems at home, she let her grade point average slip from her usual 3.8 to a 3.0—Autumn has kept her vow to make the most of what Berkeley High has to offer. But she can't have another bad semester. To qualify for the full academic scholarship she needs, she'll have to get all As and Bs this year, even in the three AP classes she's taking.

An hour after she joins the line Autumn gets her schedule and sees that she'll need to have it changed. They didn't put her in CAS, and she's been scheduled for a seventh-period class when she can only stay at school through sixth. Autumn has to be finished at Berkeley High by 1:30 in order to make the rest of her day work: her internship at Youth Radio, the broadcast training program near Berkeley High; her hostess job at Applebee's restaurant in Alameda, where she's been working all summer to help her mother pay the bills; then home to pick up after her brothers and get her homework done.

Autumn walks over to the B building, takes one look at the line in the counseling department, and decides to get her schedule changed some other time. She glances at her watch, sees that she's got three hours till she's due at Youth Radio. She thinks about going home, doing the laundry, seeing about Michael and RaShawn. Then she imagines the dishes piled in the kitchen, the sound of the big-screen TV filling every corner of the tiny apartment, and decides to go to the library instead. She's got to get an A in Patterns in Black Literature, the AP English class she's taking this semester with the notoriously strict Mr. Miller. That means doing her summer reading—*Invisible Man* by

Ralph Ellison—before next week. *Mom will be mad I didn't get the house cleaned,* she thinks. *She won't understand if I tell her I had to get some schoolwork done.*

Autumn's mother Pamela is proud of her daughter's success, but unaware, for the most part, of what it takes to make it happen. Working two jobs, with two younger children and now a husband to worry about, Pamela has left Autumn's upbringing pretty much to Autumn. Sometimes Autumn wishes her mom would come to meetings at school, get more excited about her report cards, ask about her plans for college. Sometimes Autumn resents having to "lend" most of her paychecks to her mom, and feeling as if she's going to get yelled at if she stops doing housework for two seconds and sits down in her own house. But then Autumn tells herself to thank God and count her blessings. *I have a bed to sleep in and a house to live in. And I might not be the strong person I am if I hadn't had to make it on my own.*

Autumn hates to eat on the street—that's something homeless people do. But as she walks up Shattuck toward the library her stomach is twisting into hungry knots. She passes Mel's Diner and Taco Bell, determined to get something healthy. Working at Applebee's all summer, with her employee discount and nothing but greasy food on the menu, she's been eating far too much junk. She crosses the street to the EZ Stop Deli. She shops there often because the guys who work there are nice to her and her friends—unlike a lot of the stores around campus, where they follow the black kids around, waiting for them to steal something, if they let them in at all.

The Middle Eastern clerk smiles at Autumn as he takes her money. "The summer went by fast, eh?" he says, slipping her orange juice, two bananas, and a napkin into a crisp paper bag.

"Heck of fast," Autumn agrees.

"What are you now? Junior? Senior?"

"Senior." Autumn likes the taste of the word on her tongue.

"Big year for you, 2000," the clerk says.

"You got that right," Autumn says as she heads out the door. "Well, you have a nice day."

MR. MILLER

As vice president of the Berkeley Federation of Teachers and union rep for the teachers of Berkeley High, Alan Miller is not at liberty, as are his colleagues, to blame principal Theresa Saunders for the myriad crises, daily indignities, and general screw-ups that regularly frustrate, enrage, and immobilize them. It is Alan Miller's job to work effectively with the new principal, and work with her in good faith he does.

But even to the eternally philosophical Alan Miller, looking ahead to the new school year shortly before it begins, the picture is not pretty. Bad enough that the campus is still a mess, the staff parking lot a construction site, debris strewn everywhere. Worse, after calling endless staff meetings last year to gather (and presumably to incorporate) teacher input, Theresa has, as of mid-August and unbeknownst to the staff, radically restructured the school administration. Four of the five vice principals, the head counselor, and the school secretary are gone, and five of the six counselors have been replaced—a move sure to infuriate teachers, students, and parents, all of whom have been arguing for *more* administrative support. And the restructuring will entrust to a shrunken, inexperienced staff the massive, first-week-of-the-year demand for class schedule changes, an ever-shifting Rubik's cube that brings Berkeley High to its knees even in the best of times.

Under these circumstances, Alan predicts glumly, it could take weeks to get the kids into the right classes, the teachers seriously teaching. "Theresa should have convened a meeting this summer, at least, to warn the teachers about what they're going to be up against."

Alan has been up against some challenging conflicts himself this summer, renegotiating the contract between the teacher's union and the Berkeley Unified School District. Of the nineteen Bay Area districts, Berkeley's pay scale fluctuates between seventeenth and nineteenth. "It's always framed as a choice between programs for the kids or salary for us. That's true in every district, but in Berkeley it's complicated by a public budget-development process. They invite the community to create a wish list—which they do, without knowing the cost of things. It's good for PR but bad for education. The people doing the dreaming aren't thinking about who's doing the work."

Alan is frustrated by the pay scale not only for the obvious reason— he's a forty-year-old single man trying to keep up with escalating rents in his middle-class Oakland neighborhood—but also because it hinders recruitment of talented teachers of color. He's currently the only African-American teacher in the English department (as well as the only out gay male teacher in the school). In his eight years at Berkeley High, he has often been one of two or three black teachers. "We need a diverse group of teachers because we have a diverse population of students. But competence is important too. When I started here, being a male role model was always close to my consciousness, especially for black kids. So many of them are starved for that. But I've rethought the issue over the years. I'm more interested in performance now. I'm interested in getting our SAT scores improved."

To that end, between negotiating the contract (for which Alan was paid a stipend he calculates as amounting to a dollar an hour), attending a one-week union conference, and responding to the queries and complaints of the teachers he represents, Alan has spent the summer doing the part of his job he likes best: reading books. "In Black Lit I do a new novel every year, and I like to include several major black poets. This summer I read *Invisible Man* and *Betsey Brown,* and I fine-tuned the poetry selection.

"I can't control what the administration does: how many kids we'll have wandering the halls because they can't get their schedules right. I can't control what the kids get at home, what they come to school needing from their teachers. All I can control is performance—mine, and my students'. No matter what else happens at Berkeley High, in my classroom, that's what we're going to be focusing on. Performance."

KEITH

Keith Stephens is running from the BART station on Shattuck to the football field at Berkeley High, trying to get to practice on time, when suddenly he remembers: he forgot to look for his math book. Again. He checks the twenty-dollar "Rolex" on his wrist. 6:57 a.m. Practice starts at 7:00. Keith considers calling home, asking his mom to see if she can find the book and bring it to him. Then he remembers that this is his mom's first week on her new job. Just yesterday, when she gave him the cell phone and pager she'd bought him so they could still stay in touch during the day, she warned him that she wouldn't be sitting at home any more, ready to bring him his lunch money or anything else he forgot. *I know I brought that book back last year anyways,* Keith tells himself. He keeps on running.

He already wasted half his day on Tuesday, waiting on line to get his ID card and schedule. When he finally got to the front, a white lady told him he had a book debt and couldn't get his schedule till he turned in his math book. "But I went to the Junior Prom last year," Keith argued. "Ain't no way they let you go to the Prom if you ain't turned in all your books." The lady acted like she was scared of him. She told him to go see his counselor, and went on to the next kid in line. Keith didn't even know who his counselor was. Now it's Friday and school starts on Wednesday and Keith still doesn't know if he's got the classes he needs to make sure he graduates in June.

Without his schedule in hand on the first day of school, Keith knows he'll spend days, maybe weeks, hanging around the counseling office, missing classes, falling behind. Keith can't afford for that to happen this semester. If he fails even one more class he won't graduate. If he doesn't graduate he won't be eligible for a football scholarship. If he doesn't get a football scholarship he won't go to college—his mom's dream. His dream. Keith passed the two summer school classes he took when he got back from football camp in July, but he's still got some catching up to do.

7:01. His schedule will have to wait. Keith's priorities are clear. As one of his T-shirts says, "Football Is Life. The Rest Is Just Details." School is one of those details. Football is his way out.

Good thing Ms. Russ has my back, Keith thinks. Ever since Ms. Russ got him into the Computer Academy two years ago—she'd had Keith's sisters before him, and made sure to send Keith a Computer Academy application when it was his turn to go to Berkeley High—she and the other Computer Academy teachers have been staying on him, trying to keep him from falling too far behind. *She'll hook me up next week.*

Keith rounds the corner onto Channing Way, intending to cut through the teachers' parking lot. But what he sees freezes him in his tracks. The parking lot is full of police cars, fire trucks, and ambulances. Police and SWAT teams in riot gear, carrying shields and rifles, are marching in formation toward the school. Ambulance drivers run, pushing blood-spattered gurneys.

Littleton! Keith thinks. And then: *Did some Prozac fool in a black trench coat shoot up Berkeley High?*

Scenes of last year's shoot-out at Columbine High flash through his mind. The boy jumping out the window. The screaming girls. The father of the murdered black kid crying at his son's funeral. Ever since the massacre, whenever Keith and his friends see some freaky-looking white kid—and you can't go a day at B-High without seeing at least one of those—they always say "Littleton" just to remind each other: they killed that black kid 'cause he was black. If there'd been any more black kids at Columbine High, Keith is certain, they would've killed them too.

Keith's heart is pounding. *Should I get the hell out of here while I still have a chance?* He's been shot at before, but never by some crazy white kid.

He peers over at the football field. A bunch of white girls in red-and-gold sweats are doing jumping jacks at one end; the coaches are gathering the football team at the other. Littleton or not, if Keith doesn't get to practice in the next thirty seconds he can tell the season good-bye. "Please, God, don't let them shoot me," he prays as he sprints across the Astroturf.

"What's up with the po-lice, Coach?" Keith pants, grateful to have made it alive.

"Littleton practice," Coach answers without looking up from the attendance roster.

"Say what?"

"Like a fire drill," Coach says. "In case what happened at Columbine High happens here."

"Well da-a-ang," Keith says, relieved. "They coulda tole us ahead of time."

"They never tell us nothin'," one of his teammates says.

"Dang," Keith says again. "I was hella scared."

"Berzerkeley High," Coach shrugs, and starts handing out the breakfast bags. The football team gets free Burger King breakfast and lunch every day of this pre-season "Hell Week": twelve-hour days of running, weight lifting, push-ups, and sit-ups.

Keith pulls a pastry out of the bag, swallows it in two bites, and shoves the bag aside. *Burger King is hella played out,* he thinks. Working there every night, eating breakfast and lunch from there every day . . . *Like the song says,* he thinks, *I could use a break today at McDonald's.*

"Coach, I need to get my schedule. When you want me to go?" Keith asks.

Coach raises an eyebrow at him. "Wasn't Tuesday the day for that?"

"I got some, uh, special business to deal with."

"Take care of your business then. On your lunch break. Just make sure it doesn't become my business."

The head coach is new this year, but Keith knows that he and all the other coaches have heard about his past. Coaches talk. And the last coach had a nickname for Keith. "Fuck-up," he called him. At first he wouldn't even let Keith try out for the team. "Get lost, fuck-up," he kept saying, until Keith got his GPA up from 1.0 to 2.5 and kept coming to practice, uninvited and unwelcome, every day for a month. Even after Keith proved himself to be one of the team's best running backs, the coach kept calling him that same name. Sometimes when the coaches talk to him now, Keith still hears it in their voices. "Fuck-up."

"Pick up the pace," Coach calls from the sidelines. Keith puts his head down and runs a little faster. Keith is used to carrying more than his own weight when he runs. From the time he was little, his mom has told him he's her hope—the last of four children, first in the family with a chance to go to college. His grandmother, his mother and father, his older sisters, and his brother all graduated from Berkeley High. His parents got together there. His grandmother still tells stories of being smacked with a ruler when she talked back to a teacher. That was back in the day. No one gets hit at school any more—at least not by the teachers.

"It's on you, Keith," his mother tells him all the time. Keith feels the pressure, but he feels lucky, too. His mom doesn't just push *him*. She pushes anything and anybody who tries to stand in his way. Most of his friends' moms have never even been to their kids' schools. His mom just about lives at Berkeley High. If Keith gets in trouble, if Keith gets an F that should have been a D, if a teacher even thinks about speaking disrespectfully to Keith, Patricia is at school the next day, acting like a fool if that's what it takes.

"Ten more laps," Coach calls. "Move it!" The greasy pastry flops around in Keith's stomach. *Do it for Moms,* Keith tells himself. This is the mantra that has driven him around this track a thousand times, the mantra that has kept him sitting in classes when his friends cut school to kick it on Shattuck, the mantra that keeps him getting up at 5:30 a.m. in Richmond to get to Hell Week at Berkeley High by 7:00. *Make Moms proud.* Keith feels a burst of energy. He knows he could run another hundred laps if he had to.

MR. GIGLIO

"I like my classroom. It's got character." Greg Giglio (pronounced "Jillio") grins wryly, pulling staples out of the butcher paper–covered wall that serves as his bulletin board. But as he goes through his book closet, trying to find twenty-five copies of *Caucasia* intact enough to hand out to his Computer Academy English class tomorrow, Greg can't help but compare it to the friend's classroom he visited yesterday. "She and I went through the credential process together. I wanted to teach someplace diverse, so I applied to Oakland and Berkeley. She went to Pleasanton, a very white, very wealthy area an hour from here—the town where I live, actually.

"At her school they've got grass. Places to sit and eat. The school is clean. In her classroom she's got brand new white boards, a TV and VCR, a computer hooked up to the Internet. She told me she just asks for things and they magically appear." His shaved head furrowed in thought, he looks around at the painted-over walls, chipped plastic desks, broken blinds.

"The taxpayers in Berkeley are awesome. They say, 'Tax us more, we'll give you more.' But all we ever hear from the district is, we can't find the money for this, we don't have the budget for that. So where's all that money going?" This is a question asked often by the teachers of Berkeley High. Indeed, the Berkeley electorate has consistently approved one of the highest per-pupil spending rates in California, yet the town's 113-year-old high school looks more like an underfunded inner-city school than the suburban campus where Greg's friend waves her magic wand.

This will be Greg's third year at Berkeley High. For the past two he's been teaching in the Computer Academy, Berkeley High's original "school-within-a-school." Ten years old, serving 200 students, 80 percent of them African-American and all of them considered at-risk, the Computer Academy is known as "the ghetto" of Berkeley High—the polar opposite of advanced placement.

The program's believers—especially Flora Russ, its founder and director—claim that the Academy saves lives by keeping its kids in school, off the streets, and on the path to graduation. Its opponents accuse the program of sacrificing discipline and achievement in favor of social promotion. Greg Giglio's opinion is somewhere in between. "I didn't want to work with AP kids. They're on their way; they've had good teachers all their lives. I want to work where I'm needed.

"But Computer Academy is a bang-your-head-against-the-wall kind of thing. The philosophy is to get them through, give them the D, and say they can go. Flora has tons of success stories of graduates who went on to get a degree, started their own business—all because they got that diploma. I want to get them through, but I want them to learn something while they're here. I have the seniors. I'm the last stop."

Greg has spent the summer teaching two English classes a day to the Computer Academy Class of 2000, including Keith Stephens. "They were nearly remedial classes, full of kids who have had no success in school. Both classes were out of control. It was summer; the kids didn't want to be there. I'm actually a laid-back person, but if you're nice you're seen as weak. So I was an asshole. And it worked. The majority of the kids passed the English proficiency test in August, so there's a chance they can graduate in June."

It's a long way to the Computer Academy from the all-white neighborhood where Greg Giglio grew up (and now lives with his five-year-old son), the all-white private high school where he was turned off by "this strange anti-gay, anti-black, Republican thing," his fast-track job in an all-white advertising agency, and his "Yuppie marriage." Determined to change his life at age twenty-eight when his marriage ended, Greg quit his job, moved in with his parents, got his teaching credential, and started applying for jobs in "problematic" districts. "And I got one," he laughs ruefully.

"When I drive down Shattuck on my way to the freeway every night, I see all these guys hanging out, drinking forties, smoking cigarettes and weed, and I think, 'That's where my kids are gonna be.' One time I saw one of my sophomores walking down the street with a forty in his hand at 3:30 in the afternoon. On the other hand, I've seen kids who have gone from absolutely nothing to being proud of themselves by the end of the year. Something clicked; they turned into adults all of a sudden; they went on to junior college.

"The lack of faith they have in themselves is the worst for me. It tears me up to hear them say they're stupid, they can't do it. That's my challenge with the seniors this year. When you read the stuff they write, they're a million miles from coherent. But I know all they need is a little bridge." He sighs.

"I just don't know what that bridge is."

September 1999: What's Up

By 8:00 a.m. the Berkeley sky is cornflower blue, its air summer-warm, its commuters entangled in the morning transbay rush to the towers of San Francisco. Today's a big day in Berkeley: the first day of school. All over town the schoolchildren—six-year-olds with Lunchables in their Pokémon lunchboxes and sixteen-year-olds with Master P in their Discmans; children chattering in Spanish or Tagalog or Farsi and children who don't talk at all; sons of janitors and daughters of judges; kids who will surprise no one by going to Harvard and kids who will surprise no one by going to Juvenile Hall—are tying their shoelaces, shrugging into their backpacks, setting off to see their old friends, to meet their new teachers, to start their new school year.

In the hills, kids are climbing into their parents' cars, or their own. In the flats they're walking along San Pablo Avenue or Martin Luther King Jr. Way, descending into BART stations, climbing onto city buses flashing crisp new September bus passes. (Those whose families can afford only one will run to the back of the bus to toss them out to waiting siblings.) And although where they come from, how they get to school, and what happens to them once they get there may be—is, in fact—very different for each student, the citizens of Berkeley have ensured that this, at least, is true: all of the 9,500 children in Berkeley's thirteen public elementary schools, two public middle schools, and one public high school will be educated—will go to school, at least—*together*.

No bus passes were needed on the September morning in 1968 when Berkeley became the nation's first city to voluntarily desegregate its schools. Across the country, school districts debated how (or whether) to obey the 1954 *Brown v. Board of Education* Supreme Court integration edict that overturned *Plessy v. Ferguson,* the "separate but equal" ruling of 1896. But in Berkeley—harbinger of social change, then as now—reporters' pencils flew, experts speculated, and towns-people argued as the bright yellow buses rolled. Up the steep incline of Cedar Street they wheezed, north on Sacramento, west down University, south across San Pablo until small, eager faces were pressed against each window: white professors' children being carried down from the hills where the schools were 98 percent white; black factory workers' children being carried up from the flats where, until that day, the schools were 90 percent black.

"I wonder whether the people of Berkeley really understand what we are trying to do," a Berkeley school administrator told Dr. Robert Coles, who was visiting from Harvard, on that day. "Perhaps most of all we wonder what will happen to these children later on. Will a substantial amount of fine, sensitive schooling be the prelude to a more decent and honorable life? Or will splendid early lessons later be seen as illusions . . . ?"

Thirty-one years later these questions seem eerily prescient. The nation's public schools are more segregated now than they were two decades ago and are steadily becoming more so, with one-third of America's black public schoolchildren attending schools that are 90 to 100 percent minority. The Berkeley Unified School District (BUSD) is an island of integration, with a student body that is 38 percent African-American, 31 percent white, 14 percent Hispanic, 8 percent Asian, and 8 percent multiracial. Next door in Oakland, whites constitute 7 percent of public school students; in Lafayette, an affluent suburb ten miles away, white students comprise 87 percent of the public school population. "The civil rights momentum of the 1960s is dead in the water,"

Harvard School of Education professor Gary Orfield says in Jonathan Kozol's *Amazing Grace,* "and the ship is floating backward."

Still, Berkeley floats doggedly forward. Former resident John Kenneth Galbraith called the 108,000 people of Berkeley—where Indigenous People's Day replaced Columbus Day, Martin Luther King Jr. Way replaced Grove Street, and the public schools close annually for Malcolm X's birthday and International Women's Day—"the most intelligent constituency in the nation." Certainly in the realm of school integration they are among the most progressive. Swimming against the tide of resegregation, in 1995 the Berkeley Unified School District implemented a complex plan to rectify the growing imbalance in its elementary schools, decreeing that each school's demographics must reflect the city's mix of 59 percent white, 18 percent African-American, 14 percent Asian, and 8 percent Latino, Native American and "other."

In the mission statement taped to every classroom wall, the BUSD designates itself "the beacon for a diverse community" charged with "offering . . . alternative learning experiences in a racially integrated, pluralistic environment." To that end, Eurocentrism has been purged from the curricula. The Berkeley schools celebrate Christmas, Hanukkah, and Kwanzaa in December, Chinese New Year in February, Cinco de Mayo in May. And Berkeley's public high school is the only one in the country with African-American and Latino/Chicano Studies departments and a mandatory Ethnic Studies class for all incoming freshmen.

Each year several hundred non-Berkeley residents apply for intradistrict transfers to Berkeley High. Widely regarded as one of the nation's top public high schools, the school consistently produces above-average SAT scores, impressive numbers of National Merit Scholars (twenty-one in 1999), and multiple acceptances to prestigious universities. Seven Berkeley High seniors were accepted to MIT, five went to Harvard in 1999. Yet, a century after *Plessy v. Ferguson,* nearly half a century after *Brown v. Board of Education,* six years after the *New York Times* pronounced Berkeley High "the most integrated high school in America," Berkeley High continues to bequeath two separate and distinctly unequal fates to its 3,200 students.

Most of the school's white kids graduate and go off to four-year colleges. Most of its black and Latino kids drop out, flunk out, or go off to junior colleges, low-wage jobs, or jail.

By 8:30 a.m. downtown Berkeley is teeming with students headed to Berkeley High. African-American and Latino seniors cruise down Milvia in muscle cars with rap music blaring, then hunt for residential parking several blocks away. White seniors pay eight dollars to park their SUVs in the private garage across the street. Terrified-looking freshmen slip out of their parents late-model Volvos; students with intradistrict transfers and "borrowed" Berkeley addresses pour onto Shattuck out of AC Transit buses and BART trains pulling in from Richmond, Albany, Oakland, Alameda.

They stream through the gates in the perimeter fence erected in 1991, when a rash of stabbings and shootings at the school finally trumped the Berkeley penchant for freedom: six-foot-five seventeen-year-olds and baby-faced thirteen-year-olds converging on the courtyard like supplicants arriving at Mecca. "What's up?" is their invocation, and they say it to each other, hundreds of them, over and over: "What's up!" Girls rush into other girls' arms, squealing with excitement; boys exchange high fives, stylized handshakes, barely discernible nods. " 'S'up." Most of the African-American kids wear sharply pressed, brand-new-looking clothes: the boys wearing thick-linked gold neck chains, FUBU caps, T-shirts, and gargantuan jeans with color-coordinated, fresh-from-the-box Nikes; the girls in delicate, tattoo-like chokers, tight striped knit tops, long knit skirts, black platform slides. Most of the white kids wear faded, no-brand T-shirts or batik-print tank tops, hip-hugging bell-bottom jeans or denim cut-offs, New Balance running shoes or flip-flops or Adidas beach sandals. "What's *up!*" The biracial kids can, and do, go either way—borrowing this from one culture, that from another.

Roaming through the pumped-up crowd, their faces expressionless, walkie-talkies pressed to their mouths, the school's five safety monitors—three young black men with prizefighters' bodies and two kindly faced elderly black women, all supervised by the dread "Wiggins," Barry Wiggan, rumored to be an ex-CIA operative—watch and listen, sniffing for the sweet scent of marijuana, the sour smell of trouble.

In the B building Principal Saunders has been in her office for hours, struggling to uncoil the knot of angry parents who have occupied her tiny waiting room since seven this morning. In their offices down the hall the counselors are engulfed by a throbbing mass of teenagers waving printouts of their schedules: all wrong, wrong, wrong. The counselors stare at their computer screens and find them blank.

As the kids demand service, jockeying for position in the sweltering corridor, the news seeps through the staff like a bloodstain: a contractor, working late into the night, has cut a critical power line. The school's clocks are motionless, its bells silenced, its computers useless. It will be days before the counselors can begin the byzantine task of rebuilding several hundred students' schedules; weeks before anyone at Berkeley High will know when it's time to start or end a class.

"Keith Stephens." Greg Giglio calls Keith's name as he reads off the attendance roster in his Computer Academy senior English class, although he knows Keith isn't in the room and didn't really expect him to be. Not with all the scheduling chaos, and Keith's name still on the book debt list. Mr. Giglio goes on, marking fifteen students present—half of those who should be here: nine African-American boys, three African-American girls, one white girl, one Latino boy, one Chinese boy.

"So, what'd everybody do this summer?" Mr. Giglio asks. When he gets no answer, he walks over to one of the five boys who are wearing Walkmans. "Rasheed!" he says loudly. "What'd you do this summer?"

"Nuttin'," Rasheed answers without removing his headphones. "You had to do something," Mr. Giglio says. "How 'bout you, Nimani?"

"Laid up on the couch," Nimani says. "Watched soaps with my mom," says the boy next to him. "You know what I did, Giglio," a tall boy volunteers. "Sat my butt in your damn class all morning and got my butt kicked by the football coaches all afternoon. That's what."

"LaRique! Stay in your seat, please!" Mr. Giglio says. "What about you, Crystrial? Anything more inspiring to report?"

"I went to an all-girl computer camp at Stanford," Crystrial answers. "And then I went to the God's Women Conference and got more blessings."

"KMEL Summer Jams," says another girl, examining her long, curved, purple-painted fingernails.

"Taliah?" Mr. Giglio prompts the third girl.

"Worked two jobs and went to summer school," she says.

"All right. Thank you. Now we have some business to take care of. First, I need your contact information." Mr. Giglio walks around the room passing out forms. "Make sure you give me your *real* phone number. Not your pager, not your cell phone, not your grandmother's number or your cousin's. And your real address—the one where you'd want me to send a big fat check."

"You gon' pay us to come to class this year, Giglio?" LaRique calls out.

"Dominic! Come back in here, please. Thank you. Now—Ms. Saunders has some new rules for us this year," Mr. Giglio continues, ignoring LaRique's question as well as the five to seven students wandering the room, the constant drone of side conversations, the tinny cacophony of rap music leaking from several sets of headphones. He reads from the paper in his hand. "There will be no disrespect. No profanity. Pagers and cell phones must be set on 'vibrate.' You're allowed to return calls at lunch only. And last but not least"—he raises his voice—"any Walkman worn in class will be confiscated and kept till the end of the semester."

Two of the three girls in the class poke the boys next to them. "Take it off, fool," Taliah tells her neighbor. One by one the boys remove their headphones.

"You should know my rules by now. But let me refresh your memory," Mr. Giglio goes on. "If you need to leave the room, ask first and take the pass." He holds up a laminated yellow sheet with "Giglio—

Room B207" written on it. "You'll get in trouble if they catch you in the halls without it. And we don't want any extra trouble, do we? Next: my voice mail number is written on the board."

"How's your girlfriend, Mr. G?" a girl calls out.

"Fine. But I don't get to see her much. I'm pretty busy with my son since my—"

"Divorce," two boys in the back stage-whisper to each other.

"Divorce." The boys slap each other's palms, hooting. "Thanks for your concern. Okay, one last thing. Listen up, please."

The buzz in the room goes on unabated. "You guys! This is important!" The noise dims imperceptibly. "You're all seniors now," Mr. Giglio shouts above it. "I want you to graduate. I don't want you to be missing points for being absent or not turning in assignments. If you need help, talk to me. If you need tutoring, you can get it free. Berkeley High has a new Student Learning Center on the fourth floor of the C building." He goes to the blackboard and writes, "Being good is not good enough when you have dreams of being great!"

He turns back to the class. "I want you all to be great," he says. "So please, take out your notebooks and write down three things you want to get out of my class this semester. I'll come around and help you . . ."

Keith meant to make it to Mr. Giglio's class. He really did. But while he's in the counseling department, trying to figure out which of the new counselors is his, Ms. Russ comes up to him and says, "Don't bother trying to see your counselor, Keith. Your name's on the book debt list. You have to take care of that before they'll give you your schedule." Then she walks away without even offering to help. *Like we ain't always been tight,* Keith thinks. *Like we ain't even on the same page.* Hurt, he heads for the gym, where the list is taped to the doors.

"S'up, Black." His teammate, John, greets Keith by his Berkeley High nickname—a reference to the ebony skin Keith inherited from his mother. "No wonder they put the list up on the gym, man," John says, running his finger down the printout. "Half of these dudes be on the team."

"Am I on there?" Keith asks.

"We *all* on here," John answers.

Mr. Boone, Keith thinks. *He'll hook me up.* The assistant coach knows Keith; he and Keith's family go way back. Sure enough, when Keith finds Mr. Boone in the locker room, explains that he *couldn't* have a book debt—"Now, how I went to the Junior Prom last year if I ain't gave back my books?"—Mr. Boone walks Keith over to the office, marches right through the crowd, gets the debt off Keith's record, and hands him his schedule. Just like that. But by the time Keith gets upstairs to Mr. Giglio's room, the students are pouring into the hall. "Startin' the year off right, Keith?" Taliah chides him. He throws his arm around her, bumps his hip against hers. "I'll start your year off right if you let me," he offers.

"Talk to us! Tell us what you're feeling!" Amy Crawford and Dana Richards, team teachers of the CAS seniors, exhort Autumn and Jordan's second-period class. In response, forty students—white and black, biracial and Latina, Asian and Latino, advanced placement students and marginal students—smile and smirk at their teachers, who look like a set of salt and pepper shakers in their T-shirts, shorts, and sandals: Ms. Crawford with her blonde, cheerleader-pretty looks; Mr. Richards with his short dark hair and football player's body.

"I have no schedule," one boy reports glumly. "I have no counselor," says a girl.

"This *is* the most disorganized year in Berkeley High history!" Mr. Richards announces, and the class breaks into sarcastic applause. Students keep trickling in, most of them stopping to exchange hugs with the teachers and with several classmates before finding a seat in the crowded room, a semi-converted teachers' lounge.

Autumn, in a tight, square-necked knit top and long gray knit skirt, sits beside a refrigerator, knee-to-knee with Darnell. Jordan, in a plaid button-down shirt, baggy black jeans, and DKNY running shoes, hangs his head in his hands. "Too early," he mumbles to no one in particular. "It's too hard to think after the summer! This sucks."

"Anyone have a summer story?" Ms. Crawford asks.

"I went to Trinidad and Barbados with my family," says an African-American boy. "I went to a kibbutz in Israel and to Greece and Damascus," says an African-American girl. "Washington, D.C.," says Finnegan, a red-headed white boy who turned his E-mail correspondence with a Kosovar girl into a seven-part NPR series last year. He holds up a photo of himself beside a limo. "I was famous for fifteen minutes."

"I did the five-day, eight-state college tour," says Jordan. He considers telling the rest of the story; decides against it. Mr. Richards is really big on the deep-sharing trip, but it's too early in the day, too early in the semester for that.

"I did the one-state, no-college tour," Autumn says, and everyone laughs. "Worked at Applebee's. Took care of my brothers. Same old same old."

"KMEL Summer Jams!" exclaims an African-American girl with hair extensions trailing down her back. "Yeah, an' you left me there!" a girl in corn rows shouts back at her. "I saw you down to the 7-Eleven buying condoms with that scrub you dissed me for!" The whole class laughs again.

"Okay, you guys. Listen up," Mr. Richards says. "The theme of this class is social justice, building a multicultural society. The heart of it will be your internships. They should reflect that theme. We'll talk more about the internships next week." A sudden rumble from the vending machine in the corner, its neon sign advertising chicken strips and cheeseburgers, interrupts him. "I know that machine says 'Hot Choice,' " Mr. Richards says, "but there are no men or women in there. Just terrible food. We're having it removed."

A safety officer pokes his head into the room. "No bells today," he murmurs to Ms. Crawford in the sotto voce adults use to talk about children behind their backs. She nods and turns to the class. "In case you hadn't noticed, the bells aren't working," she says in a conversational tone. "Let's synchronize our watches so we'll all get here on time, okay?"

"We're gonna use the garden as part of the classroom," Mr. Richards continues, nodding out the wall of windows at the patch of towering wildflowers, baseball bat–sized zucchinis, and compost piles that he and his students carved a few years ago from a former strip of cement. "Bring mugs from home; we'll have coffee and tea. And we're gonna make a chilling nook in the corner."

"If no one has anything else to say about the summer—" Ms. Crawford picks up a piece of chalk and goes to the board, "we'll get started on an exercise to get you thinking about the focus of your internships. So tell us: what do you think are the top issues facing our community, the country, the world?"

"Health care," a girl calls out. "The environment," says a boy. Ms. Crawford writes each phrase on the board, next to her home phone number and Mr. Richards', which are already written there. "Race." "Gender." "Capitalism." "Religion." "Education." "Class relationships."

"Great," Ms. Crawford says. "Now I want you to divide yourselves up into six groups. Pick one of these problems, and create a poster that illustrates three things: where the problem came from, where the problem is now, and what you think will solve it." She glances up at the motionless clock on the wall, then down at her watch. "Go! We'll get back together in twenty minutes."

Receiving this, the first assignment of the school year, the CAS class fractures along the fault lines of its diversity. When the students have sorted themselves into groups, two—including Jordan's—are mixed; the other four are segregated by ethnicity.

The teachers walk around the room, nudging several nonparticipants into participation, handing out paper and markers. Jordan, Finnegan, another white boy, and an African-American boy take on "Class Relationships." Autumn, two other biracial girls, and one African-American boy choose "Gender." The "Education," "Environment," and "Health Care" groups are all-white; "Teens and the Cycle of Crime" is a mix of white, Asian, African-American, and Latina students. As the kids set to work, the hum in the room quickly escalates to a low roar, punctuated by outbursts in English, Spanish, Ebonics. "Remember," Mr. Richards announces, "we're trying to do something big and deep here: launch lives that change the world and change us."

"Are you guys gonna grade us on the posters?" a girl asks.

If Alan Miller, Autumn's Advanced Placement English teacher, has rules in his class, or a laminated bathroom pass, or warnings about wearing Walkmans; if he is interested in how his students—most of whom are strangers to him, many of them strangers to each other—feel, or how they spent their summers, none of that is in evidence this morning. Five minutes into their first meeting on the first day of school, Alan Miller's AP Black Literature class is well into a discussion of the semester's curriculum and requirements.

"We're going to have a pretty traditional reading list—*Invisible Man, Betsey Brown, Song of Solomon*," Mr. Miller announces, his striped button-down shirt tucked tightly into his black jeans. "As usual I'll supplement the readings with some really interesting guests. For starters, I'm hoping to get the local writer who just reviewed the new Ralph Ellison novel for the *New York Times*. Did anyone read the review?"

A white boy raises his hand.

"What did you think?" Mr. Miller asks him.

"Well . . . my dad wrote it," he says.

"Oh, good," Mr. Miller says in his characteristic near-monotone. "You can remind him that he promised to come speak to my class."

Autumn, one of six black or biracial girls in the class of twenty, sits surrounded by four of them—her best friend Lillian, their good friend Emily, and Jamilah and Brittany, both of whom are in Autumn's Advanced Placement Anatomy class. There are three Asian girls, too, and one big surprise: Reggie, an African-American guy who's on the football team. Autumn's never seen an African-American male in an AP class before—not counting Daveed Diggs, which she doesn't. Daveed is mixed, black and white, like Autumn. Autumn calls him "my other half." "When it's me and Daveed in the room," she says, "we make one."

Like all AP classes, Mr. Miller's Black Lit classes are famous for being nearly all-white. But this one's pretty good, Autumn thinks. *For once I won't be the only one trying to explain black folks to a bunch of white folks.*

"You'll be required to attend at least two book readings during the semester and to write an essay about each of them. I'll keep the events schedules posted and current." Mr. Miller points to several mailers from local bookstores tacked up on the back bulletin board, under the Alice Walker quote that's handwritten across the wall: "Each of us has a best self and a worst self. It's up to the individual to realize that BEST SELF and aspire to move toward it."

"Since you're an AP class, I expect you already have at least two study buddies. Use them. This year as seniors you'll be juggling a lot more than you did before. You'll need to keep track of SAT dates, and ACT dates. If you're going to need scholarships next year, you need to start looking for them right now. Try the Internet for that information. And it's never too soon to start working on your college essay.

"This is the first year of your lives you can no longer say it's your parents' fault. If you're late to your job, your boss won't ask if your mom dropped you off late. Seek out the help you need at home, in the community, to make sure you graduate and get into your top-choice college."

"Lay a little pressure on us, why don't you, dude?" Autumn whispers to Lillian. Day One and she's already stressing. Normally she likes the contrast between CAS and her AP classes—"In the real world," she says, "you need to learn to deal with both situations: the freedom of CAS and the structure of AP." But Ms. Crawford is obviously planning to make CAS harder this year, and Mr. Miller isn't about to cut them any slack either.

Autumn receives a stack of papers from Lillian, takes one, and passes the rest on to Emily. "This is a poem about the Jazz Age," Mr. Miller says. "Anyone have an opinion of Louis Armstrong?"

Hesitantly, a couple of kids raise their hands. "My mom loves his music," one boy says. "I've started to appreciate it, too."

"He may have been a good musician, but he was a real Tom," Mr.

Miller responds flatly. "A lot of black people hate him—like me." The other kid puts his hand down. "D-a-a-ang," Autumn murmurs under her breath. "He's heck of harsh."

"Take a minute to read the poem," Mr. Miller instructs the class. "Then we'll discuss it further."

The room falls silent, the students' brows wrinkled with concentration as they bend to the task at hand.

Berkeley High isn't the only place in America where one group of high school seniors is instructed to put their pagers on "vibrate" and another is instructed to critique the *New York Times Book Review*. "Tracking"— defined by the U.S. Education Department–funded Educational Resources Information Center as "categorizing students according to measures of intelligence, achievement, or aptitude, and then assigning [them] to hierarchical ability- or interest-grouped classes"—happens in almost all of our nation's schools, and always has.

"The rigid academic 'tracking' so common in American high schools," write Coalition of Essential Schools co-founders Theodore and Nancy Sizer in their 1999 book *The Students Are Watching,* "has been demonstrated to be harmful in research study after research study, but it nonetheless persists. It is attractive to families who want their children segregated by race, class, or other stereotype within a larger school . . . the evidence is overwhelming that categorical tracking into faster classes doesn't necessarily improve learning, and tracking into slower classes becomes a self-fulfilling prophecy."

Tracking and public schools are twins conceived together—by none other than that father of democracy (and, apparently, several biracial children) Thomas Jefferson. In his 1781 *Notes on the State of Virginia,* Jefferson advocated the creation of public schools "to diffuse knowledge more generally through the mass of the people" ("the people," of course, being white males only). Proposing that "every person [be] entitled to send their children three years gratis, and as much longer as they please, paying for it," Jefferson stipulated that "Of the boys thus sent in any one year, trial is to be made at the grammar schools . . . and the best genius of the whole selected . . . and the residue dismissed. By this means twenty of the best geniuses will be raked from the rubbish annually . . ."

In 1909, declaring that "schools should give up the exceedingly democratic idea that all are equal and that our society is devoid of classes," Harvard University president Charles Eliot defended tracks in schools as producing necessary tracks in society: "A thin layer of managers and leaders, two larger layers of skilled workers and merchants, and a great thick layer of manual workers."

Tracking at Berkeley High has its own twists and significance. Cities Berkeley's size often have more than one high school, each, typically, as economically and racially segregated as the neighborhoods and middle schools from which its students are drawn. As other cities do, Berkeley has a "good" public high school for rich white kids and a "bad" school for poor kids of color. The difference is that in Berkeley, both schools exist under one roof. All the children together, as they were on that sunny September day in 1968: this is as it should be in admirably idealistic Berkeley, where the ideal is often mistaken for the real, and an integrated school can masquerade as an equitable one.

"Every two or three years someone writes this story, and the city of Berkeley drops everything and draws in its breath with a single, appalled gasp," Chris Thompson opened his June 1999 *East Bay Express* cover story on Berkeley High. The article included these facts about the class of '98: six out of ten black students dropped out, flunked out, or otherwise disappeared before their senior year. White Berkeley High students scored in the top fifteenth percentile nationally; black students scored in the bottom fortieth. Only eighteen black male graduates (compared to 111 white males) had the grades and credits to qualify for a four-year college.

The city of Berkeley gasped, too, when a published chart showed that Berkeley students' grades rose in direct proportion to their parents' income. The ninth graders from Berkeley's poorest, least white "flatlands" neighborhoods had the lowest grade point averages; the children in the affluent, mostly white hills, the highest.

Over the years, efforts to deny, ameliorate, eliminate, and justify the effects of tracking at Berkeley High have arisen, subsided, and arisen again, fueled by the conflicting interests of the town's diverse populace. For the wealthy white hills parents, Berkeley High serves as a messy, complicated, but cut-rate private school—and they consistently invest large amounts of time, money, and political influence to keep it that way. For Berkeley activists of all races and classes, and for Berkeley's poor, tracking is a blot on the town's progressive image; proof of its hypocrisy and betrayal. As Berkeley High parent, former Berkeley School Board member, and UC Berkeley professor Pedro Noguera wrote in his 1995 article, "Ties That Bind, Forces That Divide: Berkeley High School and the Challenge of Integration," "Critics of the practice have argued that tracking conflicts with most of the values that Berkeley and Berkeley High claim to cherish." One of those critics is Principal Theresa Saunders, who calls tracking "a system that prevents students from gaining their potential."

The long-term positive effects of throwing kids as different as Keith, Jordan, and Autumn together on the same campus, if not in the same classrooms, are desirable in the abstract ("Can't we all just live together?") but not yet embodied nor measurable in the real world. The long-term negative consequences of the differences between the "education" that Keith is receiving at Berkeley High—the same education that hundreds of thousands of Keiths are receiving at ghetto schools across America—versus the education that Autumn has fought for, and Jordan has been granted as his birthright, will be evident in the number of jails we build, the fortitude of the fences we erect around our gated communities, the grim determination with which the "geniuses" separate and protect themselves from the "rubbish."

The immediate social repercussions, on the other hand, are visible daily at lunchtime.

"You look pretty good for a white girl," an African-American boy calls to a blonde in a tank top and tight bell-bottoms crossing the Slopes—running right over the red, black, and green map of Africa painted on the ground there, as it happens—as she hurries out the Milvia gate for lunch. The boy and his friends watch, grinning, as the girl spins around, her face crimson, her mouth sputtering with anger. She plants her feet, looks up the incline of the Slopes at her harassers: five guys, jeans slung low on their hips, gold chains, gold teeth, diamond earrings glinting in the sun. Berkeley High has well-publicized, aggressively enforced school rules against sexual harassment, hate violence, intimidation. Still standing within spitting distance of the principal's office, the boys stare mockingly at the girl, daring her, challenging her. The girl's face grows redder. She opens her mouth, closes it. She turns away from the boys, breaks into a run again as soon as she gets through the gate. The boys laugh, then saunter across the street to Top Dog for a hot link.

Between the poles of black and white a multitude of hues coexist at Berkeley High. Forty-five languages are spoken here; nearly 10 percent of the students are immigrants, and traversing the campus at lunchtime is like taking a walking tour of the world.

In Berkeley High's high-rent central district—the steps of the Berkeley Community Theater—English only is spoken. "Senior Step," the top one (whose lofty view of the campus is reminiscent of the sweeping bay views enjoyed at home by many of the hills kids who populate it), is reserved for white seniors and invited guests only. Jordan is welcome here for the first time this year, and despite his ambivalence about identifying, or being identified with, the hills kids, he spends a couple of lunch periods here each week, sharing bottles of Evian, plastic bags of carrot sticks, Head Royce gossip. The lower steps are claimed by the other white cliques: the crew team, preppies, housers, and skaters.

Elsewhere on campus—on the periphery, invisible from the center—the "ghetto kids," mostly boys, kick it on the Slopes, where the language is straight-up Ebonics, incomprehensible to the uninitiated. Although Autumn knows many of the guys who hang out on the Slopes, including Keith ("All the black kids know each other; don't ask me how"), she doesn't have classes with any of them and doesn't associate with them at school. Autumn's academic success depends in part on her good reputation with her teachers; she doesn't want to risk the attitude shift she's known teachers to make when they see their students hanging with the wrong crowd. So at lunchtime she and her friends run up to Shattuck for a burrito or a Jamba Juice smoothie, or do their homework together in the library. On Thursdays they go to Black Student Union meetings in the African-American Studies department.

Latino kids gather beneath the Mexican history mural across from the gym, passing bags of Doritos and bottles of Coke, flirting and teasing in Spanish. The Southeast Asian students crouch on the floor outside the ELL (English Language Learner) classrooms, eating with chopsticks from plastic containers, speaking to each other in Cambodian, Vietnamese, Laotian. Chinese and Filipino kids hang out on "the Bricks" on the outskirts of the courtyard. In the park across the street—in full view of the Berkeley Municipal Courthouse and one block from Berkeley Police headquarters—white and biracial Deadheads, Goths, punks, and stoners kick hacky sacks and pass the pipe, coughing and gasping down lungfuls of marijuana.

The defining paradox of Berkeley High is that the very "complications" that make the school (and lunchtime there) so problematic also make life (and lunchtime) there incomparably rich. There *are* kids of different races who choose to hang out together at lunchtime. And even those who keep to their own kind get the benefit of the high-spirited, high-volume, oftentimes delicious lunchtime celebrations of diversity that happen at least once a month.

September is no exception. In the second week of school, Raza Unida—one of Berkeley High's seventy-five school clubs—transforms the courtyard into a fiesta. Mexican flags fly; streamers wave; $3.50 tostada plates are served by Latina students wearing *huipils*. The white seniors displaced for the day, Latino boys in serapes and sombreros dance ecstatically on the Steps to salsa music blasting from giant speakers. Summoned forth from the sidelines, hands waving ecstatically, Latinos and Latinas toss each other into the air as Azetc dancers in feathered headdresses perform ancient rituals for the curious crowd gathered on the courtyard below.

The next week the Hapa (biracial Asian) Club sponsors an International Food Sale: "Various Foods from Around the World to Promote UNITY." Filipino kids serve *lumpia;* Chinese kids serve stir-fry; Japanese kids serve soba to a diverse, hungry lunchtime crowd.

Later in the month flyers mysteriously appear everywhere on campus: "It's Time To Get FUNKED UP! Courtyard. Lunch. Be there." On the designated day the mammoth speakers reappear on the steps, pounding out a something-for-everyone mix of rap, reggae, rock, and hip-hop that draws a dancing crowd from all corners of the campus and all camps of the student body. Keith is in the thick of it, dancing with two girls, then three. Autumn, Lillian, and Lauren watch from the steps of the C building, their heads nodding to the beat but their feet staying put. Jordan is eating last night's pasta dinner, cold, in Mr. Ayers' room while he does his Statistics homework.

Except on days when a club sells food on the courtyard, lunchtime at Berkeley High is not about eating lunch. The school has no cafeteria; the campus snack bar sells candy bars, microwaved burritos, and lukewarm, beige "hamburgers" of dubious content, engulfed in doughy white rolls. Still, many students and just about all the staff are choosing, now, to stay on campus for lunch: one of the changes Theresa Saunders has made is the reduction of last year's already unworkable forty-five-minute lunch period to forty minutes. Those who are hungry and haven't brought lunch from home have limited choices—all of them indigestion-inducing. Some leave campus the instant lunch starts at 11:15, then stand on a fifteen-minute line, as Keith often does, at Top Dog, the only place nearby. Others run several blocks to Shattuck and stand on even longer lines at the one-dollar Chinese place, at McDonald's, or at the EZ Stop Deli. Either way, by the time the students have their fried rice or Big Mac or avocado-on-whole-wheat sandwich in hand, it's time to swallow it down while running back to Berkeley High before the safety officers lock the gates at 11:55.

Normally a five-minute warning bell blasts through the halls, across the campus, and into the neighborhood, summoning students back after lunch from wherever and however they have spent it. Since the bells aren't functioning, lunch now ends with a mass emigration that begins around 11:55 and goes on, most days, until well past noon. Students returning late from lunch are sent to OCS, On-Campus Suspension, where they are required to spend the next period doing nothing, and doing it in silence. The administration defends this new policy as necessary to keep the halls and campus cleared while class is in session. The students see it differently.

"Brilliant," Jordan says sarcastically. "Punish kids for being late by making them miss all of fifth period instead of missing a few minutes of it."

"We have 3200 kids," Theresa Saunders announces, her opening words to the first staff meeting of the year. "And we might get more."

A collective groan rises from the nearly two hundred teachers in the school library. The campus was bursting at the seams last year with 3,100. Even this room isn't big enough to hold the staff; many teachers are sitting on the floor, leaning against the walls. "We'll hire as soon as we can. But let's keep things in perspective, people," Saunders adds. "Oakland has 60 percent of its teachers on emergency credential, a lot of them with no training whatsoever. Teachers are hard to find."

She hands out a thick sheaf of papers—stapled lists of the rights and responsibilities of district staff, administrators, teachers, parents, and students—then continues her rapid-fire delivery, sounding and looking like a hyped-up TV news anchor in her tailored black suit, neatly trimmed Afro, and minimal but effective makeup. "Next item: I need you to hold the line on ID cards. We've found numerous kids without Berkeley addresses. And keep a stronghold on attendance. By Tuesday afternoon any kid who hasn't showed up and whose parents haven't called is dropped from the system. Is that clear? I don't care if they bring their attorneys. I don't care if they hang from the rafters. Now, don't rush home and call your friends and tell them to show up. We have moved the piano out of the music room. We are using the costume room in the theater as a classroom. We are done! Full! Do I make myself clear?" She pauses for a few seconds. "Good. Now I'll introduce Beverly Jones from the attendance office."

An African-American woman—one of many who staff the back offices of Berkeley High—stands and announces that parents of absent students will now receive computer-generated phone calls from the attendance office every night. "Save the kids' lives at home. Save the kids' lives at Juvenile Hall," she entreats the teachers. "Mark them absent when they're absent. Tardy when they're late. Our records are subpoenaed regularly by social services and by the kids' probation officers. They *must* be accurate. And don't you ever assume anything about a kid. We've got con artists who rip off every form we print. Any questions?"

"Is it true that seniors are allowed to write their own notes once they turn eighteen?" a new teacher asks. Beverly Jones nods.

"Then what's gonna keep them from getting themselves out of class?" the teacher asks.

As one voice the group answers in a shout: *"Nothing!"*

Theresa Saunders' voice rises above the laughter. "We hope that what's happening here is compelling enough to keep them in class." The teachers shake their heads disbelievingly at the principal's naïveté.

Saunders perseveres, holding up a black T-shirt. "This is our new school slogan," she says, pointing to the back of the shirt. Emblazoned there are the words "Believe-Achieve-Succeed" in three-inch-tall red letters, with the letters "B," "A," and "S" in yellow. She turns the shirt around. On the front in bold letters, yellow against a red background: "Achievement is for EVERYONE."

"We're going to provide each of you with one of these shirts. I'm encouraging you all to wear them every Friday. I think this will help set the tone for the year.

"I want to acknowledge the new staff, and then we'll get out of here. New people—please stand and introduce yourselves."

About twenty people—one, a clerical worker, is African-American; two teachers are Asian; the rest are white—rise from their seats, each offering his or her name, department, and former position. Each is dutifully applauded. Like most schools with majority "minority" student populations, Berkeley High suffers a chronic shortage of teachers whose ethnicities and backgrounds match those of their students. This year, the student body is comprised of about 30 percent white and about 35 percent black students; the teaching staff is 75 percent white, 16 percent black, with seven Latino, six Asian, and three Native American teachers. Although Theresa Saunders tells the *Berkeley High Jacket,* "There has been a thirty-year effort to hire teachers of other races," that effort, it appears this afternoon, has not yet been fruitful.

Greg Giglio leaves the library feeling frustrated. Last year he was a big fan of Theresa Saunders. He saw strength in her, the kind of heart and drive he thinks Berkeley High needs. He empathized with her, too; he knew she wasn't married, had no family nearby, was a deeply religious person, and he'd seen her in her office until late at night. His least favorite thing about Theresa was, and is, the way she leads meetings— reading memos to the staff as if they were kids, babbling on without taking feedback. This meeting has been a perfect example. "Let's face it," he tells himself as he gets into his car for the long drive home to Pleasanton, "the honeymoon's over."

Amy Crawford is fuming as the meeting breaks up. "I can't believe how condescending that was," she tells Dana Richards. "We spent hours last year talking about the daily schedule. About restructuring the administration. And then we get here today and *why did we bother?* We've got a shorter lunch, one vice principal left. Nothing we said we wanted. And these rules!" She flips through the lists of "Rights and Responsibilities." "Now we're supposed to be the rubber stamp, present these to the students as if we've okayed them, when we've never even seen them before."

"So much for thinking things are gonna get better," Dana agrees.

"Starry Plough?" Amy suggests, naming the South Berkeley Irish pub the CAS teachers frequent. "Starry Plough," Dana affirms.

"It's going to be a long night," Alan Miller thinks as he drives home to Oakland. The teachers had started out feeling great about Theresa Saunders, hopeful and energized. But that didn't last long. By last June, when a large number of grade sheets turned up missing and Theresa put out a memo that seemed to blame the teachers, her fate was sealed.

Today's events—the scheduling madness, the broken clocks and bells, and now these new school rules—are sure to trigger a new wave of complaints.

Principal Saunders' first meeting with the senior class goes no better. She appears on the stage of the Community Theater, where the Class of 2000 is assembled, and without preamble begins a recitation of new, stricter, state-mandated attendance policies. "The school is only paid each day," she explains, "for students who are marked present."

"She sayin' they gon' kick us out for bein' absent!" Keith announces from his seat in the balcony.

"What kinda bullshit is that?" his teammate John says loudly. And then all around them the chant begins. "BULL-SHIT! BULL-SHIT!" booms from the theater rafters.

Autumn frowns at the boys in the balcony, puts her finger to her lips to shush them. She doesn't want to miss any college information that might be forthcoming—although she agrees with the boys' reaction. "Is *that* the only reason she wants us to come?" Autumn whispers to Lillian. "So the school can get paid? You don't say something like that to a bunch of seniors!"

As the chant spreads, Saunders shouts into the microphone, "This disrespectful behavior will *not* be tolerated! You are all dismissed!" and storms off the stage.

"And *she's* supposed to be the mature one!" Lillian says, rolling her eyes.

"Fifteen people out of six hundred seniors and she couldn't handle it," Autumn agrees. "She could have just sent someone back there to quiet things down."

In the middle of the theater Jordan sits in his seat, waiting for the crowd to thin, shaking his head with disgust. "Saunders is like thirty years old. If she can't handle a few loud football players, she's got problems. And now *her* problems are *our* problems. She got rid of the college counselor, so how are we supposed to get the information we need? I heard Cornell is visiting this week and I don't even know when."

"It wasn't us," Keith says later, when the rumor circulates that the whole football team will be disciplined for the incident. "They just blame the football team for everything 'cause we black."

Black kids are blamed, too, for the violence that breaks out after the Unity Dance, the first one of the year. And who else could be blamed? As usual, there are almost no kids of other races there. "Except for the Prom, white kids don't go to Berkeley High dances," Jordan says. "I don't know why. Black kids go to dances; white kids put out the *Jacket*. Black kids play basketball; white kids play lacrosse. It's tradition. My first semester, before I knew better, I made the mistake of going to the winter ball. I was the only white kid there."

The dance is tense from the start. Although the flyer announcing it specified "No pagers or phones," very few of the kids in line seem to know about the ban, or that each of them will be individually searched at the door. This means an hour-long wait for the students who do get in, and the expulsion of those who don't want to relinquish their cell phones and pagers. After a half-hour on line Autumn, Lillian, and Lauren decide it's not worth the wait. They walk up to Shattuck and buy tickets to see *Blue Streak*, the new Martin Lawrence cop movie, instead.

When Keith finally gets into the gym, he heads right for the DJ table and puts in his song requests. Berkeley High dances are famous for being boring. "In Oakland and Richmond they let anybody in. At Berkeley dances they only let in Berkeley students. So you end up kicking it with the same people you just saw in class that day." Keith never misses a dance, though, and he always takes it upon himself to liven them up with tight music and tight moves.

At around eleven, sweaty and thirsty, Keith is waiting to buy water at the refreshment stand with about a hundred other kids. Suddenly the police assigned to the dance close in on the refreshment stand and tell the kids there that they have to leave the campus. The kids try ignoring the cops. Then they try arguing. But the cops don't relent.

By 11:10 there are a hundred hot, thirsty, angry teenagers on Milvia Street with the gate to their school padlocked behind them, guarded by a phalanx of police. By 11:15, about fifty of them—including some non-students from Oakland and Richmond who were kicked off campus earlier—migrate to Shattuck Avenue and descend on EZ Stop. Keith retreats to the movie arcade across the street and watches as a group of boys punch the employees who are closing up the store, steal food and candy, and throw a bottle through the front window. As sirens wail and cop cars converge on the scene, Keith walks briskly—heeding his mom's repeated warning never to run from the police—to the BART station a block away. "No sense getting caught up in that mess." By the time he arrives in Richmond, $3,000 worth of damage has been done and several arrests have been made.

Autumn, Lillian, and Lauren have a three-way call about the "riot" the next morning. "That is *scandalous*," Autumn says when Lauren tells her what happened. "They are so nice to us at EZ Stop."

"We've been seeing the guys that work there every day for years," Lillian agrees. "They call us by our names and everything."

"People steal heck of stuff from them every day," Lauren adds, "but they still let us in at lunch. They say only seven students at a time, but they're not discriminating. Only seven people can *fit* in there."

"Some people just don't know how to act," Autumn sighs.

"The owner and employees of EZ Stop deli are furious over the fact that they were not informed of any dance at Berkeley High," the *Jacket* reports the following week. "All calls by the EZ Stop deli to the principal's office have gone unanswered so far."

Despite perennial efforts to break the stronghold of the hills parents and involve parents of color in the school, this year's first Back to School Night once again earns its nickname: "White Night."

By day the halls of Berkeley High echo with the boisterous laughter of the black students, who occupy the top rung of the school's social ladder as firmly as they occupy its academic bottom; the other kids emulating their language, their music, their style. But by night it is the white parents, as Jordan says, who "rule the school." The genteel sound of Back to School Night is that of affluent white parents having happy reunions outside their kids' Advanced Placement classrooms, hugging each other, promising to get together for dinner sometime soon, their laughter tinkling gently against the school's scarred walls like ice cubes against cut glass.

In his classroom Greg Giglio greets a total of five parents: two African-American couples and the father of the one Chinese boy in the class. The boy is there, too, translating for his father. Keith's parents are not here. "Whether they think they're going to college or not," Mr. Giglio tells those who are present, "we're going to write college essays as if they were." Near the end of the fifteen-minute period, a white mother sticks her head into the room. The people in the room gape at her; everyone realizes she couldn't possibly belong here; she ducks her head and leaves.

The diversity of Alan Miller's Advanced Placement Black Lit class is not reflected in his classroom tonight. Sitting at their children's desks are eleven white mothers, three of them accompanied by their husbands, two white fathers, two Asian couples, and one Asian mother: Lillian's. There are no black parents here to meet their children's Black Lit teacher—Autumn's mother, for one, has never yet set foot on the Berkeley High campus—but Mr. Miller is used to that by now.

"I'm a very opinionated person," he introduces himself to the parents. "Sometimes I'm just picking a fight, but I'm also teaching them to step up and meet a challenge. We're really lucky we have such significant arguments going on right here in Berkeley. This class will take a lot of those arguments on."

"Will you be reading any contemporary fiction?" a white mother asks.

"*Invisible Man, Betsey Brown, Song of Solomon, Black Boy, Their Eyes Are Watching God,*" Mr. Miller recites. "And Terry McMillan, before she started writing the trash that made her rich."

Even in the CAS room Amy Crawford and Dana Richards make their presentation to twenty-four white parents, two Asian mothers, one Latino man with a young boy in tow, and UC Berkeley professor Pedro

Noguera, whose son Joaquin is a CAS senior. Jordan's mom, who normally attends every Berkeley High function, is out of town on a business trip.

"We talk a lot about making history," Dana tells the parents, "but we really feel we are doing that on a daily basis with this group." Amy, having traded in her T-shirt, sneakers, and scrubbed face for a long black skirt and red lipstick, nods as Dana speaks. "So many classes at Berkeley High do not have the kind of diversity and texture we have in this class," he tells the nearly all-white group.

In the last week of September Autumn finds a flyer on the floor of her Anatomy class, announcing the first meeting of a group called "Youth Together."

> Circle All Statements that Apply to You:
>
> - Wasted time in line trying to get your schedule
> - Don't know graduation or college requirements
> - Don't have access to the Internet at home
> - Sick and tired of being just another number at BHS?
>
> If one or more of these statements apply to you then you're already knowin' BHS needs serious change.

All of the above, Autumn thinks, and decides to check it out. After school she heads upstairs to the Student Learning Center, where she finds the meeting being led by Jamilah, Brittany, and Pam from Mr. Miller's class. Joaquin from CAS is there, too. They're talking about going to a Berkeley City Council meeting and getting the council to take a stand against the Juvenile Justice Initiative, a state ballot measure that could send kids to jail for life just for writing graffiti. Autumn has to work the night of the council meeting, but the next day Pam tells her they got the council to agree. Pam shows her an article she's written for the first issue of *Conscious Seed,* the Youth Together insert that's going into the next *Jacket.*

It's time that students and parents start making some changes, instead of sitting back and complaining. We have not succeeded in providing a service to the community until all of us are achieving. We must create a change and leave a legacy on Berkeley that will be remembered.

"That's *deep*," Autumn tells Pam.

"You should come to the next meeting," Pam responds. "Help us put out the next *Seed*."

"I'll try," Autumn says, thinking as she says it: *One more thing to feel bad about. One more thing I can't find time for in my life.*

October 1999: Bling, Bling

Lunch is over—Keith can tell by the kids running past him and his friends on the Slopes. His friends are in no hurry to get to class, but Keith's getting his senior pictures taken at 12:30, so he has to get out the gate before they lock it at noon. "How do I look?" Keith asks before he goes. The boys check him out—his hair sectioned and coiled into tiny twisties, his arm muscles bulging through his skimpy white undershirt, his new gold necklace glistening against his neck, the gold grill (removable gold tooth covers) he bought for the photo session gleaming in his mouth.

"You flossin'," Dimitri says approvingly. "Bling, bling," John agrees. "You showin' you hard, wearing all that gold to school," Dominic adds. "You showin' you won't let no one take it from you."

Satisfied, Keith saunters off the Slopes and onto Milvia Street, where he runs into Jamal and Bo. Bo shakes a pair of dice invitingly at Keith. "Naw, man," Keith shakes his head. The last time his mom found money in his room, before he had the job at Burger King, she went off on him, crying and yelling about her baby dealing drugs. He couldn't stand to see her like that, so he told her the truth: he'd been shooting dice at lunch once in awhile, just to keep some change in his pocket. She kept crying until he swore he'd never gamble again. Keith meant to keep his promise, but when Bo and Jamal duck into an alleyway between two apartment buildings a block from Berkeley High, he goes with them.

They've only been in the alley a minute or two when Keith hears someone shout, "Okay, guys—break it up!" He sees two white cops standing at one end of the alley. He sees Jamal and Bo run the other way, hit the fence, scale it, and keep running. "Whatever you do, Keith, *never* run from the police," he hears his mom saying. So Keith stands still.

"We was just shootin' dice," he tells the cops as they approach him. The bigger cop puts one hand on Keith's shoulder, reaches for his handcuffs with the other. Keith panics. "I ain't goin' to jail for shootin' *dice!*" He takes off running. He doesn't get far. The cops grab him from behind, throw him up against the fence. "Spread em!" they yell, pushing his legs apart with their clubs, mashing his face into the metal. The cops handcuff him, jam his wrists up behind his back, knee him in the backs of his legs.

"Ow!" Keith screams in pain. The cops twist his wrists up higher. "You crazy motherfuckers!" he starts to curse. "Why you doin' this to me?" The cops throw him to the ground face down, hog-tie his ankles and start kicking him in the back. Not just two cops now, but a bunch of them, all of them white. "Fuck you!" Keith shouts. "Get off me!" The more Keith curses, the harder they kick him. They wrestle him into a body bag. A cop holds Keith's mouth open, pulls out his gold teeth. They throw him into a van.

When they get to the police station four blocks away, the cops carry Keith inside and dump him, still hog-tied, onto the floor. "Keith!" the black desk cop says, looking down at him. "What happened?" Keith recognizes Officer Jones from the Twilight Basketball League he used to play in. "What's this about?" Jones asks the white cops. "Gambling," one of them answers.

"Gambling? All this for *gambling?*" Jones cuts Keith loose, takes him into an office, asks Keith who he should call. "My grandma," Keith says, and gives Officer Jones her number. He doesn't want to bother his mom on her new job. He doesn't want his mom to know about this at all.

Officer Jones goes away, comes back. "Your grandma's on her way," he says. "The charges are gambling, trespassing, resisting arrest, and assault on a police officer. That's what the arresting officers say you did, so that's what you're being charged with. I'm going to read you your rights now. Ever had cause to hear them before?" Keith shakes his head. He's been stopped a few times, hassled a few times, but he's never been arrested. "I didn't think so," Officer Jones says. "Well. You have the right to remain silent . . ."

Keith's grandma takes him to her house in West Berkeley. Keith's mother shows up right after work. "You told me you were *never* gonna gamble again!" she yells. "Now look how you gone and messed up your life! And just when you were all set to go to college!"

"I know I got a gambling problem, Mom," Keith says. "But it can be fixed."

"It might be too late to fix it! You think you gon' get a college scholarship with a po-lice record? Do I need to quit my job and keep running down to Berkeley High to keep track of you like I used to?"

"Patricia . . ." Keith's grandma says. "The boy is hurt."

Patricia peers at her son. "They kicked me in my back *hella* hard," Keith says. "And I don't even know how *this* happened." He holds up his right hand, cut and crusted with dried blood.

"We're goin' to the hospital right now," Patricia says, snatching up her keys. A few minutes later she deposits Keith in the emergency room at Kaiser Hospital in Richmond, where she works the day shift as a nurse's aid. "I been in this place eight hours today already," she tells her son. "You got your cell phone?" Keith nods. "Call me when you ready to come home."

"Nothin' broken," Keith reports when Patricia picks him up several hours later. As they're walking to her Saturn, Patricia says, "Now I'm even madder at the police than I am at you. A PE teacher from Berkeley High called me just now. She saw the whole thing. The kids in her class did, too. She says she'll testify for us if we sue. Which we are most definitely going to do. Our lawyer is looking for another case like the last one." Two years ago, when Keith's older brother Kenneth was tear-gassed and beaten by police in the melee that followed an Oakland street festival, a well-known local African-American civil rights lawyer won them a $40,000 settlement.

"I did something stupid," Keith says. "I shouldn't of been gambling. But the po-lice shouldn't of jacked me like that."

"Yes you *did* do something stupid," his mom replies. "And trust me on this: they *will* be sorry that they did you like that."

When Keith shows up at second period the next day, his teacher sends him to the vice principal's office. Ms. Wallace-Tanner tells him he's suspended for three days "pending investigation of your arrest." Keith tries to talk her out of it, even though he knows he might as well argue with his shoes. Like his mom says, "Ms. Wallace-Tanner don't take no mess."

"Berkeley High has a new reciprocal agreement with the police," Ms. Wallace-Tanner tells him. "Any student who is arrested is automatically suspended."

"You know my mom gon' be down here in a quick minute," Keith warns her.

Ms. Wallace-Tanner nods calmly. "I'll speak to your mother later today." She hands him a pass to leave the campus. "Remember, Keith: you'll be expelled if you're seen on campus before Tuesday."

"But I got practice every day after school!" Keith protests. The season's just getting started, and already Coach is steadily riding his ass. Coach didn't even seem to care that Keith's 78-yard touchdown was just mentioned in a *San Francisco Examiner* story about Berkeley High's first win of the year: "If I hadn't of done that our team would have been down," the story quoted Keith as saying. "Returning kickoffs is something that's always in my mind because I'm competitive like that. I don't even have to think about it, I just do it." Keith and Coach are like oil and water. Missing practice isn't about to help.

"Your coach will be informed of your suspension," Ms. Wallace-Tanner says, and escorts Keith to the door.

. . .

While Keith is on his way home on BART, Autumn, Jordan, and twenty-six other CAS seniors are on a bright yellow school bus, bound for a two-day CAS retreat at a youth hostel overlooking the ocean in Marin County. Rap blares from a boom box in the back of the bus, where most of the African-American students are sitting, seemingly oblivious to the symbolism. Several girls are standing up on their seats, singing and dancing to the music, until the bus driver asks the teachers to make them sit down and turn it down. "We're gonna take turns with the music," Dana Richards announces from the front. "We'll have one kind till we're halfway there. Then we'll switch."

"Can we have Jewish music?" a white girl named Sarah calls from the middle of the bus.

"You guys work it out," Amy Crawford answers, swigging on her bottle of Rooty Fruity, the organic smoothie she drinks in class every morning.

All of the black and biracial kids, some of the white kids, and none of the Latinas rap along to "Back That Ass Up," a detailed, graphic tribute to anal sex. "Can you imagine what Maria's dad would say if he heard them singing *this?*" Mr. Richards whispers to Ms. Crawford, who rolls her eyes in response. A few of the Latinas' fathers needed some convincing before they allowed their daughters to go off overnight in a group that included boys. Ms. Crawford grits her teeth through a few more rap cuts played at full volume, then kneels backward on her seat to face her students. "Please," she begs them, "can you play something that's not *quite* so misogynistic?"

Someone stops the rap and puts on Bob Marley. "Thank you," Ms. Crawford says as the lilting strains of reggae fill the bus. Rap is popular across bounds of race and class, but reggae—even Marley—appeals mostly to middle-class white and biracial kids. There aren't many middle-class kids of color at Berkeley High; their parents tend to send them to Catholic or private schools. So it's not surprising that most of the white and biracial kids, none of the Latinas, and only a couple of the black kids sing along to Marley's "Redemption Song."

"Public education is so big and impersonal," Mr. Richards declares after the kids have thrown their sleeping bags into the one big room they'll share tonight and gathered in a huge circle on the hostel lawn. The white, Latino, and biracial kids sprawl on the grass; most of the African-American kids are standing. "This is a chance to do something one on one."

"We need you to pair up," says Ms. Crawford. "Find a partner. Someone who moves you out of your comfort zone."

"A partner, not a patna," Mr. Richards clarifies, and the kids nod at his acknowledgment of their word—one of many ghetto expressions that have become youth expressions—for "friend."

"Then go for a walk. The ocean is that way." Ms. Crawford points west. "The woods and the mountains are all around you. Find a spot where you feel good. Sit there for twenty or thirty minutes and write in your journal about your strengths, your gifts. Then write down three weaknesses and how you're going to work through them this year in CAS. Everyone be back here at 4:00 to share your journals and start making dinner. Okay?"

There are nods and murmurs of assent. "Before you go . . . let's see if I can find a good way to talk about this," Mr. Richards says, grinning. "Umm . . . rules . . . drugs . . . sex . . ."

"Nuff said," Jordan interrupts him. All the kids and both teachers laugh. The kids do, in fact, find "partners, not patnas": Jordan tromps off into the woods with Darnell; Autumn heads for the hills with a white boy named Steve.

At 4:00 the kids are still scattered. At 4:30 only a few students, including Jordan and Autumn and their partners, are back. The teachers are in a huddle, talking strategy. As usual, Ms. Crawford is the one advocating discipline; Mr. Richards plays "good cop." "Should we try to round them up?" Ms. Crawford asks. "We did say 4:00. We can't start out like this. I want them to connect with each other, but they have to understand there are rules."

"If they break the agreement, dinner's late," Mr. Richards says. "Hunger's a great teacher."

"I guess," Ms. Crawford agrees reluctantly. The teachers join the ten kids in the circle. "Anyone want to share your writing while we're waiting?" Ms. Crawford asks.

Jordan pulls out his notebook and starts to read. "Inevitably my father pops into my head when I do an activity like this one. Memories and lost hope are the main thoughts, flanked by the rare and vivid dreams I've had about the two of us.

"The first one came a few weeks after his death. He walked up and told me that he was all right, but his face looked sad. I tried to ask him questions but he didn't respond, as if he couldn't hear me. He started to walk away and I woke up in my bed, tears rolling down my cheeks. I still believe that even through all of the drama that we had together, I would rather have had him for the sixteen years that I did than anyone else for more time with less shit to deal with."

The group is hushed and still. Then Mr. Richards crawls across the circle and throws his arms around Jordan. The two of them embrace for a long moment, their heads buried in each other's shoulders.

"Mario?" Ms. Crawford prods gently as Mr. Richards returns to his place. "Would you like to share?"

"I'm not following Jordan!" Mario exclaims. Everyone, including Jordan, laughs.

"Hey! What about dinner?" Autumn asks.

"We said be back by four," Ms. Crawford answers. "So, whatever . . ."

Autumn jumps to her feet. "Ex*cuse* me? What*ever*? I'm hungry! I'm going to go get done what needs to be done! Who's coming with me?" She gathers a few recruits; they stride off toward the hostel kitchen.

After dinner—bags of premixed salad, garlic bread, and a choice of vegetarian or sausage frozen lasagna, all purchased by one of the CAS hills moms, who also procured a free garbage bag full of day-old pastries from Berkeley's most upscale bakery—thirty kids and teachers form a circle in the hostel living room and settle in for the retreat's main event. The kids sink into overstuffed couches, squeeze in pairs into easy chairs meant for one, stretch out on pillows tossed onto the floor. Many of the girls play with each other's hair, feet and heads nestled in each other's laps. "Bring a cultural artifact to share," Mr. Richards had instructed the class a few days ago. "Something that reflects your background."

Immediately an African-American girl's hand shot up. "Does it have to be from our parents' culture?" she asked. "Or can it be from our own?"

"Your own," Mr. Richards answered.

"Why do we have to do that?" another girl asked. "So we can bond with each other," Mr. Richards answered. "Don't trip," Joaquin leaned over and whispered to the girl. "You can just pick up a rock or something when you get there."

"Catherine—will you start?" asks Ms. Crawford. A pretty girl with a café-au-lait complexion holds up a wooden statuette. "This is a carving from Ghana,' she says. "My mother is white. I never got to know my African-American culture. Having this in my house reminds me of that part of myself." Her classmates begin to applaud; Catherine holds up her hand. "Don't clap, y'all. I'm trying to share myself with you guys here." The students snap their fingers in the air approvingly instead. "Oh—and my mom doesn't know I took it," Catherine adds. "So don't step on it, okay?" She nods at the Latino boy sitting on the floor at her feet.

"Most of you don't know me," says Luis, who astonished the group before dinner, playing brilliant Mozart on the hostel piano. "This is my first year in Berkeley and my first year in CAS. I brought this sheet music because it's just like me. It looks easy, but it's almost impossible to play. Like this music, once people know how to read me, they see what's in me."

The students listen attentively, their faces soft and open. "Music is my one true passion. It's kept me going through everything I've been through. I'm quiet in all my classes because I don't know anybody. But I hope you'll try to read me." Ms. Crawford and Mr. Richards exchange a pained look. They and only they know that Luis's mother left the house one day when he was twelve and never came back. He's been living in foster care and with relatives in different states ever since.

Luis turns to Malik, a tall, baby-faced boy with an Afro pick sticking out of his hair and a huge boom box in his lap. "This box is like my damn son," Malik says ardently. "Malik Junior and I have been through a lot together." He bends over and kisses the boom box. His classmates nod seriously. "Next," Malik orders, shifting the group's attention.

"This belt buckle is the only thing I have of my dad," says Maria, who's scrunched into a love seat with two other Latina girls. "My mom burned all the pictures."

Ms. Crawford holds up a framed letter and a brooch. "A letter from my great-aunt to my mother. And a brooch that was made by her great-great-aunt."

"My teddy bear," says Elizabeth, a blonde girl in a red T-shirt and tight bell-bottom jeans, clutching a worn brown bear to her chest. "I slept with him every day of my life, until last year. When my friend Gabe got his bone marrow transplant I loaned it to him. He kept it until he died. Today's Gabe's birthday, by the way." Elizabeth's best friend Susi puts her arm around Elizabeth's shoulder; across the room, Elizabeth's identical twin sister Jessica watches intently.

If the magnitude of these revelations, the enormity of the issues these teenagers are dealing with is surprising to anyone in this room, that is not evident in their responses. Only Autumn acknowledges her emotion. "Every time someone talks I want to cry," she says. "I'm going to try to say this without breaking down. Even though I don't know everyone here, I can relate to everything people said.

"The ring I'm wearing was given to me by this boyfriend I hate now. I keep it because it's three dolphins and their tails become one. I love dolphins—they're free, friendly, sleek, and long. The ring makes me think of me and my two best friends, Lillian and Lauren. In the last seven months we've all become really close. We've formed a special bond that no one could ever take away from me. The things I've learned from them I'll pass on to my kids.

"I'm hearing a lot of people talk about their family. Well, Lillian and Lauren are the most important ones to me. I don't know who I'd be if I didn't have them to love and do nice things for. So if you see me walking down the hall with them, give them a smile. Because those are my girls!" Autumn beams at the group, then gestures to Jordan, who's sitting on the next couch with Steve and Finnegan.

"I wear three rings," Jordan says, holding up his hands. "One is my dad's wedding band with his name and my mom's name engraved on it. One is a design my dad made twenty years ago. The third one I got from one of my best friends, a girl who's always been there for me. I wear them to keep these people close to me." He turns to face Ms. Crawford and Mr. Richards. "It's cool that you guys are down with this," he tells them. "I like to know teachers are people too. It's like we're all equals."

"This day was damn near the shit for me," Malik agrees. He has to shout to be heard above the roar of the Blue Angels, the Navy fighter jets that put on an air show over San Francisco Bay each October and have been noisily soaring overhead all day.

"Why don't they have one less Blue Angel and make Berkeley High right?" a boy named David asks.

"They could just take a wing, and CAS could be funded forever," Mr. Richards responds.

Three hours after it began, the sharing ritual ends—with fifteen pints of Ben & Jerry's donated by a friend of the CAS program. "That was *too deep* for high school," Autumn says, licking cookie dough ice cream off her spoon.

"Welcome to *high* school," Mr. Richards replies.

"Look inside a high school," reads the introduction to a special issue of *Time* published two weeks after the CAS retreat, "and you are looking in a mirror, under bright lights. How we treat our children, what they see and learn from us, tell us what is healthy and what is sick—and more about who we are than we may want to know."

Mortified by what they see, shaken to their collective core by Columbine, Americans are clamoring for change. "The debates over what policies we need to adopt to fix our schools are heating up in Washington and in state capitals from Sacramento to Madison to Tallahassee," writes Maureen Steinbruner, director of Washington's Center for National Policy in a *San Francisco Chronicle* editorial. "[Parents] ranked safety, discipline and organized activities high on the list of priorities . . . [in opposition to] elected officials and business leaders [who] are concerned about public schools' ability to prepare children for the challenges of a fast-paced, highly complex global society. . . . Their prescriptions for school improvement run the gamut from ending social promotion, to more authority for principals, to longer school days and school years, to wiring all classrooms for Internet access."

In the *New York Times Magazine* James Traub writes, "Nobody believes in school the way Americans do, and no one is more tantalized by its transformative powers. School is central to the American myth of self-transcendence, whether it's Thomas Jefferson's seedbed of the republican spirit, or the one-room schoolhouse that propelled Abe Lincoln out of frontier backwardness . . ."

In the name of school reform, potential remedies such as charter schools, the privatization of public schools, vouchers for private schools, graduation exams, and "small schools" like CAS are being invented, implemented, and analyzed. Books and research studies are being compiled and published, politicians elected and defeated, grants funded, bake sales held—all so that our schools might accomplish what *The Students Are Watching* calls high school's "three core tasks: to prepare young people for the world of work; to prepare them to use their minds well . . . and to prepare them to be thoughtful citizens and decent human beings."

At Berkeley High at the turn of the millennium, the reform process manifests not only in the day-to-day do-si-do of teachers, students, parents, and community coaxing and demanding more, better, *now* from each other—but also in two entities that are simultaneously offering Berkeley High its redemption, and challenging its existence.

One is the UC Berkeley-sponsored, foundation-funded Diversity Project, a four-year study of Berkeley High launched when the class of 2000 entered the school in 1996. "We felt *all* kids should be able to get a good education here," DP cofounder (and father of CAS student Joaquin)

Pedro Noguera explains to the twenty Berkeley High teachers who turn out for the project's October meeting, called to kick off its final year. "Our goal is to transform this school, to make the community feel better about this school."

Besides producing volumes of chilling data that render undeniable Berkeley High's "dirty little secret"—the failure rates of the school's black and Latino students—the Diversity Project has also helped to create some programs to address it. DP committees on English as a second language, discipline, and parent organizing engendered the Student Learning Center, where kids like Keith can (and do, whether they want to or not) get free tutoring from UC Berkeley grad students before, during, and after school; and the Parent Resource Center, designed to make the school more welcoming and manageable for parents of color. "Taking on the issue of equity is never easy," Pedro tells the teachers as they munch on carrot sticks and cookies, "but we've been persistent in keeping the issues on the table."

If the Diversity Project is, as its published report claims, "like the rock that lands in the middle of the pond, disrupting and transforming the scenery with its ripples," then WASC—the Western Association of Schools and Colleges, the auditing agency that grants or denies schools' accreditation—is a boulder poised to leave a crater where Berkeley High now stands.

The WASC auditors last came to Berkeley High in May of 1999. When they left, the school had been granted a two-year accreditation instead of the standard six-year term, and issued a clear warning. If Berkeley High fails to solve key problems, and soon, its accreditation will be revoked, its diploma rendered meaningless. "If this was Fremont High," says Rick Ayers, referring to one of Oakland's ghetto schools, "we'd have gotten six years. But because we've got low-achieving kids of color in the same building with high-achieving white kids, WASC says, 'What the hell are you doing?' We have a horrible equity problem at the school. WASC is where it bleeds."

Sure enough, "Achievement Disparity" tops the WASC list, followed by "School-Wide Safety," "Planning and Decision Making," "Attendance and Discipline," "School-Wide Communication," "Tracking," "Technology," and "Staff Development." In response to the audit, every Berkeley High teacher has been assigned to a work group, each group focused on one of the WASC-identified issues. Sitting in their students' seats in eight C building classrooms every Wednesday from 3:30 to 5:00, the teachers drink their lattés and struggle to solve the problems that currently wrack high schools across the country.

"Politicians and reformers can talk all they want about standards and vouchers and academic performance," the *Time* cover story comments, "but the people on the front lines worry about a lot more than test scores . . . Is it worth renouncing homework if it keeps struggling kids in school? . . . Is it worth busing 161 black kids in from St. Louis if parents and some teachers quietly argue that because of busing, overall achievement has fallen? . . . Is it worth turning the principal and her deputies into sentries, equipped at all times not with books or rulers but with walkie-talkies if it keeps the lid from blowing off?"

On the front lines indeed, the Berkeley High teachers are now charged with deciding whether they should solve the attendance problem by dropping kids who cut class, and if so, how many cuts; or by making the curriculum more engaging, and if so how, and to which kids; or by breaking Berkeley High up into several smaller schools more capable of maintaining accountability on all ends?

Should they solve the tracking problem by testing students regularly to allow for movement up or down; or by eliminating Advanced Placement classes or the eligibility test for AP classes; or by "letting students pick their own tracking groups with people they get along with," as one teacher suggested in a meeting of the WASC Committee on the Achievement Disparity? And to solve that disparity, should Berkeley High expand its mentoring and tutorial services? Or reduce the size of its classes? Or hire reading specialists, or create "back-up" English classes? And if so, from where might the necessary funding come?

"WASC is the single biggest problem we face, and the achievement disparity is the biggest issue for WASC," Principal Saunders reports to the 150 parents—herself and six parents the only people of color—

assembled in the school library for the year's first meeting of the PTSA, Berkeley High's student-inclusive version of the traditional PTA.

"The auditors don't want dialogue. They want action. There's no maybe about this. If we don't do the work they could take our accreditation away."

"Is it my imagination," a white father asks, "or is the high school being held accountable for discrepancies that started in kindergarten?"

"The short answer is 'yes,'" Saunders says. "I don't mean to dump on you people, but you let this happen a long time. Now we're saying that this school does not work—for kids, for teachers, for parents, for the community. Is that the fault of the children? No! It's the fault of the adults who know to do and don't do. There's not a teacher on this staff who doesn't know what it takes to help children learn. It's not about knowledge. It's about having the will to do."

"Maybe we should focus more on the successful kids," another white man says, "and not focus so much on the others."

"I'm looking at fifty ninth-graders who can't read," Saunders replies evenly. "It's my job to see that in the four years I have those children I give them the best education I can. I feel a moral obligation to do that.

"If a kid can't read or write, the truth is, he's going to eat, sleep, wear, and drive something. How he does that is a question. I'm not saying they're all going to be criminals, but this much is guaranteed"—her dark eyes are flinty against her bittersweet chocolate skin as she turns them on one, then another of these affluent white parents—"every one of them is going to eat, sleep, wear and drive something." She pauses, lets the words sink in.

"I'd rather be on the helping side than the victim side. Wouldn't you?"

Saunders doesn't wait for an answer. "Understand this," she concludes. "I know what I believe. I stand for what I believe. And I tell you honestly: what we are trying to do here is rebuild a high school from the ground up."

"Educational inequality is rooted in economic problems and social pathologies too deep to be overcome by schools alone," asserts *New York Times Magazine* writer James Traub. Indeed, it seems unlikely that some

Berkeley High students, like Keith, will be able to "believe, achieve, succeed" until the school—or society, perhaps—is rebuilt. Some, like Jordan, will do just fine (academically, at least) whether the school is rebuilt or not, because it operates to meet the needs (the academic needs, at least) of kids like him. Others, like Autumn, will transcend the fate that was bequeathed to them and "go get done what needs to be done" regardless.

"On this question—whether you're the first in your family to go to college," Autumn asks the UC Berkeley recruiter who's leading an application workshop in the Berkeley High library. Autumn points to a line in the fifty-page UCB application. "What if you don't know your dad so you don't know if he went to college?"

"Just say you don't know," the recruiter answers.

"Where it says 'father,' " Autumn points to another line, "is that where you'd put 'stepfather'? "

"It's whoever claims you."

"What if no one claims you?"

"This form isn't really geared for the kinds of family structures we see today," the recruiter answers with a shrug, and calls on the next student. There are fifty-three aspiring UC Berkeley students in the room: twenty-five white kids, eighteen Asian kids, five Latinos, three African-Americans, Autumn, and Daveed Diggs, Autumn's biracial "other half." Last year Berkeley High sent thirty-two graduates to UC Berkeley, the flagship campus of the University of California system. Three of them were African-American.

"Are there any advantages to applying on-line?" an Asian girl asks.

"No. But if you do have E-mail you might want to indicate that. If we have a quick question for you, it might speed up the process." Autumn, who does not, smiles the unhappy smile she calls "lookin' silly to keep from crying."

"How many students apply and how many get in?" a Latino boy asks.

"Last year we got 31,000 applications and accepted 8,400."

"No more affirmative action, right?" Autumn asks.

The recruiter, a young Latino man, nods ruefully. "Right."

"But if you have a 4.0 . . ." a white boy begins.

"We turn away hundreds of kids with a 4.0," the recruiter says. "That's why we encourage you to take AP classes, to have a full extra-curricular load, to do community service, and to put all of that into your two-page college essay."

"They need to reevaluate their whole system!" Autumn declares to no one in particular as the meeting is adjourned. "Put my life down in two pages? I could write a novel 'bout my life and still be leavin' out most of it. I ain't gon' beg nobody to go to they school! I'm Autumn! Why don't they just let me in?"

There is an answer to Autumn's question, and it is Proposition 209. In 1996, after a heated, divisive campaign that sparked national contro-versy, Californians passed Prop 209, thereby abolishing affirmative ac-tion throughout the prestigious UC system. The impact was immediate and dramatic. The number of African-American entrants to Berkeley, the top UC school, was cut in half—from 7 percent in 1997 (the last year minorities were admitted under affirmative action) to 3.5 percent in 1999. Admissions of "underrepresented" (non-Asian) minorities were reduced from 20 percent to 13.6 percent.

"If they don't take me, that's on *them,*" Autumn says, zipping up her backpack, grinning that same unhappy grin. "I'm gonna get mine some-how because I have to."

The teachers get theirs somehow, too. In early October, a petition is circulated and quickly signed by 115 of them, demanding "the tools we need as professionals in order to perform our jobs": repair of the still-dysfunctional bells and clocks and replacement of the school's iffy-at-best copy machines. Although the petition doesn't mention it, everyone knows that there's a move afoot to boycott staff and WASC meetings until the teachers' demands are met. The petition is handed to Theresa Saunders, with copies sent to all school board members. Within weeks the bells are working, some broken clocks have been repaired and others have been inventoried for replacement, and Saunders has written a memo promising to buy two new copy machines and make them available to teachers.

"The petition drive was successful," says union vice president Alan Miller. "We got lots of signatures, many teachers said they'd be willing to boycott staff meetings, and it looks like Theresa's making an effort to fix things.

"Still, it took too damn long and it took too much effort on our part. We're talking about things basic to the functioning of the school. If teachers can't use copiers to supplement their curriculum, we can't do interesting things spontaneously. If we don't have bells or clocks we can't hold kids accountable. Basic stuff! And it's the kids who lose the most when we don't have it."

"What's your story, Keith?" asks Officer Jamison. A young African-American woman in a short-cropped Afro, white linen shirt, and neatly pressed khakis, she faces Keith and Patricia across her tiny office in the Berkeley Police Department's Youth Services Division.

"Wrong place, wrong time," Keith answers. "I should of been somewhere else. I was with the wrong guys."

Jamison nods. "I did a check on you. You don't have a juvenile record, Keith. You'll be eighteen next month, You need to take from this experience what my mother used to call 'food for thought.' If the police come for you, don't run. Don't fight."

"I told him not to run," Patricia concurs. "He could have got shot."

"Most of the officers here know you, Keith, from Twilight Basketball," Officer Jamison continues, her tone conciliatory. "The officers who arrested you are new. They didn't recognize you.

"The most serious thing you did was resisting arrest. That's a felony. That could have sent you to Santa Rita. Next time this happens—and we hope it doesn't—just stand there. Don't run," she says, and stands up. "That's it. You're free to go."

Patricia and Keith stand, too. "Now I'm going over to Berkeley High and get his school record cleaned up," Patricia tells Jamison. "Because this boy is going to college. Either he's gonna get a football scholarship or he's gonna go some other way. Wherever they'll take him, that's where I'm gonna send him."

"You really want to get his juvenile record sealed when he turns eighteen," Jamison tells her.

"I'll do that. Because this young man is going somewhere," Patricia repeats.

Where Keith is going now is around the corner to the courthouse. Patricia leads him past the "Traffic" window to the one labeled "Criminal." Keith studies the sign; after several minutes his face creases into a frown. "I am *not* a criminal," he blurts.

"I'm only at this window because they won't know nothin' 'bout you at the Traffic window," his mother reassures him. "As soon as we leave here," she goes on, "I'm gonna reschedule our appointment with the lawyer. I've got to deal with those people at the school first. Even though I'm working now, they need to know they're still gonna see me when I need them to."

"I had a case number and charges," Doris Wallace-Tanner says when she looks up from her desk and sees Patricia and Keith in her doorway. "That's why I suspended him."

"The charges are dropped. I don't want this on his record," Patricia answers, taking a seat. The vice principal picks up her walkie-talkie, rubber-bands its cracked halves together, calls Barry Wiggan, and asks him to check on the disposition of Keith's case. "That's another thing— that Wiggins," Patricia grumbles. "I don't like him. Your staff doesn't like him. He shouldn't be here."

"No one likes him. But before he was here the teachers complained they didn't feel safe. Now they feel safe but they want us to get rid of him." Wallace-Tanner shrugs. "Six of one, half a dozen of the other." She stands up. "I'll call you as soon as I hear anything," she promises Patricia. She turns to Keith. "You need to get to class now, Keith. Ms. Russ tells me you're in trouble in English and World History. And your coach isn't too pleased with you either. He says you're off the team unless you stay out of trouble and start showing him some respect."

"We'll handle all that," Patricia says. "It's just all this mess with the police—it's got him feeling moody."

Keith's mood improves greatly the next day when he finds his picture—gold grill and diamond earrings flashing—in the *Oakland Tribune,* naming him one of four Athletes of the Week. Despite the constant arguments with his coach and all the pressure he's been under, he played a good game Friday night. Patricia reads him the caption over breakfast. "Stephens, a 5-foot-11, 175-pound running back and defensive back, played a big role in the Yellowjackets' 41–21 victory over Granada."

Relieved by the news that the police charges have been dropped, bolstered by the attention the *Tribune* story earns him in the halls—girls are jocking him even more than usual—Keith decides to go all out for the last Spirit Week of his high school career.

Perhaps the most unusual thing about Spirit Week at Berkeley High is how unusual it isn't. For one "Homecoming" week in October, in high schools everywhere, the pursuit of education bows to the pursuit of school spirit—here, with particular "Berzerkeley" flair and universal participation unrivaled by any other Berkeley High event.

Monday is the first-ever Superhero Day—an attempt at a new ritual that doesn't quite take. But Tuesday is Sixties-Seventies Day, a Berkeley High tradition. Nanoseconds after the lunch bell rings, "Play That Funky Music, White Boy" is blasting from the speakers on the Steps and three thousand white, black, Latino, and Asian kids and teachers in glittering headbands, Afro wigs, platform shoes, and skin-tight polyester are writhing to the beat together, singing along to every word. "Peace, Love and SOOOUULL" reads a black girl's picket sign; five boys, a perfectly composed multiracial replica of the Village People, lead the crowd in arm-miming to "Y-M-C-A."

Jordan is resplendent in a leather jacket and psychedelic-print shirt, both sporting the wide lapels of his parents' hippie heyday. Autumn, Lillian, and Emily are almost unrecognizable in their dark granny glasses, tie-died bell-bottoms, fringed fur jackets, and scarves corralling their Afro-puffed hair. And Keith—well, Keith is Superfly himself in his white wool fedora, white fur-trimmed ankle-length coat, white vest and pants, and black platform shoes. His arm is draped around the ultimate accessory: the bell-bottomed, bare-bellied body of CeCe, the first girl ever to play on the Berkeley High football team, her long, center-parted blonde hair blowing in the wind.

Student activities director Jamie Marantz has one tricky job to do this week: keep it fun and keep it safe. Experience has taught her how to ensure the former; past years' drunken fights, arrests, and hospitalizations have made her grimly determined to prevent the latter. So every time a chant breaks out—"Oh-Oh" from the Senior Steps, "Oh-One" the retort from the courtyard below—Ms. Marantz stops the music to break it up.

"Trouble starts every time that starts." Ms. Marantz nods at the seniors. "The reality is, they're white, they're privileged, they're seniors, they're in the center of the action. It's like they're saying, 'Here I am, hate me, throw something at me.' " She gestures toward the mostly black kids on the Bricks. "The black kids are on the periphery, as usual. After a while it just builds up in them: all that class and racial anger. Last year we had kids throwing bottles at the kids on the Steps." The chanting starts again; Ms. Marantz races to the speakers and changes the song again.

Greg Giglio, in a huge black Afro wig and shocking-pink acetate shirt, is laughing and dancing to "Brick House." Amy Crawford is dancing with Dana Richards, whose pile-lined sheepskin vest provokes the same comment from several students, who say they can't tell whether he's in costume or not. "What would it take," Ms. Crawford asks Mr. Richards, surveying the wildly creative costumes and high-spirited performances all around them, "to inspire this much brilliance in the classroom?" "That," he replies, "is the $64,000 question."

Alan Miller is at his desk, periodically observing the scene from his classroom overlooking the courtyard. This is his eighth Spirit Week; at this point he finds the goings-on amusing at best, distracting and dangerous at worst.

"Go back to class now, please," Ms. Marantz announces at 11:55. "You've all been great! Please clear the courtyard so we can do this again tomorrow." Amidst a few scattered boos, miraculously the students disappear into the buildings, leaving the resident seagulls to their daily post-lunchtime feast.

On Wednesday, Tropical Day, Keith outdoes himself, strutting around the courtyard wearing a yellow plastic pineapple in his hair, turquoise swim trunks, a white plastic lei, and the day's show-stopper: a Hawaiian-print bikini bra tied around his naked chest. "Go ahead—I'm secure enough in my manhood so I can dress up like a woman," he tells the steady stream of boys who come up to squeeze his "breasts" and the steady stream of admiring girls who take his photo with their disposable cameras. Meanwhile Lance, a gay African-American boy who is regularly tormented (by Keith and his friends, among others) for his unashamed effeminacy, has a rare moment in the sun: he is a finalist in the limbo contest, his schoolmates shouting his name just this once with admiration instead of contempt as he bends over backwards, clutching his ankles and slithering under the pole to the reggae beat of "96 Degrees in the Shade."

And then it is Friday, the grand finale: Spirit Day. Brightly colored, hand-lettered posters have appeared, taped to the courtyard bricks.

> ALCOHOL IS THE #1 DRUG PROBLEM
> AMONG YOUTH

> 2.6 MILLION TEENS DON'T KNOW THAT A
> PERSON CAN DIE FROM AN ALCOHOL OVERDOSE

> HIGH SCHOOL STUDENTS SPEND $6 MILLION
> ON ALCOHOL EACH YEAR

"We're just gonna try and keep a lid on it," says Walter, one of the school safety officers patrolling the campus at 7:30 a.m. "We're making 'em go to class but there ain't really no classes."

"The teachers were told to go home at noon," says Amy Crawford, wearing her red Berkeley High jacket and bright red lipstick. "Jamie

Marantz says they're gonna bring tons of cops in. Maybe they want us gone so they can impose martial law."

As she speaks, a van drives by on Milvia with "00 Rules!" and "Class of 2000!" painted all over it and CAS girls hanging out the sunroof, honking and yelling, "Oh-oh! Oh-oh!" Another car follows, but this time the kids are yelling, "Oh-one!" and then the students start arriving, almost all of them wearing their school colors: hair, faces, and torsos painted half red, half yellow; red shoes, yellow-and-red striped knee socks, red Berkeley High gym shorts, red-and-yellow Berkeley High T-shirts, each emblazoned with the appropriate graduating year. And suddenly the courtyard is a thronging mass of red and yellow, "00," "01," "02," and "03" signs waving, those dangerous chants erupting.

Barry Wiggan stands at the Milvia gate shouting over and over, "Young people! You must go to class or leave the campus! You may not hang!" Doris Wallace-Tanner is on the Slopes with her walkie-talkie, monitoring the safety monitors as they boom into bullhorns, "You must clear the courtyard! You must go to class!"

"We're hoping to keep things under control," Ms. Wallace-Tanner says. "We've got good support from the community and from Berkeley Police Youth Services. We've warned the local merchants and we've got undercover officers at every store—we know the kids give money to homeless people to buy alcohol for them. We don't want that happening today.

"The police got information to us on thirty kids who are known users of controlled substances. We called those kids' homes. Not one of the parents was surprised to hear from us. That was pretty telling." The walkie-talkie in her hand spits code. "We'll have the campus on lockdown all day. No lunch period. Anyone who leaves is *gone*. We've even got the A-hole closed off," she says, using the students' name for the hole in the fence near the A building, a kind of deer path through the chain link for latecomers and cutters.

Ms. Crawford and Mr. Richards have proclaimed the CAS room a "substance abuse–free zone" for Spirit Day, but they don't have many takers. The room is empty except for Mr. Richards, who's writing a fund-raising grant on the computer, and Ms. Crawford, who's helping a few CAS Latinas apply gold eyelashes and yellow jacket tattoos to each other's faces. "I wish we had some decent school colors," Amy mutters to Dana. "Maybe something in a nice pink and mauve."

Mr. Giglio's Computer Academy English class is a party. A boom box pounds out the rap song "702," kids eat Cool Ranch Doritos and drink Cokes and work together on Class of 2000 posters, stopping to beg for pens, glitter, paper, *anything*. "They cleaned me out first period," apologizes Mr. Giglio, looking fittingly goofy in a red knit cap, red shorts, and Berkeley High T-shirt.

"If they were this intent on schoolwork," he says, watching them diligently lettering their posters, "miracles could happen." When the bell rings he sends them off with the warning, "Be safe! Have fun!" Keith, in street clothes ("I had my picture taken more this week than I did in my whole life. I'm takin' a break"), counters, "Get drunk! Get hurt! Have fun!"

"Here's what we're going to do today: nothing," Mr. Miller tells his Black Lit class. "But we're going to do it in the classroom. No one can leave." He spends the period tutoring an African-American boy who's not in the AP class, while girls practice their Spirit Rally dance routines, boys take each other's pictures with disposable cameras, and Autumn tells Lillian and Emily about waking up her baby brother for school this morning. "He told me just like this," she says, " 'You interrupted my shut-eye.' " The three girls crack up. "He told me he hates me because I make him get up. Where's the love?" "Nowhere. He's five," Emily answers.

At 1:00 the rally opens with two African-American girls standing in the center of the gym facing each other, singing a cappella: "I believe the children are our future/teach them well and let them lead the way . . ."

As the girls sing, Barbara Mitchell, the newly appointed college counselor, moves through the crowd slipping packs of earplugs into each teacher's hand. And then suddenly it's clear why. The freshman dancers, in yellow Old Navy T-shirts and yellow rubber overalls, explode onto the gym floor to deafening rap music. In the stands the freshmen bellow the class cheer, and then the sophomores, then the juniors and the seniors—each chant more unintelligible, each dance more incredible than the one before, while the full-blast beats of Snoop Doggy Dog and "Like a Genie in a Bottle Baby" shake the gym walls.

Autumn, Lillian, and Emily scream "Oh-oh" until their voices are gone; Lauren, a sophomore, screams "Oh-two" at them from the next section. Jordan has no trouble sneaking his girlfriend, Kristen, a UC Berkeley freshman he met at a crew meet, into the gym: her face is painted half yellow, half red to match his. It's too loud for them to talk, but they're happy to be here together. With their conflicting crew schedules and separate social circles, they haven't seen much of each other lately.

The Class of 01 howls triumphantly when the senior tug-of-war team is disqualified for having too many nonregistered contestants on the floor—including Keith. "The football team did that!" he yells as teachers shoo him back to the stands. "Blame it on the football team!"

Nearly all of the dancers are African-American; all of the student government leaders at the mike are white. The homecoming queen and king from each class are crowned, all of them African-American; all of the student leaders holding signs directing the crowd to "SCREAM!" and "QUIET DOWN QUIET DOWN!" are white. As Principal Saunders and Barry Wiggan pace the gym nervously, seeming to be having no fun at all, and as the Berkeley Police amass their forces for the homecoming football game and dance to follow, all of the students of Berkeley High— a picture-perfect diverse group, as their foremothers and forefathers had decreed they would be—do together what Keith's sign urges them to do: "GO WILD!" They holler out their class cheers; they pound the bleachers to the beat of their class dance; they throw glitter at each other and blow noisemakers. And then, when Jamie Marantz tells them to go home, that is what they do. In the end only ten kids are suspended, one hospitalized, two arrested.

That evening the Berkeley High varsity football team—with two wins, one loss, and one tie for the season—beats Monte Vista in the homecoming game. It's an exciting two hours, made more so by the two touchdowns scored by #4, Keith Stephens, whose mother, sisters, brother, and four-year-old nephew cheer him on from the stands. Keith's father, his dreadlocks tucked inside the down jacket he wears against the cold October night, works the gate, as always; a soft touch, as always, for a kid with a good story and no ticket.

"Of course I did good," Keith says after the game. "See what happens when they finally give me the ball? I coulda done even more if they gave it to me more." He emerges from the locker room, having shed his red-and-yellow uniform for the outfit his mom bought him for the homecoming dance: a dark green denim Girbaud jacket and matching jeans. Along with his teammates he heads over to the gym.

This time the kids lined up for the homecoming dance—most of them African-American, as usual—expect to be searched, metal-detected, and ID-checked at the door, so they are more tolerant of the one-hour wait than they were at the Unity Dance last month. Barry Wiggan and his assistant, Billy Keys, run scanners over each student; Doris Wallace-Tanner patrols the doorway, keeping the students inside from agitating the students outside.

On the dance floor the kids are clustered in the center of the gym. The lights are dim, the $10 photo booth empty. As Keith and his friends negotiate with the DJ, the white school-board president watches from the sidelines. Summoned here in response to rumors that at the Unity Dance some of the dancers were "simulating intercourse," she peers through the darkness at a few kids slow-dancing butt to groin. "Why do they *do* that?" she wonders aloud.

When everyone who's allowed to be inside has been admitted and everyone who isn't (those without a ticket and/or school ID) has been swept out the Milvia gate by the Berkeley Police, a scene reminiscent of last month's "Unity Riot" starts to simmer. "Why you actin' like we don't even go here?" one of the fifty locked-out boys yells through the fence at the cops. "I want my five dollars back!" "You treatin' us like animals!"

Once again an angry crowd of teenage boys descends on Shattuck Avenue. But this time they find every street corner, every store, every bus stop guarded by Berkeley Police in cars, on foot, on bicycles. An hour later the crowd dissipates, the dance ends, and the kids go home.

November 1999: Stressing

College Essay

Jordan Etra

My father had an addictive personality, and it showed in whatever he did. I guess that's why I wasn't as surprised as I think an average eighth grader would be to discover a pharmaceutical and narcotics addiction.

I remember it hitting me, suddenly and hard, an epiphany of sorts. It was right before Christmas in '94 when I brought this up with my mother. She was standing on a ladder in the living room hanging Christmas lights. When I told her what I knew, she burst into tears and slumped to the floor where she stood. She told me through sobs that his problem was one of the main reasons for their divorce and that she had hoped I wouldn't find out until I was older. She was very supportive after that and agreed to help me deal in whatever way I decided to. I wanted to see a therapist and started considering confronting my father as an abstract possibility.

In the next few months, I grew closer to the therapist and felt more detached in school and with my social life. I wasn't sleeping at night and I was tired in class during the day. Dr.

Walrod helped me to get my courage up, in the early spring I decided that something had to be done, for my sake at least. I decided to bring the issue to my father. He was scheduled to visit in the coming weeks, so I made an appointment with Dr. Walrod and waited, hoping for the best and expecting something worse.

I was more scared than I can ever remember being, but I wanted to go through with the intervention. When we talked with Dr. Walrod I received a lot of promises and apologies, but I felt that nothing had changed. Sadly for both of us, I was correct.

He actually died in August of 1998, sadly bringing some closure to this chapter of my life and opening a new one without the worry of losing one of my most important role models, mentors, and friends. A father has a big job, and it is tough for even a strong support group to take up the slack that has been left behind.

This sadly forced me to mature far beyond my years and deal with problems that I wouldn't wish on anyone, much less on a young teenager. I was trying to be the parent in my relationship with my father and it really didn't work. Now that he has gone, I feel very at peace with my relationship with him and with the mistakes that he made in his life, but this has come after a lot of personal reflection and inner turmoil. I now know more about myself than I probably ever would have if I had a "normal" relationship with my father and I am glad for at least that. This has begun to prepare me for life on my own in ways that I probably can't even see yet.

"Can I get a copy of my transcript?" Jordan asks his counselor, Guillermo Barcenas. It's a month before UC applications are due, two months before the deadlines for private colleges. At Berkeley High, Jordan always says, you need to leave plenty of time for them to screw up and still not hurt you too badly.

"You're ahead of the game. That's great. What's your ID number?" Guillermo asks. He punches the number into his computer. "Jordan Etra. Hmm. There's a whole line missing from your transcript. That's been happening a lot lately. What are your SAT scores?"

"1,280. I'm taking them again."

"They're almost guaranteed to go up. Are you in a sport now?"

"Crew."

"We have a new college counselor, Barbara Mitchell. You should ask her about getting into UC Berkeley on early admissions for crew."

"I'm seeing a college counselor outside school. And I'm hoping to go to a private college. UC is actually my backup school."

"Well, then," Guillermo shrugs. "Just get your transcript corrected and give it to Ms. Mitchell with your applications when they're ready. She'll send them on. Your grades are good; your SATs are good. You should have no problem."

I better not have a problem, Jordan thinks as he leaves Guillermo's office. Between the $90-an-hour college consultant he's been going to since last summer—recommended by a crew team mom, Joanne is supposed to be the best in Berkeley—and his private SAT tutoring, he and his mom have already spent more than $1,500 of his inheritance making *sure* he doesn't have a problem.

On his way to lunch Jordan takes a quick detour, as he often does, past Memorial Grove. What used to be a patch of concrete behind the B building was turned into a sanctuary by some Computer Academy teachers and students last year, after five Berkeley High students died within a few weeks of each other. Two of them died in car accidents, two were killed in fights, and one was found floating in the bay. There are a couple of benches there now and some landscaping, and a boulder inscribed, "This Memorial Grove is dedicated to the students and staff of Berkeley High School who have passed away. May They Never Be Forgotten." The rock serves as a makeshift altar. Today, the Day of the Dead, someone's put a plate of Halloween cookies on it between a pair of votive candles. "I didn't really know any of the kids who died," Jordan says, "but I figure the memorial isn't just for them—it's for people who loved people who have died. That definitely includes me." Jordan bends to light the candles, thinking of his dad, then heads out the Milvia gate.

As Jordan crosses Shattuck he notices a gigantic plastic banner that's been hung across the top of an office building.

> ## JUST IN CASE THE ROCK STAR THING DOESN'T WORK OUT
> Kaplan: World Leaders in Test Preparation
> kaptest.com

Jordan frowns up at the sign. It's not that he didn't know college admissions would be just like everything else in this capitalistic society: "Money talks." It's just that recently he's had so much disgusting evidence of it. Some kids in CAS can barely afford to *take* the SAT test—forget prep classes or private counselors—and they're applying for fee waivers to cover their application fees. Meanwhile a lot of his friends' parents have spent thousands of dollars making sure that their kids get into Harvard and Yale and Columbia. Jordan hates how unfair the whole thing is, but doesn't know what he can do to change it. *Even if all the rich kids refused to go to private counselors, what good would it do?*

Except for last year, when his dad died, Jordan has always done well in school. The truth is, it's never been hard for him. He developed solid study habits early, going to small private schools in New York, and then, after the divorce, in the Bay Area. His classes were intimate enough, his teachers interested and interesting enough to keep him from slacking off too much, even when he got lazy or distracted. And with his mom being a computer consultant, he's always had the latest software, the coolest machines, the fastest Internet hook-ups. When he was at Head Royce he took all that stuff for granted. Not anymore. Now he sees what kids go through at Berkeley High trying to get time on the school's funky old computers. They're all in one room in the library, with all kinds of warning signs on the locked door.

Last year school started a month after his father died and Jordan's academics tanked, along with the rest of his life. He'd always heard people talking about kids "falling through the cracks" at Berkeley High— that was one of the reasons he'd had to talk his mom into letting him go there. And that's exactly what would have happened to him if it hadn't been for CAS. The teachers cut him all kinds of slack, and Mr. Ayers—with all those phone calls "just to check in" and Saturday night movies when Jordan felt like he'd go nuts if he didn't get out of the house—had probably saved his life.

Jordan explained all of that to Joanne, his private college counselor, at their first session last summer. Joanne suggested he apply to small, personal schools: Skidmore, Bard, Bates, Vassar, Hampshire. After this summer's East Coast tour and his meeting in early November with the Bard recruiter, Jordan has pretty much decided on Bard.

"Bard students get a fantastic amount of attention from their teachers," the recruiter tells the five seniors, all of them white, who meet with him in the Berkeley High college counseling office.

"How's your photography program?" Jordan asks. Since his dad's death he's been losing himself for hours in the darkroom he built in his basement—he poured the cement floor, installed the plumbing and wiring, built the fixtures himself. Jordan set up a computer room in the basement, too, where he scans his best shots into his PC, creates special effects in Photoshop, prints them out on his color printer, and E-mails them to his friends.

"It's excellent. And getting better." The recruiter smiles at Jordan. "One thing about Bard is, you can put together the program you want. We put a lot of emphasis on community service. The Hudson Valley is a fascinating area, dotted with small, struggling inner city communities. We're interested in dealing with poverty issues, racial issues—the kind you guys are familiar with."

Only at Berkeley High, Jordan thinks, *would a recruiter brag about his college being close to a ghetto.* "Bard is not a campus that's overly policed.

We don't want you to kill each other, but you have a lot of freedom to make your own thing happen. And it's not terribly competitive academically. If you want to float you can float at Bard. No one will be in your face."

Float. The word settles over Jordan like a warm quilt. He imagines himself floating at Bard: no pressure, no worries, three thousand miles from home. When he drives up to Joanne's home office in the hills the next Saturday, just after taking the SATs for the third time, he tells her he's made up his mind. "I think Bard's a wonderful choice for you, Jordan," Joanne says warmly. "We'll get you into a few other schools, too, just in case. But I'm sure there won't be any problem."

That again. Jordan thinks of the kids he knows who *will* have problems—are already having problems. In CAS he overheard Autumn, a girl he doesn't know well but has always respected, telling another girl that she hasn't been able to get an appointment with Ms. Mitchell. She was trying to get her application fees waived and didn't know how to do it. An idea comes to him. "I was wondering," Jordan asks Joanne, "if you'd ever consider seeing one of the, um, less affluent kids in my class. For free. Kind of like community service."

And that is how Autumn—who has been paying for her SAT tests and her application fees (plus two root canals) with her Applebee's earnings; whose mother reminds her often that she does not have a penny to contribute to Autumn's college education—is able to retain the services of a private college counselor.

Autumn Morris

Personal Statement

My apartment on 545 Sunnyview Drive was completely empty. In my mom and dad's bedroom my father layed on nothing but an exercise mat with one blanket. As we began to leave my mother forced me to go into the room and tell my father good-bye. I did not want to see my father looking so depressed and pathetic. "Bye dad," I called from the doorway to the room. "Come give me a hug," he asked faintly. His tight embrace was one of finality. "I'll see ya soon," I said. I looked deep into my father's tearful face as he replied, "No you won't." I did not know it then but he was right.

When my mother began working three jobs, I had to take on a tremendous amount of responsibility at home. I was now the woman of the house, which meant I had to keep it clean and watch after my younger brother everyday. I was ten going on fifteen. In order to help my mother be strong, I had to be strong. This meant covering up my pain, disappointment and heartache. At ten years old this was difficult to do.

As I entered high school life became harder. I found myself slipping into spurts of depression. This terrified me because I did not want to turn into my father. Now my family had grown with the addition of a stepfather and another younger brother. When it came to school I was expected to be perfect. My mother or stepfather had not attended college and knew nothing about what it took to get there. On my own I had to try to get information here and there. Attending a large high school such as Berkeley High where it is easy to slip through the cracks did not help either.

Junior year I overdid it. I was in several clubs, class president, attending a community college at night, and playing basketball. This eventually backfired and I found myself mentally, physically and spiritually tired. I felt that any chance for me going to a good college was out the door. I was trying so hard to live up to everyone's expectations and trying desperately to be everything my father was not. During my junior year I learned so much about Autumn, and I count this self knowledge as my greatest achievement thus far.

Although I have been through many trials I have found a strength and discipline within myself that along with my education and background give me full confidence that I will thrive in college. Beyond all the pressure my family and the rest of society puts on me as a woman of color, I have learned to set my own goals and standards. I no longer feel the need to try to make myself seem better than I am. I see some people trying to make themselves seem intellectual by using big words that do not even know the meaning of. I believe you do not need big words if you have big ideas because your thoughts will be evident if you are clear and precise.

I not only have been preparing myself academically but spiritually as well. I have joined my church's youth group where I am surrounded by people my own age who are trying their best to do what is right. I no longer have to doubt myself because my faith has empowered me to keep striving even when the times get hard.

I have learned to deal with my past and use my experiences as motivation. I see the future as a stage in which my generation will act out its role as an agent for change. My main goal is to be one of the stars in this production.

"Go home and ask your parents if they have some money hidden from you. If not, don't bother applying to a college in New York. You won't be heard from for four years because you won't have plane fare." Deirdre Johnson, the one longtime counselor who made it through the summer cutbacks, has been asked by the CAS teachers to get the students started on their applications. "Don't apply to Maine if you don't like cold. Or Texas if you don't like heat. You're Berkeley kids. You have that attitude—diversity and all that. But the rest of the world isn't like this. They won't accept you the way they do here."

"How do we make an appointment with the new college counselor?" Sarah asks.

"I don't know," Ms. Johnson answers flatly.

"How do you get a letter of recommendation from your counselor if you never met your counselor?" asks Finnegan.

"Wait on line and *get* to know them."

"I'm stressing hard over the essay," Autumn says. "Do you have any tips?"

"You guys are teenagers. You're fun. You're not stiff like an adult, so don't try to sound like one," Ms. Johnson replies. "I had a girl in my office yesterday who used to be an A student. Her mom got diagnosed with breast cancer last semester, so of course she got Ds and Fs. Everyone's got a sad story, but bottom line, how did it make you a stronger person?"

Autumn's only question is how much of her sad story to tell. Can she make college admissions officers understand, let alone value, the unmeasurable, untestable changes she went through last year, when her grades reflected her worst academic performance ever? Will college admissions officers forgive her first dip below a B average, in a lifetime of signing herself up for enrichment programs and pushing herself to win spelling bees and essay contests and pass AP admissions tests, if she explains the reasons for it? Or does she need to tell the deeper story: how depressed she was that year, living with a new stepfather whose morals were abhorrent to her—who didn't go to church and married her mother only after he'd gotten her pregnant? Does she need to explain how it broke her heart the day she stepped onto a city bus, sat down opposite a homeless man stinking of alcohol, mumbling incoherently, dressed in rags, and realized that she was staring into the blank, unseeing eyes of her father?

After struggling with her essay for months, Autumn takes it as a godsend when Jordan comes up to her in class, gives her the phone number of his private college counselor, and invites her to call and make a free appointment. "She'll see me for free? For real?" Autumn asks. Jordan nods, avoiding her eyes. Both of them are embarrassed; both of them are thrilled. Autumn asks Ms. Crawford if she can use the CAS phone.

"If it's about your internship," Ms. Crawford answers.

"It's about college," Autumn says, and Ms. Crawford tells her to go ahead. Autumn makes an appointment for the following Monday.

Joanne greets her at the door of her home in the Berkeley hills—a mansion, it seems to Autumn, with gardeners planting purple flowers in windowboxes and picture-postcard views of San Francisco from every room. Autumn arrives fifteen minutes early, her transcripts and essay drafts gathered in a plastic Gap bag. To her surprise Joanne doesn't even ask to see them. She spends the whole hour asking Autumn about her life, coaxing forth her wildest dreams like a fireman luring a cat down from a tree. *No one's ever listened to me talk about myself like this,* Autumn thinks. "What an amazing, accomplished young woman you are," Joanne says when the hour is up. "You should feel really proud of yourself." Autumn goes home feeling exactly that way, and writes her essay in two hours.

When Autumn shows it to her at their next appointment, Joanne beams. "This is great, Autumn! Perfect! Now—I researched scholarships, as I promised you I'd do. I haven't had much experience with financial aid, but I've gathered some information." Joanne leans forward, pushing aside the vase of flowers on her desk. "With your grades and community service record, and given how hungry the colleges are for diversity, I think you can get a scholarship at pretty much any school you'd like!"

"Even . . . Columbia?" Although she's always fantasized about going to Columbia, about living in New York City, Autumn never dared to say it out loud until Joanne insisted that she should "aim higher" than her top pick, UC Santa Cruz.

"Even Columbia. Or Brown. In fact, I'd say that UCSC should be your fallback school."

Autumn glows, walking down the hill to the bus stop. She glows, riding the bus to the BART station. She glows on the train to Alameda, imagining Lillian and Lauren's excitement when she tells them the good news. But then she walks into her apartment. Hears Michael and Ra-Shawn fighting. Sees Skittles wrappers and dirty clothes strewn all over the floor. And feels like the worst kind of fool.

What was I thinking? I can't go to Columbia! Who's gonna look after these boys, keep them off the streets, make sure they get into all those after-school programs I got myself into, if I'm three thousand miles away? "Turn that TV down!" she snaps at her brothers. *No one, that's who.*

What's kept Autumn sane this far is a delicate balance of aspiration: believing in the dreams she knows she *can* achieve, even if she doesn't know exactly how, and not allowing herself to be defeated by dreams that are just plain unreachable. She sees now that going to Columbia, living in New York City for four years, belongs in the latter category. The next time Autumn takes the bus up into the hills, she tells Joanne she's decided to apply to UCSC only. Joanne tries to argue her out of it, but Autumn stands firm. "No offense," she tells Joanne, "but I'm not sure you can understand why for me, for someone from my family, going to college at all is a really great accomplishment."

Keith Stephen

College Essay

The most significant Experience I had was personal training camp with my uncle, Ronnie Lott. As a child I played pop warner football, but it seemed to effect my grades in school. In the second grade I was considered slow by my teacher because I wouldn't do work or even function in class. I wasn't even expected to graduate from the third grade on time. When my mom got my second grade report card, she demanded a conference with my teacher and the princible. When my mom got home she told me that her and Ms Johnson came to an agreement that every time I was to slack off in class, I would have to spend a night in training camp. I thought to myself, is this a joke because football camp with NFL players was the best thing that could happen to a kid. I was very excited, well at least until I found out the camp was ran by my uncle Ronnie Lott, starting safty for the San Fransico 49ers. He was a son of a gun and you could tell by the way he played football.

I never remember being so scared before in my life. I still can remember the felling I felt when the doorbell rang and my mother opened it. But in my mind I was thinking, never have I seen a man so big and strong standing in the doorway. He gave me a hard look for a minute then said lets go. My name never sounded so powerful until I heard it from his mouth. Are you ready" he asked, Yeah" I replied trying to have bass in my voice like him. I felt afraid walking to the car with him, and He noticed it because he said "loosen up, It will be fun".

Arriving at the camp I saw heaven. NFL players playing football with kids and all types of play structures filled with children. As soon as he parked I ran out the car and ran towards the football field. Right when I got 10 feet with in the football field I heard him yell "Hey, why are you running to the field. That field is for kids with good grades only. Do you have good grades?" he asked knowing I didn't. "No" I said feeling bad about myself. "Where this is where kids with bad go. He pointed at a little cabin with 1 window. You are not to leave this room until it's time for you to go to school Which was the next morning. "I'll leave you and your bed alone know".

He left and locked the door on the way out showing that he meant business. I looked out the window and saw all my favorites Joe Montana, Jerry Rice, Kenny Norton and of course my so-called uncle Ronnie Lott who locked me in a cabin like a slave. When morning came he opened the door and said "You Know, there was a point to why you had to spend the night in this cabin. This summer your going to spend a month a this camp and your grades will determine weather or not your in the cabin or on the field" From those words on I've never had trouble in school again, until he died in 95.

"About your college essay, Keith," Mr. Giglio says, stopping beside Keith's desk as he walks around the classroom handing back the first drafts. "It wasn't supposed to be a made-up story." *And you weren't supposed to have someone else write it for you,* Mr. Giglio does not say, finding himself in the position he so often feels strangled by: wanting to challenge laziness and dishonesty, not wanting to be accused of making disparaging (or worse yet, racist) accusations.

Knowing what he knows about Keith's academic history, and the likelihood that his race has played a part in it, makes Greg Giglio's dilemma even thornier. Like his father before him, like many of the kids in the Computer Academy, and like so many other bright, unruly African-American boys, Keith spent the eight years of his pre–high school life in special education classes. Experience has shown Greg Giglio that when white kids are difficult to teach, teachers tend to call the parents. With African-American boys like Keith, teachers are quicker to send the kids into special ed. From there they often become caught in the hopeless cycle that's brought Keith to where he is today: knowing all his life that everyone thinks he's stupid; coming to believe it himself; acting out to conceal the fact that he's not learning.

Although Keith's "essay" is light-years better than his usual writing, Mr. Giglio can almost convince himself that Keith wrote it. It does ring with Keith's ironic, hyperbolic style and passionate condemnation of injustice. But then Mr. Giglio notices that Keith's last name is misspelled on the upper right corner, leading him to believe that Keith must have dictated the essay to his mother or to Taliah, Keith's classmate and self-appointed private tutor.

"How'd you know it ain't true?" Keith asks, grinning.

"For starters, you've never mentioned that your uncle was Ronnie Lott," Mr. Giglio answers. "And in case that didn't clue me in—"

"—Ronnie Lott ain't dead," Keith finishes, his eyes sparkling mischievously. "Right," Mr. Giglio says. *I could give him credit for a short fiction story and let him slide on the essay,* Mr. Giglio thinks. *He's never going to need a college essay anyway. And he did put some work into this.*

No. "We've been working on college essays for weeks now, Keith. You can't pass this class without writing one. A real one." Mr. Giglio started them off slowly, in October. Step one was a list of personality traits: "Communicative (Like to Talk), On Time (Punctual), Shy, Fun,

Athletic." Each student was to check all traits that applied to him or her. As simple as the task seemed, it took several days to get through it. Many of the kids couldn't read the words on the list. Without even glancing at the sheet of paper in his hand, Keith had complained immediately, "They don't have 'sexy' on here."

"You're not just your GPA," Mr. Giglio explains to the class now. "Sometimes schools take a chance on people. Maybe you've had a hard life up to now. Well, short of visiting colleges, the essay is the best way to present yourself. Even if you're going to a junior college or into the army, you'll need a personal statement."

"I'm going to work for Taco Bell," Dimitri announces.

"Even if you don't think you're going to college, you must do the assignment. I know there are writers in this class. I've heard you in the poetry slams."

Keith gets up and walks toward the doorway where the hall pass hangs on a hook. "Where you goin'?" Taliah demands from across the room before Mr. Giglio notices.

"To talk to a teacher," Keith answers.

"You filled out all your college applications already, huh?" Taliah challenges him.

"Oh yeah. I sent ten of 'em in last week."

"You believe in God, don't you?" Taliah spits back. "You know it's a sin to lie."

"Thank you, Taliah," Mr. Giglio intervenes. "But don't worry: Keith *will* write his college essay."

"I don't need to be stressin' over no college application." Keith gets in the final word from halfway out the door. "Wait till after the football season. Them Division One scouts gonna be comin' round jockin' me."

At Berkeley High the achievement disparity is glaringly visible to the naked eye: one need only follow Jordan, Autumn, and Keith through their respective college preparation processes to witness it. In other American cities, in more segregated schools, the contrast is less readily apparent within any single high school's walls—but no less insidious to the students, the community, the nation. "What is the most important educational challenge for the United States?" asks *Reaching the Top,* the 1999 report of the National Task Force on Minority High Achievement, a blue-ribbon panel convened by the College Board, the agency that administers the SATs. "Many would say that it is eliminating, once and for all, the still large educational achievement gaps among the nation's racial and ethnic groups."

Why? Because "America is a diverse society in which educational differences have the potential to become a progressively larger source of inequality and social conflict."

What the Diversity Project studied at Berkeley High, the Task Force studied nationally—uncovering equally appalling patterns. Only 17 percent of black and 24 percent of Latino high school seniors were found to be proficient in reading. Four percent of black students were rated proficient at math and science; no black students and one percent of Latinos were rated as "advanced" in those subjects. Black, Latino, and Native American students combined comprise one-fifth of students nationally with SAT scores high enough to be admitted to top colleges and universities.

Reaching the Top names five factors that affect students' educational outcomes: economic circumstances; level of parents' education; racial and ethnic prejudice and discrimination (not only segregation, but the "rumor of inferiority" that "continues to take a toll on the academic performance of many minority students"); cultural attributes of the home, community, and school (including the "tendency among some minority students to view doing well in school as "acting White"); and the quality, amount, and uses of school resources. The report recommends a number of remedies: making schools smaller, lowering student-teacher ratios, spending staff development money to provide students with better educated teachers, and offering students an academically challenging curriculum.

Certainly all of these factors are present and all of these solutions needed at Berkeley High, about which Diversity Project cofounder Pedro Noguera wrote in *Ties That Bind, Forces That Divide,* "On almost every negative indicator of student performance and behavior, black students are over-represented. This is true with regard to suspension and expulsion rates, drop-out and absentee rates, enrollment in remedial classes and special education."

There is one American school system in which the usual rules do not apply: the U.S. military's. In the seventy-one schools operated on domestic military bases, *New York Times* writer Anthony Lewis reports, scores on writing proficiency tests are almost as high among low-income children as among their more affluent classmates. Twenty-six percent of black children and 32 percent of Hispanics scored at or above passing level, compared to 7 percent and 10 percent nationally. More than 80 percent (compared to 67 percent nationally) of the military schools' high school graduates go to college.

Why does the military succeed where civilian schools fail? Lewis attributes the difference to some of the same factors cited in *Reaching the Top*. One is money. Base schools spend 23 percent more per pupil than public schools do, fund music and art programs, and are well endowed with computers. Another is parent involvement. The military gives parents an hour off a week to volunteer in the schools. Also, Lewis says, "The gap between high and low incomes is less stark among military personnel, and less distorting . . . Military families are not likely to live in the desperate ghettos that exist in our inner cities . . . there is a deeper sense of community among military families."

In his *New York Times Magazine* cover story, "Schools Are Not the Answer," reporter James Traub asks, "How powerful can this one institution be in the face of the kind of disadvantages that so many ghetto children bring with them to the schoolhouse door, and return to at home?" Citing such statistics as the persistent 200-point difference between the College Boards scores of black and white students, Traub says, "there is little evidence that any existing strategy can close more than a fraction of the overall achievement gap," and advances a radical proposal: "The most effective solution is to move families out of the ghetto environment altogether."

In resolutely progressive Berkeley, such a politically incorrect idea as this—not to mention a prohibitively impractical one—would never fly. But something must be done now that everyone, including the WASC auditors, knows just how wide the achievement gap is. Desperately seeking ways to align its egalitarian vision with its not-separate-but-unequal reality, in September of 1999 the Berkeley Unified School District became one of fourteen multiracial school districts in the United States to join a national consortium on minority achievement. "This is really a national problem," school superintendent Jack McLaughlin tells the *Berkeley High Jacket*, whose reporter comments, "Although Berkeley has been working on the achievement gap problem, it has not had much success. Now, however, Berkeley knows that it is not alone with its difficulties."

"If we truly wish to change the 'achievement gap,' " a student tells the *Jacket*, "it must be attacked on all levels: from Kindergarten on up, in the home, in the workplace, etc. . . . The problems that our school faces surrounding race will probably be around as long as Berkeley High remains a microcosm of America."

But the WASC auditors have said that Berkeley High's achievement gap must be closed now, not later; and so the WASC Committee on the Achievement Disparity task force goes on meeting throughout November. "Everything I'm reading tells me that the more contact kids have with teachers who know them, the better they do," says an art teacher. "Can we expand the tutorial program?" suggests a new math teacher.

"One-third of our students are being screwed by the school, and we think major resources should go to fix that, and we don't have the power to tell the administration to spend the money!" Annie Johnston, a teacher of Keith's and a white, out lesbian known for her militant antiracism, blurts in frustration. "At least let's ask the students what they think we should do!"

In mid-November a Youth Together delegation meets with the WASC committee and then with Principal Saunders, protesting the lack of student input to the WASC process and offering its own Equal Opportunity Program to address the achievement disparity. Saunders agrees to hold student forums—in second-period classes, not those risky school-wide assemblies—on each WASC topic.

"Does anyone know what 'academic disparity' means?" Ms. Johnston asks Keith's history class—most of the students African-American, most of them Computer Academy students—a week later. "No," several kids answer.

"It means African-American and Latino students do worse than white students," Ms. Johnston says in her street-preacher cadence. "Do you know that by the second grade, 80 percent of African-American students are reading below grade level, and 90 percent of white students are reading at or above it? Do you know that 90 percent of African-American males in this school get a D or F on every single report card?"

"What!" several kids shout. Unmoved, Keith goes on eating the doughnut he just bought from Mr. Collier, the history teacher who sells doughnuts and fruit for fifty cents apiece. "A lotta teachers here say 'Hey, they came to me that way. I try not to make it worse but it ain't my fault,' " Ms. Johnston goes on. "But the WASC people have told Berkeley High, 'You can teach a wider range of people than you're teaching and you can teach them better.' What do you-all think about that?"

"If you live in Berkeley you're gonna do a lot better than if you go to Oakland schools," an African-American girl says. "I think the problem is, there are too many kids here from other places."

"I came from Oakland," snaps another girl. "I think it's about your parents, how much they stay on you."

"I see so many black kids three and four years old, still not knowing how to talk," says another. "White parents read to their children. For some reason black parents don't."

"Not being able to read in third grade," one of the two white boys in the class says, "that's not about the school. That's about parents."

"In the African-American community parents are working two or three jobs," a girl argues, "so you don't have your parents with you, staying on you. Anyway, by the time you get into eighth or ninth grade . . ."

"It's on you," Keith finishes her thought.

Thanks to Annie Johnston's determination to keep her students engaged—sparking debates daily about race and class with provocative news stories, guest speakers, and videos—hers is always the most spirited of Keith's classes. Today, especially, the students are falling all over themselves and each other to be heard.

"My friends go to Oakland Tech," an African-American boy says, "and our work is hella harder. I'd be a straight-A student at Tech!"

"Some white people have Internet access in they own house," a girl says. "At the Berkeley Public Library it's like a week wait. I be running around to all the libraries looking for Internet access. Then if the teacher's prejudiced I don't even get a good grade."

"If you have teachers who primarily make eye contact with white students," Ms. Johnston interjects, "who put African-American males in the back of the room . . . who say stuff in a way you might not understand because they don't know how to talk to kids of different backgrounds . . ."

"Then why she a teacher," Keith asks, "if she can't talk to black kids?"

"If you can't teach black kids you need to teach in an all-white school," a girl agrees.

"I think it's the attitude of the kids, not the teachers," a white boy says. "If you want to learn you can learn in this school."

"If a teacher stop teaching 'cause a few kids are acting crazy," a black boy says, "what can you do? Go see your counselor?" The class howls with laughter at the thought.

Down two flights of stairs and in a different universe, David Bye's AP English class is discussing the achievement disparity, too. Here, the racial balance is exactly the opposite—biracial Daveed Diggs is the only student of color—and so is the ambience. Mr. Bye is as famous for his staunch defense of "classic education" and his elite classes as Ms. Johnston is for her rough-and-tumble radicalism; his classes are as sedate and erudite as hers are boisterous and gritty. In Mr. Bye's room, students wait to be called upon, speak quietly and politely one at a time, and never use curse words or the bathroom pass.

"There's nothing being done to ignite kids here," Daveed says, calmly explaining to twenty-five white kids why black kids cut school. "Why should they come?"

"That's exactly why WASC is so irritating to me," Mr. Bye says. "They're telling me I have to have balance in my classes. But wouldn't it be bad if they put kids who aren't even interested in learning into AP classes, just to achieve balance?"

"I was reluctant to be in AP classes because I didn't want to be in the all-white AP clique," a girl says.

"Hopefully you guys spread out, hang out with different kinds of people, once you leave this room," Mr. Bye responds.

"No!" a girl tells him, her cheeks flushed with anger. "*All* our classes are like this! We're all in the same classes with all the same people. And it's *boring!*"

"Maybe this isn't entitlement," says another girl. "Maybe this is *worse*."

"Can't there just be one class where you work really hard," Mr. Bye asks pleadingly, "and everyone's mind works well?"

There is a sharp collective intake of breath. The students stare, horrified, at their teacher. "Everyone's . . . mind . . . works . . . well?" a girl repeats, her voice shaking.

"I don't expect to be on the varsity football team," Mr. Bye defends himself. "I'm lousy at football. Why should someone who's lousy at English expect to be in AP English?"

"We all say we love diversity, but everyone in this class prefers classes where everyone has something interesting to say," a boy agrees.

"What!" "No!" Outcries of indignation erupt around the room. "You're saying someone who's not white has nothing interesting to say!" a girl accuses him.

"I went to private schools, not Oakland public schools. That's why I do well in school," another girl says grimly. "There's so much dishonesty at Berkeley High. The administration won't admit that the teachers teach at different levels. And the kids whose parents are in this one little group get everything they want."

"Do the 'Mothers of Excellence' still exist?" Mr. Bye asks with a nervous smile. "They used to terrify me when they came down from the hills. You know, the very mother who was responsible for balancing the classes came to me demanding that her daughter be placed in my class."

The bell rings. For a long moment no one moves; teacher and students seem slightly stunned. And then the moment passes, and the teacher sinks into his chair, and the students gather their things and go on to their next class.

In its November 10 issue the *Jacket* reports three recent alleged assaults on students by teachers: one, a science teacher on hall duty who pushed a student against the wall in a choke hold when he refused to go to class and "mumbled negatively" at the teacher; another, a football coach who "roughed up" a player on the team bus when he wouldn't stop singing "disrespectful" songs in front of the team's female statisticians and made fun of the coach.

In an editorial that's surprisingly supportive of the teachers, the *Jacket* comments, "While a teacher laying a hand on a student is never morally acceptable and always illegal, it is more important to find the root of this problem than to simply punish the teachers involved. The staff was greeted at the beginning of the school year with dire warnings about the possibility of an incident similar to the one at Columbine High School. It should come as no surprise that after being so frightened by threats of student violence, teachers find themselves more ready to react to a perceived threat in a rash manner. Too often, the chaotic environment of the school leaves teachers crying or throwing things in frustration. Some of those involved in recent incidents were enthusiastic and well-loved teachers. Can the school afford to waste this talent?"

That same week national news headlines are captured by violence at Eisenhower High in Decatur, Illinois. "Zero Tolerance Brawl," *U.S. News and World Report* calls the fistfight that erupted during a football game, physically injuring no one but resulting in the expulsion of seven African-American students. ". . . this midsize factory town became a case study of the nation's post-Columbine angst over just how to handle school-related violence."

Captured on videotape and aired repeatedly on national TV, the fight seems to have been an unremarkable high school happenstance—until Jesse Jackson comes to town, leading marchers demanding that the students be reinstated. Claiming the issue is "not race but fairness," Jackson nonetheless compares Decatur to Selma, pointing out that the last Eisenhower student caught fighting was punished with a ten-day suspension, and the student who threatened to blow up another Decatur high school the previous summer was only expelled for a year. "Where do seventeen-year-olds go when they're expelled from school?" Jackson asks Bryant Gumbel on the *Early Show*. "If we marginalize these young people now, what will become of them in the future?"

"If [the expelled students] don't get back into class fairly soon," agrees a November 22 *Time* editorial, "they will in all likelihood become permanent dropouts—which, for young black men, often translates into a one-way ticket to jail."

"I told you your college essays were due Friday," Mr. Giglio announces. "But I'm going to extend that, due to the fact that not many of you are anywhere near done."

No one seems particularly grateful for the reprieve. In fact, no one seems to be paying much attention to Mr. Giglio at all. Today is Keith's eighteenth birthday, and amidst side conversations about whether Beeper City or Pager One has the better deal and which fast-food chain is the worst place to work ("When they drop the food where I work they make you put it in the bag anyway," Akila confides. "So when they call it 'ground beef,' they mean what they say," Dominic quips), the boys in the class are busy passing around and reading the cards that the girls in the class have given Keith.

Keith opens the one from Taliah and studies it closely. "Happy Birthday you bum!" she has written. "May you get every thing you wish for (except Leisha!) and then some. Enjoy life, try being more . . . tactful, & do your work. The world needs more smart, intelligent Black males out here; not just another 'great athlete.' Thanks for keeping me laughing on both my sad and happy days. Stay cool. Much love, Taliah B."

"Thank you," Keith tells Taliah dully. The birthday attention does nothing to lift his low spirits. "I woke up this morning and I didn't feel happy," he says. "All my life I thought this would be such a big day. But now it's nothin'. My dad left me a fifty-dollar bill on my bed but he does that every year. Last year my mom brought a cake onto the field for the football team. She wasn't working then."

It isn't just birthday letdown that's bothering Keith. Life itself is starting to feel like one big letdown. Friday was the last football game of the season and the Yellowjackets lost again, ending the year ineligible for the play-offs. The next morning Keith was eating his Cap'n Crunch when his mom called to him in the kitchen, "Keith! You're on TV!" After waiting the whole season, he'd finally made it onto *Sports Highlights* on ESPN. "You look strong," his mom said, watching number 4 darting across the big-screen TV. Keith knew she was just trying to make him feel good. "Shoulda had a touchdown," was all he could say.

Then yesterday he'd gotten into it with Josh in Mr. Giglio's class. Josh was giving the class one of his speeches about being elected president of the Black Student Union. Keith got tired of listening to him brag. "You look like New Kids on the Block," Keith called out to shut him up. Keith and Josh trash talk each other on a regular basis, but this time Josh went *off*.

"Your football dreams are shot, Keith," he spat from the front of the room. "You've got junior college written all over you."

"My dream is *alive!*" Keith shot back. The other kids in the class straightened in their seats, anticipating a fight.

"You go to college and I'll give you fifty dollars." Josh stomped across the room, planted himself in front of Keith's desk. "Everybody hear me?" Josh shouted. "I'll shake your hand and give you fifty dollars." He grabbed Keith's hand and pumped it, hard. Keith was about to fire on him when Mr. Giglio pulled them apart.

The truth is, Josh hit a sore spot. With all the ups and downs Keith's been through lately, his last high school football season hasn't ended the way he always believed it would. Plus, in the past few weeks every one of his teachers has warned him that he's failing their classes. Keith keeps telling them that he's trying: he's gone to the Student Learning Center at lunch a couple of times; he even went to the public library to try and get a paper off the Internet for Ms. Johnston's class. But with football practice every day and working at Burger King on the weekends, Keith is falling so far behind, he doesn't know how he'll ever catch up. The worst part is, his belief in himself—the faith that's always kept him going—is starting to slip too.

December 1999: Crackdown

Principal's Office Memo
12/09/99

To: All Staff
From: Theresa
Subject: Information Items

Yesterday afternoon a fight occurred between two male students and erupted into a major altercation that included four students. In the process of attempting to defuse the situation a teacher was allegedly threatened and a School Safety Officer was allegedly hit and kicked. This is sent to inform you that the students involved have been arrested by the Berkeley Police Department and suspended pending a hearing for expulsion. It is also sent to let you know that assaults on adults at this campus will not be tolerated.

Ms. Crawford puts down the memo she's been reading and looks around at her CAS seminar. "I'm sure you guys already knew about this," she says.

"I saw the whole thing," Amaya reports. "Billy Keys was on the ground. There were hella kids kicking him."

"There are so many kids in this school who are so pissed off at Wiggins and Billy Keys," Jordan says, "I'm surprised it hasn't happened before."

"Expelling kids for fighting is ridiculous," Autumn adds. "Billy Keys is on a phat power trip. Wiggins too."

"Before we go any further with this conversation," Ms. Crawford says, "it happens that today's the day for the student forum on school safety. We need to choose a facilitator. And a recorder. Then we can keep talking. Lynndra?" She encourages a girl with long hair extensions who rarely speaks in class. Lynndra takes Ms. Crawford's place. Melania offers to take notes.

"So . . . what do you all think?" Lynndra asks hesitantly.

"It wouldn't have got that big if it was white kids fighting," says Rena, a biracial girl who always sits in the front row, always participates actively in class discussions. "Some white kids were caught smoking weed during Spirit Week. They weren't expelled. That Billy Keys is wack. Wiggins too."

She snorts derisively. "On Spirit Day me and Melania had the van painted up with '00' all over it. Before school we're driving around on Milvia and this cop car pulls us over. Guess who pops out the passenger seat: Wiggins! He's like, 'Open the door—NOW!' And the cop says, 'Have you been smoking weed?' We were like, 'Yeah, we smoked four blunts earlier.' "

"Mr. Wiggins, he walks around here like *Men in Black*," says Christian, the only CAS student who's also in one of Keith's classes. "One time we were coming back from our internship and Wiggins sent us to on-campus suspension for being late to class. We weren't even late. Mr. Richards had to come bail us out."

"The security force gives the illusion of safety," Julien says, "but they're actually making the school more prison-like."

"The people who should be intimidated aren't. And the people who shouldn't be intimidated are," Malik says. "But as far as Berkeley High being a jail: not compared to the other schools around here! In Oakland they got metal detectors, barbed wire fences—"

"Do you know how many kids walk around here with guns and drugs?" Mario interrupts him. "We *need* security officers! There are some bad kids at this school!"

"I heard that Mr. Wiggins is requesting the power to actually arrest us and take us across the street to jail," Daniel announces. "Is that what you want at Berkeley High?"

One flight up and one building away, Annie Johnston is recruiting a student facilitator, too. "Keith! Keith!" the students chant. "I don't wanna be up front," Keith mumbles. Sitting beside him in a fuzzy pink sweater, Taliah tugs at the sleeve of his Girbaud jacket. "Do it," she urges him. "You'll get extra credit." But Keith won't move, so Marcus goes to the front of the room.

"Do we get a grade for participating in this?" Taliah asks. Ms. Johnston shakes her head. "This is for *you*. Student leadership uses the notes from these forums to pressure the administration to do what you want." She writes on the board, "Personal Experiences with Campus Security," and nods to Marcus.

"How do you feel you've been treated by campus security?" Marcus reads from the sheet in his hand.

"Fair," a girl answers.

"That's 'cause you a girl," a boy says.

"What improvements could be made to improve campus security?" Marcus reads.

"Get rid of Wiggins!" the kids shout in one voice.

"He gave up his Corvette to get a hair transplant," Keith volunteers.

"It's an implant," Taliah corrects him. "It cost $40,000,"

When the jeers and laughter subside Charley says, "Billy Keys got jumped yesterday."

"I was right there when it happened," Keith says. All eyes turn to him. "Three kids jumped one kid. Those three ran away. Then Billy Keys came and started harassing the kid who got jumped. The kid got mad and pushed Billy Keys off him. Billy Keys fell on the ground and one kid kicked him. Not me," he concludes. "I wanted to but I didn't."

Billy Keys gets no more sympathy in this class than he did in CAS. "Last year I had my bike stolen and I saw some white boy ridin' it and Billy Keys didn't do shit," a boy says bitterly.

"That's 'cause you a black man in a black leather coat with an Afro," Keith replies.

"So he needs to get twisties like yours if he wants to be safe?" Ms. Johnston asks sarcastically.

"They be sayin' let me see you ID to people they see every day. They be racist," says a girl. "Uh-huh," several kids agree. "Hella racist."

"Are you feeling oppressed by security?" Ms. Johnston asks.

"They beat down the little guys but they leave the big guys alone," answers Taliah.

"Who are the big guys?" Ms. Johnston asks.

"The trench coat Mafia!" yells Dimitri. "After Columbine, Berkeley High had a rule: you couldn't wear no leather coat. And who wears most of the leather coats at Berkeley High? *Black people.* But there was males *and* females wearing they hair dyed black, they faces lookin' all weird with that black make-up the trench coat Mafia people wear. No one did nothin' to *them* cause they was *white.*"

"When all those people in trench coats were around here I didn't feel safe," Taliah says.

"You clearly have some concerns," Ms. Johnston interjects. "We need to write them down if we want things to change."

Taliah hands Keith a piece of paper and leans over him, correcting each sentence as he writes it. "Keith wants to read his statement," she announces when they're finished.

"I don't want to read in front of the class," Keith says. Taliah takes the paper and reads what's on it.

> "Since I been at BHS all I every had was problems. A Man
> by the name of Billy Keys is the biggest loser of them all he's
> just 25 years old. and he went to school with my brother

and they talked about him ever day. When Billy Keys got out of BHS he came right back to get every one who used to teas him and he would later be campus monidur and get all the kids that used to talk about him and there bother and sister. A nother man that should not be at BHS is a man by the name of Mr. Wiggins I would call him a loser but he's a . . ."

Taliah hesitates. "Fag."

"What!" Ms. Johnston explodes. "Keith! I told you if I ever heard that word from you again I'd—"

"Fake!" Keith interrupts her. "I wrote 'fake'! She read it wrong!"

Ms. Johnston squints at him skeptically.

"For real!" he swears. "Keep reading," he instructs Taliah.

"He always do way to much when there a problem at school. Just last year he was bald this year he has hair. Wiggins has been herasting people since I got a BHS no one likes him and his little side kick Billy Keys."

"Billy went to the hospital but he's gonna be all right," says Officer Roosevelt "Rosie" Brown, the Berkeley police officer who spends every school day at Berkeley High, his empty police car parked beside the Milvia gate serving as a constant reminder of the BPD presence on campus. "Two sets of brothers got into a fight. Then all four of them got Billy on the ground and some other kids ran over to kick him. They just thought it would be fun to throw Billy Keys down and stomp on him." Officer Brown shakes his head. "The four brothers are under arrest. One has a broken arm. Another one needed stitches.

"None of them are bad kids, really: wrong place, wrong time, hot tempers. One boy's a senior. He was on track to graduate. But not any more. The other kickers haven't been identified yet. But we'll find them."

Keith laughs when he hears Officer Brown's version of the story. "There was like a hundred kids saw Billy Keys gettin' kicked. Everybody hate him too much to tell the po-lice who did it. That should tell the school something. But they don't care what we think. If they did, Wiggins and Billy Keys wouldn't still be here."

Notwithstanding the high-profile school shootings at Columbine and other suburban high schools, America's public schools have actually become safer in the past decade, according to an annual survey of school principals conducted by the U.S. Department of Education. The same is true of Berkeley High. "We have fewer fights breaking out at lunch time, fewer kids getting jumped in the bathrooms, less personal violence than we did in the recent past," reports Vice Principal Doris Wallace-Tanner. "The kids have seen the consequences and they don't want them."

Whether the improvement demonstrates the effectiveness of the school's beefed-up security measures—the presence of the ever-unpopular school safety officers, the intensified partnership with the police department, the expanded number of teachers on hall duty, the erecting of the chain-link fence, the militaristic "Columbine practice run" conducted the week before school opened—or the school's growing practice of conflict resolution, or some confluence of factors, is anybody's guess. But even in freedom-loving Berkeley, those whose guesses count are tending toward "better safe (safer, anyway) than sorry"—especially since Columbine.

The same is true of decision makers across the nation. The first rash of school shootings triggered the original zero tolerance law: the 1994 Gun-Free Schools Act, which may have decreased schools' "tolerance" but certainly did not end the violence that continues to dominate national headlines. December is particularly gruesome.

Early in the month a popular, churchgoing, thirteen-year-old honors student opens fire on his middle-school classmates in Fort Gibson, Oklahoma. That same day Holland suffers its first-ever "American-style" high school shooting. The following week five videotapes made by Columbine killers Dylan Klebold and Eric Harris in the weeks before their shooting spree are released to the media. "Columbine Killers Hoped to

Slay Hundreds, Tapes Show," the *San Francisco Chronicle* headline reads. "Thank God, my parents never searched my room," Harris tells the camera, leading a guided tour of the arsenal of guns, bombs, and ammunition he has hidden there.

Two days later an eighteen-year-old in Florida sends an E-mail to a sophomore at Columbine, threatening to "finish what began." Officials close the school for two days for the first time since the massacre and the FBI arrests the eighteen-year-old, who spends five days in solitary confinement facing possible penalties of $250,000 and five years in prison. "Today's arrest should send a strong message that threats, especially against our schools, will not be tolerated," announces the Denver district attorney.

Three days before Christmas, thirty-nine weapons are seized from the homes of five seventeen-year-olds in Oswego, Kansas, after the boys attempt to recruit classmates at a party to join them in killing their principal, associate principal, five teachers, and a student. "The fact that those kinds of weapons were available to kids is very disturbing," says the local school superintendent.

Even more disturbing to many is the nation's response. "Could we begin this millennium with a policy that offers kids something more than 'zero tolerance'?" asks nationally syndicated columnist Ellen Goodman. "Zero tolerance for misbehavior evolved into zero tolerance for kids themselves. . . . A tough love without the love."

The toughest love of all is reserved for the kids America loves least. A report released in mid-December by the Applied Research Center, a national education policy institute, shows that since American schools began adopting zero tolerance polices—and despite the fact that not one of the mass school shootings was perpetrated by an African-American—the policies have been disproportionately used against black students. In some districts, the study reports, African-American kids have been removed from school three to five times more frequently than whites.

"The uneasy truth," Ellen Goodman concludes, "is that children are often tragically disconnected. The schools don't really know their lives; the communities are clueless. Paying real attention to the younger generation is labor intensive. It consists of connections and discipline, expectation and second chances."

"Jordan!" Ms. Crawford summons him to her desk as he saunters into her classroom, ten minutes late, the Monday after Thanksgiving break. "What's happening with your internship?"

Jordan flushes. He looks down at his DKNY running shoes, looks up at the Audre Lorde poster on the wall, finally looks Ms. Crawford in the eye. "Not much," he admits. "Joey and I keep trying to hook up with Street Space. But they keep flaking on us."

"That's not acceptable, Jordan," Ms. Crawford says. "You need to take the initiative to make it happen. You're a senior now. I need some work from you if you want to pass this class. You need to hand in your brainstorm notes. You need to join a book group. And you need to start coming to class on time. You've earned the right to be trusted. I don't want to have to talk to you about this again. Got it?"

"Got it." Hot-faced, Jordan slinks to his seat. *I deserved that,* he thinks. *I haven't done shit all semester.* It's not just CAS, either. Except for Ceramics, his mid-semester grades were all Cs. "Once I sit down and open a book I can do anything. Even my AP classes are below where I could be working. But I just can't get into it. I already know I'm going to Bard. It's too hard to sit and do this menial, obtuse bullshit that doesn't have much to do with life at all."

CAS used to be Jordan's easiest, most interesting class. Now it's one of his hardest. Ms. Crawford keeps loading them down with all kinds of heavy-duty projects: a book journal, an "I-Search" paper, the damn internship. Jordan was highly motivated by the internship concept at first. Outraged by the rape of a friend's mom in her own house by her own brother-in-law, he tried to volunteer as a phone counselor at the rape crisis center. They didn't take males. Then he offered to help out at a local mental health clinic. They said he couldn't work there till he was eighteen.

Mr. Richards knows the organizers of Street Space, a nonprofit that's setting up free Internet access stations in Berkeley cafés and BART stations. Since Jordan couldn't seem to get anything else going, he signed up for that. It was fun for a while, wandering around Berkeley with Joey and the Street Space videocam, interviewing people coming out of movies and UC Berkeley students coming out of classes. But then he missed a few appointments, and the Street Space people missed a few, and the whole thing kind of fell apart. *Ms. Crawford won't flunk me,* Jordan tells himself now. *She's just trying to scare everyone into working harder.*

I'll feel better when I get back from Bard. Next week, right after he and his mom celebrate Hanukkah ("the honorary Jew," she calls herself) they're flying to Bard so Jordan can apply on the school's immediate decision plan. He'll spend a day in classes, followed by an interview, at the end of which he'll be told on the spot whether or not he's been accepted. *Then I'll know for sure that I don't need to be stressing about school.*

"I'm going to be straightforward with you," Ms. Crawford tells the whole CAS seminar now. "I'm disappointed with how you guys are working. I know it's a hard time—your UC applications are due, you've got senioritis. But on the day the book journals were due I had *two.*"

She pauses for emphasis, looking around the room. "I'm not seeing the kind of effort this program is all about. We're about creating something meaningful here and it's not happening. What is the problem? Where's the gap?"

Ms. Crawford waits again. The students stare at their shoes, doodle in their notebooks, take long drinks from their Snapples and Calistogas. "If you don't give me any answers," Ms. Crawford says, "I'll pile on the work. That's my way of coping. Some teachers back off on work at this time of year. I have the opposite response. I don't want to give you bad grades, but the grade has to reflect the final product. So talk to me."

Autumn raises her hand. "I'm overwhelmed. Every time I turn around I have so much to do." What Autumn doesn't say is that she's not doing much of it. Right now she's on the verge of failing AP Anatomy, she owes Mr. Miller two essays, she's getting a C in AP Statistics, and she hasn't turned any work in to Ms. Crawford in three weeks. In fact, she barely managed to get her UC application finished and mailed by the deadline yesterday. She rushed to the downtown Berkeley post office just before closing time, handed the packet to the clerk, accepted her receipt. Then she stood there in a daze until the clerk called "Next!" and snapped her out of it. "All of a sudden I realized: that's it—that's my future in that envelope! Because I'm only applying to UCSC and UC Berkeley. I don't have a chance at Berkeley, but UCSC would be just fine. I know people who are going to Santa Cruz. And I heard Angela Davis teaches there."

"Everything's due," Autumn tells Ms. Crawford now. "Everything's got to be good. I don't want to give you something crappy, Ms. Crawford, with you being so dedicated to this program. I want to be on time with my stuff. But please—" Autumn folds her hands theatrically in prayer, gazes beseechingly at her teacher. "*Please* don't give us more work!"

"I read your *Song of Solomon* essays over Thanksgiving break. There are some things I'm seeing in them that I hate. Other people will hate them too," Mr. Miller announces to Autumn's Black Lit class two periods later. *Is every teacher in this school tripping today, or what?* Autumn thinks. "Dude couldn't of hated mine since I ain't wrote it yet," she whispers to Lillian in her "second language," the one she uses with her family and friends. "I'm bilingual," Autumn acknowledges. "I talk differently in the halls and at home than I do in class."

"Your sentence structure, many of you, is terrible. Your use of punctuation is amateurish." Mr. Miller leans on his lectern, which is incongruously adorned with a Jesse Ventura wrestling poster. "There's something important that happens in your career, and the quicker you get to this point, the happier you'll be: *reading as a writer.* Write that phrase down.

"You're in AP. You should be able to see the strategies that writers use. For instance, sentence variety: simple, compound, complex, compound complex." Every student in the room is taking down every word he says. "You need to use the three-to-one ratio. For every statement you make or quote you use, you should have three sentences to say about it." Mr. Miller walks to his desk, stands below the sign that says "I don't give out grades. YOU EARN THEM."

"I'll expect better from you in the future. Now we're going to talk about the relationship between race and violence, a theme of *Song of Solomon*. Autumn: facilitate, please."

Lillian shoots Autumn a sympathetic look. Just before class Autumn was telling Lil that she hasn't finished the book yet. Autumn takes a deep breath, willing her confidence to stand in for her undone homework, and carries her book to the lectern. "For Youth Radio we had to go around and ask people what they thought of America," she begins. "This young black man told me, 'White people will kill their own families plus fifty other people—like Jeffrey Dahmer or Littleton.' Maybe it's 'cause I'm black, but I don't expect a black person to do something random and strange like that."

"Like the guy in Chicago who drove around killing blacks and Jews," says Tom, the boy whose father reviews books for the *New York Times*. "White people get mad 'cause they think blacks and Jews are taking over the country."

"But why is it always white males?" asks Autumn.

"It isn't. Black men are catching up," Mr. Miller interjects.

"I read in my Black Psychology class that black people in this country act violent because we've been forced to adapt to materialism. It's a way of life that's unnatural to us genetically," Lillian says. "Even though most black people haven't been to Africa or lived in a tribe, tribal Africa is in our blood."

"Excuse me, but blood is the red shit running in your veins," argues Chris, a blond boy. "The only way you inherit beliefs is if your parents teach them to you."

"I'm not going to speak for all black people—"

"Good," Mr. Miller interrupts.

"But my blood remembers Africa," Lillian continues. "Even if I've never been to Africa, my blood has been."

Hands are waving now all over the room. *This is about to be one of those phat Black Lit racial arguments,* Autumn predicts, relieved. She calls on Tom, her unread copy of *Song of Solomon* open in her lap.

. . .

"I'm not getting what I want from you," Mr. Giglio announces to Keith's English class that same day. "I'm gonna have to step things up to make sure you guys graduate. Ms. Russ is gonna be on you too. That's why you signed up for Computer Academy—so someone would stay on you."

"What if you call my house to talk to my mom and I'm sitting right there listening," Dimitri says. "Won't you feel kinda stupid?"

"I'm used to feeling kind of stupid. Doesn't bother me a bit. It's December, you guys. Time to stop sliding. Now: here's the seating chart for the rest of the year." He starts reading the new arrangement from the paper in his hand.

"Seating chart! I *know* you ain't talkin' 'bout no seating chart!" John yelps.

"What! I ain't sittin' next to Alex!" Keith protests. "Why you pick on me all the time, Mr. Giglio?"

"You know why—'cause you're black," Mr. Giglio responds. The students hoot with laughter.

"Mr. G—you're in charge of the yearbook, right?" asks Taliah. Mr. Giglio nods. "Is it too late to put my picture in? You *know* they need more black people in the yearbook."

"But I hate black people," Mr. Giglio replies. The class laughs again.

"That's why you stay out in Pleasanton," Dimitri says.

"Mr. Giglio act silly-o," Keith sing-songs.

"Okay. Enough!" Mr. Giglio shouts above the din.

Alan Miller's tone is flat, monotonous; he injects provocative remarks, then retreats, never raising his voice. Amy Crawford starts whispering when her students start getting rowdy; quickly, they quiet to hear her. Greg Giglio shouts nearly all the time, his speech punctuated by frequent short exclamations—"Now!" "Listen up!" "All *right!*"—that occasionally succeed in their desired effect: catching the attention, just for an instant, of a group of kids accustomed to the staccato, nonstop overstimulation of Beavis and Butthead, Eddie Murphy action movies, and homicidal video games.

Mr. Miller's English class is midway through the third book they've read and discussed this semester. Mr. Giglio's English class is less than halfway through their first.

"By last Friday you were supposed to have read *Caucasia* to page 125. I'm going to come around and check your reports now, see who did it and who didn't."

"You didn't tell us to have it today!" protests LaRique.

"It was on the board," Mr. Giglio responds. "If you don't have your report, take out your copy of *Caucasia* and start working on it."

"Can I borrow a book?" Keith asks.

"I'm out of books now, Keith. Why don't you work on your vocabulary instead?"

"Can I get the pass then, Mr. G? I'll go get my book from my locker."

For twenty minutes Mr. Giglio's classroom is relatively quiet. The twelve students who showed up today are reading, listening to CDs on their Walkmans, having whispered side conversations, or sleeping with their heads on their desks.

"I have an announcement," Mr. Giglio says just before the period ends. "Ms. Russ told me the school is going to have a special ceremony for college-bound African-American students. That can be a four-year college, a junior college, dental assistant college, anything. Who wants an application to be included in the ceremony?"

"I need one," Keith says immediately. Taliah and another girl raise their hands. Thor, the Chinese boy, and Carlos, the Latino boy, raise their hands. The other students don't seem to have heard the announcement.

"Eighty percent of the kids at this school use drugs. Ten percent of them are addicted to heroin or cocaine," Lucas Daumont, Berkeley High School's drug abuse prevention coordinator, announces to the Wednesday afternoon staff meeting. The teachers seem utterly unfazed, drinking their coffee and water, eating their sandwiches and chips. "In the last six months I had forty-eight kids referred to me. That's more than I had in a whole year at Oakland Tech."

If Daumont is going for shock value, he doesn't appear to be succeeding. "The Latino kids' drugs of choice are alcohol, marijuana, and coke," Daumont continues. "Asian kids are into coke and methamphetamines. They're using drugs to boost their academic achievement. We find that kids are using up to sixty-five dollars' worth of coke a day. And it's all bought at this school."

A new teacher raises his hand. "How do we refer a student to you?" he asks.

Daumont holds up a form. "Fill out one of these. I'll come and take the kid out of class." Most of the teachers don't look up from the papers they're grading.

"Black kids—I don't see a lot of them," Daumont continues. "Although I will say that the youngest alcoholics I've ever seen were African-American kids right out of middle school. They come here already addicted.

"Seventy percent of the kids who get referred to me are upper-middle-class kids of dominant culture. Their drug of choice is marijuana. Many of them tell me they get high with their parents every morning at breakfast. And they don't think we give a shit."

What no one in this room knows is that Lucas Daumont is about to quit his job, in part because of the school's disparate treatment of drug users. "Minority kids get nailed and stay nailed," he says. "Their parents say, 'My kid was using drugs, he should be punished.' White middle-class parents immediately come to the defense of their children with lawyers and threats of lawsuits. The kids sit there with smirks on their faces watching their parents jump through hoops to get them off. I find that attitude of entitlement very disturbing."

Even more troublesome to Daumont is what he calls Berkeley's "irresponsible liberalism: the kind of parental naïveté that brought us Columbine." "The people in this town are more concerned about homeless people sleeping in the streets than children shooting dope in the park." A long-time Oakland resident and drug counselor in the Oakland schools, Daumont blames those naive parents for "the shocking sense of entitlement of the Berkeley High student body—especially among the affluent white kids.

"The minority kids are a little more reality grounded. Their problem is cynicism: 'Why try? This is as good as it's gonna get.' But these wealthy kids, whose parents bail them out no matter what they do, manifest a preadolescent self-centeredness. You can be in the middle of a conversation with another adult; they walk in and stand there until you stop and pay attention to them. I constantly have to say, 'I'm talking to someone. Would you wait outside, please?' You just don't see that lack of propriety in the Oakland schools.

"The other thing I find *very* upsetting is the nonchalant attitude of most adults at Berkeley High—except the principal and some of the high-ranking people—about marijuana smoking. I've never seen anything like it. Kids have this sense that they have a right to get high, and something's wrong with the adult population if they criticize them for it. When kids get busted in Oakland schools, they expect there will be consequences. They accept that. In Berkeley kids become righteously indignant when they get busted for getting high in the park. 'What the hell is this about? My boyfriend was just shooting heroin! He wasn't hurting anybody.'"

Daumont shakes his head, runs his hand through his graying hair. "Irresponsible liberalism is killing these kids. They're totally unprepared for the reality of life. They believe they can do anything they want by the mere fact of their will. They're going to come into the world with a level of expectation that cannot be met."

"This is your world! You can define your own expression," says CAS director Rick Ayers, welcoming a hundred students, teachers, and parents to the monthly Berkeley High poetry slam. Cosponsored by Berkeley High's two "small schools," CAS and the Computer Academy, this month's slam is being held in downtown Berkeley's two-hundred-seat Repertory Theater. "Just give respect to the speaker and don't hate on others. This discourse should connect with everyone."

Amy Crawford is in the back row with several CAS and Computer Academy teachers and a few parents. Jordan sits near the front; he is here to be entertained, and to support his slamming friends. A prolific and talented writer, Jordan keeps his poetry to himself. "I'll say anything to people, but I don't share my poetry with anyone."

"Ayers," as he's known to teachers and students alike, recruits five student judges from the crowd, hands them pads of yellow paper and markers, and introduces the MC for the evening—Crystrial, a girl in Keith's English class. The slam begins.

CAS student Joaquin Noguera explodes onto the stage, his lean, muscular body pumping to the beat of his "Reason 4 Life."

> *"Much hope has been killed*
> *the belly of the beast has been filled*
> *We will continue to make capitalism feel us*
> *over time it will heal us*
> *It's never too late to be taught and to teach*
> *worldwide consciousness is not out of reach*
> *Understand the hocus pocus*
> *we've got to stay focused*
> *they tryin' to choke us*
> *up in the belly of the beast*
> *so I smoke my hashish*
> *far more religious than a priest . . . "*

The judges hold up their yellow pads, marked with boldly written numbers: 9.5, 9, 8.5, 9.8, and one perfect 10. The audience cheers for the highest scores, boos at the 8.5.

A blonde, baby-faced girl recites a mournful, chilling poem about her best friend dropping out of school as she "graduates" from crack to heroin: "She's got diplomas of addiction/hanging on her walls." Another girl undulates to her melodic critique of religious institutions: "getting wrapped up in devious notions/of a God created by others . . ."

An African-American boy in a FUBU baseball cap and massive sagging jeans stomps across the stage, rapping about his sixteen-year-old friend who's serving life in prison for murder. "Why/Why/Why are brothas killin' brothas." Niles, a Youth Together organizer, warns, "Teenage passions get buried in the mainstream/my passions put on trial/I became Mr. Nine to Five."

After each performance, the five judges award scores from zero to ten: five points maximum for performance; five for the quality of the poem. Most of the poets are given scores above 9; no one is marked lower than 8. Everyone in the theater cheers wholeheartedly for everyone else.

Autumn and Lauren sit beside each other until Lauren is called to perform. In ringing tones she reads a wrenching memorial to her grandmother who died recently.

> "I sit and watch the worse condition she's ever been
> Her voice fading out and in
> And yet she still finds the time to partake in the white man's drug
> The one that stops the circulation of blood
> The one that kills over one million people each year
> The type of dying you can't hear
> We are living the same lives our ancestors had
> We are free but still enslaved
> Walking over people's graves
> Not learning from the life they had to live
> The things they had to give
> For us to survive
> For them to look into our eyes
> And say this is the next generation
> This is my relation
> This is my child
> This is our future"

When she finishes the crowd is silent, reverent for a moment; then everyone bursts into wild applause. Autumn reaches up to hug Lauren as she comes back to her seat. Then it's Autumn's turn.

"Give my girl a hand," Autumn says, and extends hers toward Lauren. "She put her *heart* into that poem." When Lauren's second round of applause subsides, Autumn pulls a folded-up piece of paper from the side pocket of her cargo pants, unfolds it, closes her eyes for a moment. She isn't nervous, just excited; she's already tried her poem out on her friends, who reassured her that it's "tight." "I'm willing to put this out and let everyone know," she told Lillian and Lauren. "Because when you believe in something but you keep it a secret, it's not as good. After the slam, when people look at me they'll remember my poem. They'll know that's the kind of person I am."

"This is called 'Stimulation,' " Autumn says to the hundred people in the theater. "It's a poem about how I want to feel about somebody someday. It's directed toward the opposite sex, but it's really about the qualities I look for in anyone I love. Some of the stuff I put in here I feel about Lillian and Lauren, my best friends." She reads from the crumpled piece of binder paper in her hands.

> *"Yeah I guess you can call it infatuation*
> *Because something about you starts a stimulation*
> *And reminds me of a certain situation*
> *Where your face and soft skin get full accreditation*
> *Now I'm not just talkin' physical thangs*
> *Because although your body makes mine sang*
> *Your mind and your soul*
> *Is what I want to hold*
> *Your spirituality and intelligence*
> *Is all that's really relevant*
> *I know when I started this verse*
> *You probably thought something sexual of course*
> *But I think understanding the mind as well as the body is key*
> *Because it's going to take more than your body to satisfy me*
> *So before you think I'm caught up in the ass*
> *Look at the things that really last*
> *The love, the intellectual interaction*

The spending of time in self-meditation
Because baby that's where I find the real stimulation."

The audience applauds as Autumn folds the paper again and puts it back in her pocket. *I did it,* she thinks happily. Her score is 8.5, a lot lower than Lauren's 9.8, but that's okay. *This isn't the SATs,* she tells herself.

The night's hands-down winner is Daveed Diggs, whose "Where My Niggaz At," about being the only biracial kid in his advanced placement classes, brings roars of recognition.

"I tend to try to stay away from observing skin tones
What does it matter, right
Show sight beyond sight to look within
Yet I begin to break my self-inflicted pact because
God damn it I'm the only black one here
And I'm only half black!
So, where my niggaz at?

"I've been told that college is the most effective way to get
ahead
So my ears have bled from the shout of
TAKE AP!! TAKE AP!! TAKE AP!!
So I take AP
And now I'm sitting here feeling darker by the second
Where My Niggaz At?

"My Niggaz
I know it's not your fault
I know it's The Man
It's the Oppression
It's the fucked up system of this county
But this shit is 400 years old and I'm getting cold and lonely
As I trudge through AP land alone

So do your thing and be happy and more power to you
But meanwhile, I still want to know
Where My Niggaz At?"

In the final elimination round Daveed comes back strong with a poem about the future. "As long as poetry lives in the hearts of the young/ there is hope/force them to remember/we were all born from the same miracle."

A miracle indeed. By any measure this slam is a stellar Berkeley High moment. Multicultural, multihued, multitalented; coming to us live and very much in person, the youth of Berkeley High School—their creativity and their cravings, their passions and their pain—shine bright tonight.

"The exciting part about the Slams," a white, middle-class *Jacket* reporter comments in the next issue, "is the people who come out from the woodwork. The most unexpected people—some of whom I see at school daily—expressed themselves with a power that shocked me . . . the wide range of subjects and deliveries paid tribute to the diversity of BHS, and as a whole the poems presented a picture of a gritty reality."

The gritty reality of homelessness in Berkeley brings an equally diverse group of Berkeley High Students out from the woodwork on a Saturday in mid-December. A block away Keith is clocking in at his new job, working the fountain at Mel's Diner on Shattuck (closer to school and a little better paying than Burger King). Three thousand miles away, Jordan is waking up in a dorm at Bard College. And on the Berkeley High campus Autumn sits with a group of mostly white and Asian seniors in the basement of the C building, taking the ACT test for the second time, while her friend Lauren and the Lady Jackets play a hot game of hoops in the gym, the Berkeley City Ballet performs the *Nutcracker* in the Community Theater, and several hundred Berkeley High students gather in the school's industrial cooking classroom, preparing and serving the school's annual free holiday meal to the homeless people of their town.

Oakland kids and hills kids, Spanish speakers and Mandarin speakers, Japanese moms and white dads crowd into the kitchen from dawn to dusk, slicing thirty turkeys and ten hams (all donated by local grocers), baking cookies and stirring simmering beans, wrapping plastic cutlery in paper napkins and serving steaming cups of coffee to mothers with several children in tow, young men with matted hair, old men carrying bed rolls. "How y'all doin' this season?" a toothless man with waist-length dreadlocks asks, pointing to the Berkeley High lacrosse team jacket his blonde, blue-eyed server is wearing. "Great, thanks," she answers as she spoons stuffing and potatoes onto his plate. "Be sure to come back if you want any more."

"We did a canned food drive during Spirit Week," Jamie Marantz says, explaining why the hundreds of cans covering the pantry floor are all marked "00," "01," "02," or "03." "The class with the most cans won a pizza party. The kids did great, for the most part. Of course last night I *was* ready to kill them all. As I was leaving at ten o'clock I asked the Menu Committee if they had everything they needed for the pies. They said, 'Chill out, Ms. Marantz—all we need is pumpkin, right?' " She rolls her eyes. "Guess where *I* was till midnight!"

Theresa Saunders is here in blue jeans and a sweatshirt, delivering two cooked turkeys she brought from home. "That's more than I ever cook for myself or anyone else! Last year they ran out. I didn't want that to happen again."

The only community members missing here today are the media. Ever present when a gang fight or a fire breaks out, when dismal statistics are released or a principal is fired, the TV cameras and newspaper reporters miss this chance to report good news today from Berkeley High.

Two days later, back from Bard and shaking with anger, Jordan pounds on the door of the Berkeley High college counseling office with his right hand, clutching an empty Federal Express envelope addressed to Bard College with his left. "Ms. Mitchell!" he shouts. "Anybody! Open up!" If he doesn't get everything he needs in this package and the package to FedEx by 5:00 . . . "Ms. Mitchell!" he calls again. No one answers.

He storms through the halls of the H building and across the courtyard. There he finds his friends Finnegan and Ari, along with the rest of the student body, on line for the second-period concert that's about to start in the Community Theater. Josh Redman, valedictorian of Berkeley High's Class of '86 and a Grammy-nominated alumnus of Berkeley High's famous jazz band, is putting on a free concert for his alma mater today. "I don't *believe* that idiot!" Jordan fumes.

"Which one?" Ari asks.

"Ms. Mitchell," Jordan answers.

Finnegan starts to say something; Jordan cuts him off. "Wait till you hear this!" He keeps talking as the three of them are propelled up the steps of the theater, swept along by the momentum of the crowd. "My mom and I fly to New York. We rent a car. We drive up to Bard." The boys are standing in the lobby now, surrounded by students rushing in all directions. Despite Ms. Saunders' order that students sit with their classes and classes sit with their teachers, most of the black kids, as usual, are heading upstairs to the balcony.

Jordan, Finny, and Ari squeeze through the throng into the first empty seats they find. "I spend my first night there in the dorm," Jordan continues, as students stream up and down the aisles around them. "It's hella cool—they smoke pot in their rooms, and nobody cares. It's just like Berkeley! Anyway—I go to classes the whole next day. I go to my interview that night. Everything's cool. Bard's lovin' me. I'm lovin' Bard. I'm sitting there at the end of the interview, waiting to find out that I'm accepted. And you know what they tell me instead?"

"They don't have your transcript," Ari says.

"Or your letters of recommendation. Or your essay," Finnegan adds.

"How'd you know that?" Jordan demands.

"She did the same thing to me," Ari answers.

"And me," Finnegan says. "I applied early admissions to Harvard, Georgetown, and Yale. Ms. Mitchell didn't send my paperwork to any of them. I should have known: when I brought my stuff to her in October she said, 'Oh—I guess kids are going to be applying early.' Like she'd never heard of that before."

"She's doing this to *everyone?*" Jordan asks. Finnegan nods. "Everyone who applied early. We're gonna run an exposé in the *Jacket,* collect horror stories, see if we can get her fired."

"My mom made her write a letter of apology after she screwed up my application to Skidmore," Ari adds.

"We're all going to Laney!" Finnegan cries out, drawing curious looks from the students around him—many of whom are, in fact, likely to be going to Laney or another local junior college, if they're going to college at all.

Theresa Saunders appears on the stage in a bright yellow mudcloth tunic and stylish black hat, shouting in vain into the microphone, telling the students to sit down and quiet down. Finally she gives up and Josh Redman, indistinguishable from a current Berkeley High student in his khaki cargo pants, oversized sweatshirt, and baseball cap shadowing his biracial features, strides onto the stage. "It's great to be back at Berkeley High," he says quietly. The three thousand kids fall silent in their velvet seats, and the soaring sounds of his saxophone fill the theater.

"If Bard's too mad at me to let me in," Jordan says to Ari as Josh Redman lowers the sax from his lips and applause explodes around them, "and if Skidmore isn't too mad at you, maybe if I get into Skidmore I'll go there with you."

"That's a whole lotta ifs," Ari replies.

"Good morning!" LaShawn Routé-Chatmon, one of the five teachers of Berkeley High's African-American Studies Department, shouts to the hundred African-American students gathered in the school library. They're here to kick off Berkeley High's annual week-long Kwanzaa celebration, sponsored by the parallel universe, virtually unknown to the school's nonblack students and teachers of African-American Studies. Some, like Keith, are here because their Computer Academy teachers brought them. Autumn, Lillian, and Lauren are here as members of the Black Student Union. "I said GOOD MORNING!" Ms. Routé-Chatmon repeats. "I will wait for your attention!" This time the students put down their pagers and Walkmans and water bottles and chorus, "Good morning."

"First, a rule of the African-American Studies Department: we allow no hats, sunglasses, or electronic devices. Brothers! Let your natural hair show! You are representing African-American Studies now!"

Keith pulls the black knit cap off his head and continues leafing through a football magazine. "Does anyone know the first principle of Kwanzaa?" Ms. Routé-Chatmon asks.

"Umoja!" Autumn calls out.

"Yes! Say it back to me!" Ms. Routé-Chatmon says.

"UMOJA!" the students roar, and they are introduced to the first speaker, a woman wearing a head wrap and dashiki. She represents a group called Pulling Ourselves Together.

"Africa supplies 70 percent of the world's resources," she begins. "Does anyone know which of the world's resources come from Africa?"

"Oil!" "Gold!" "Diamonds!" "Sugar!" "Platinum!" "Everything!" the kids shout out. "Black people," Keith mutters.

"You can say that out loud," the speaker tells him. "Say it!"

"BLACK PEOPLE!" Keith shouts.

"Yes, that's a major resource of the world," she affirms. Keith takes a few bows before he takes his seat.

"Did you know the Congo has been getting robbed of its diamonds *forever?*" the speaker asks. "You think South Central is bad—in the Congo they been killin' *up* each other. The media want us to believe it's tribal, but the tribes would be wiped out by now if that were true. Why do you think we hear so much bad about Africa?"

" 'Cause they takin' so much out of Africa and puttin' so little into it," a boy with his hair carved in perfect concentric circles answers.

" 'Cause we might want to go out there and get diamonds from Africa ourselves," says Lillian.

"Right!" the speaker says. The discussion of Africa continues until Ms. Routé-Chatmon introduces Keith's classmate and nemesis, Josh Gray, the president of the Black Student Union.

"We have so many African-American males failing at Berkeley High," Josh says. "The system bringin' us down and we bringin' ourselves down. We want to step up and be leaders in our community." The girls, including Autumn, Lillian, and Lauren, applaud enthusiastically. Across the room, Keith and his friends roll their eyes.

"As far as African-American males not graduating," one girl says, "that's a personal problem. They more males hangin' outside the school than inside. You can only tell your brothers to go to class so many times."

"That's where the African-American Studies Department comes in," another girl replies. "They give us more motivation to go to class."

"I started takin' African-American Studies 'cause I get to work with African-American teachers. They understand us. It's hard when your teacher doesn't look like you," a boy adds, to much applause.

Ms. Routé-Chatmon steps up beside Josh. "The BSU is trying to tell you something. Your average GPA is 2.1," she says. "For white students it's 3.2. For Asian students 3.3. If you-all want to go to college, how come we're not seeing academic achievement from you? What do you need?"

Without waiting for an answer she continues. "We're not living in an economy where you can afford not to graduate from high school. My dad worked at Chrysler and made good money. You can't do that." The students shift in their seats, pick at their hair.

"Am I wrong to think that you-all can do better?" Ms. Routé-Chatmon continues. "Black students can do as well or better than any other group on campus! The behavior I see from you does not confirm that. I cannot care about you more than you care about yourselves!"

Throughout the week that message is hammered home by African-American Studies teachers and guest presenters in a myriad of workshops and classes: "Are You Still a Slave? Understanding Psychological Enslavement and Representing Our Race"; "Black Male/Female Relations: Respecting Each Other, Respecting Ourselves"; "Hip Hop Culture: the Men, the Women and the Message"; "Signifying: There's Power in Our Words."

The last day of Kwanzaa Week is also the last day of school before the two-week holiday break. While the white, Latino, Asian, and "other" Berkeley High School students eat, drink, and dance at their in-class holiday parties, exchanging Christmas and Hanukkah plans and shiny-ribboned gifts, hundreds of Berkeley High's black students fill the Little Theater hidden behind the Community Theater, watching each other perform breathtaking African-Haitian dance. Garbed in homemade traditional African costumes of yellow and orange and blue, in groups of ten and twenty, the hundred and fifty students of Berkeley High's seven African-Haitian dance classes pound the stage, their bare feet flashing, their gleaming bodies flung into the rhythm supplied by the young men drumming in the wings. From the audience the students hoot and clap and shout out the dancers' names, and just this once the teachers don't shush them but join them, hugging the sweating dancers as they thunder down off the stage.

When it's time to close the ceremony, the statuesque, Kente cloth–clad dance teacher known to all as "Mama" invites the whole audience onto the stage "because that's the African way." Soon the stage is packed with kids in street clothes mingling with the brightly clad dancers, their backpacks flopping, jeans drooping, Nikes stomping on the trembling wooden floor. "Come on up! Don't be afraid!" Mama keeps calling, smiling beatifically at this coming together of African and American.

In the audience Autumn, Lillian, and Lauren laugh and point as friends of theirs "act a fool" on the stage. "I'm gon' take me some African-American Studies classes next semester," Autumn vows. "Fo' sho," Lillian agrees. Now that they're seniors, with most of their graduation requirements met, they can start taking the "fun" electives that they haven't had time for before. "I can't be takin' no dance class though," Autumn adds, and the three girls laugh. Autumn always says it's her "white side" that makes her an embarrassment on the dance floor.

Keith jumps up onto the stage just long enough to shake the girls in the front row into a frenzy. "Keith! Keith!" they scream. Satisfied, he runs back to where his friends are standing in the aisle.

Then Mama steps out into the center of the writhing bodies on the stage and holds up her hand. "Umoja—Unity! Kujichagulia—Self-determination! Ujima—Working together! Ujamaa—Supporting each other!" She calls out each word of Kwanzaa and its meaning, waits for the kids to shout it back to her. Standing in the aisle, Keith flirts with

Crystrial, whispering in her ear so as to be heard above the commotion. Bouncing in their seats, their voices joined with the others, Autumn, Lillian, and Lauren shout themselves hoarse. "Nia—Purpose! Kuumba—Creativity! Imani—Faith in ourselves!"

However they end their last day of the twentieth century, every Berkeley High student goes home with a millennial holiday message from Principal Saunders, printed on festive red paper.

Message to All Students and Staff

. . . As we close this millennium with all of the celebrations, excitement, nostalgia and anticipation that come, may we remember our life together as Berkeley High School. We have had times of great joy, sorrow, hope, dreams, failures, and successes. However great the past has been, the future is still before us. Berkeley High School is a great school with a great history . . . but our best days are ahead . . .

Love, Joy and Peace in the New Millennium,

Theresa Saunders
Principal, Berkeley High School

January 2000: Scandalous

"Jordan!"

From his basement bedroom directly below his mother's, Jordan hears his mom calling him. At first he thinks she's just making sure he's awake and getting himself to school on time for a change—except for the sound of her voice: *almost like the day she told me Dad died.* Jordan gallops up the stairs.

Natalie's hand is still on her bedside phone; her face is pallid against her tousled carmine hair. "I just talked to Bard," she says. "They're not . . . you're not . . ."

"I'm not in?"

Natalie nods.

"Mom! I am or I'm not?"

"You're not."

"*Fuck!*" Jordan sinks heavily onto his mother's bed. "Because they didn't get my paperwork from Berkeley High?"

"Because they got the wrong paperwork from Berkeley High." Natalie kicks off the goose-down comforter Jordan gave her two weeks ago for Hanukkah. "Apparently Ms. Mitchell sent Bard those awful mid-semester grades of yours by mistake."

"*What?* Bard saw *those?*"

"I just got off the phone with the Bard admissions director. He said normally they don't get applicants' mid-semester grades or factor them into the decision. But once they'd seen all those Ds they couldn't ignore them."

"Bard wasn't even supposed to know about those grades! Teachers always give shitty mid-semester grades to scare everyone into working harder. I was gonna cram for finals, get my GPA back up . . ."

His mom nods. "I know. The admissions guy said they'd been planning to accept you—even with your transcript being late and all the hassles they've had trying to get your stuff from Ms. Mitchell—until they saw the Ds."

"I could throttle that stupid bitch," Jordan swears.

"Jordan!" *Ms. Mitchell didn't earn those grades—you did,* Natalie starts to say. Then she sees the look on Jordan's face and bites her lip. *No need to make him feel any worse.* Natalie climbs out of bed, yanks open her closet door. "I'm going to school with you," she says. "I'll be ready in five minutes."

Jordan's head is buried in his hands. "What's the point?" he mumbles.

"I'll talk to Ms. Mitchell. Get her to write a letter. We'll appeal the decision." She doesn't mention that the admissions director has already discouraged her from doing that.

"Jordan. Go get ready, okay? We've got to try and fix this somehow."

Ms. Mitchell's office in the H building is locked, as usual. Jordan and Natalie march back over to the B building, park themselves in Principal Saunders' waiting room, and refuse to leave until a secretary gets on the walkie-talkie and tracks Ms. Mitchell down. When they intercept her in the hall she confirms that yes, she did send Jordan's failing mid-semester grades to Bard. In fact, she says, she also sent those grades to Skidmore, Boston University, Lewis & Clark, and Pitzer: every college Jordan is applying to. Standard procedure, she says.

"I've been on the phone with every one of those colleges every day for the past two weeks," Natalie tells Ms. Mitchell, her voice shaking but controlled. "I know for a fact that they only expect to see grades through last June."

"Do you realize what you just did?" Jordan hisses at Ms. Mitchell. "You just screwed up my whole college education!"

"I'll be back to talk to you later," Natalie tells Ms. Mitchell. She grabs her son and pulls him down the hall. "Jordan. I'm angry too. But—"

"She's lucky she hasn't gotten bumped off yet," Jordan sputters. He plants himself in a classroom doorway, faces his mother. "You know she did this to a bunch of other people too?" he says. "Finnegan was supposed to go to *Harvard!* He got denied early admissions because of her. Ari's in trouble with Skidmore. The one thing this school is supposed to do—help kids get into good colleges—and they put that . . . that . . . *idiot* in charge of it."

Natalie's hand flutters toward her son, falls to her side. "Jordan—"

"That woman doesn't deserve to *live!*"

"I want you to go to class now," Natalie says. "I'll handle this. I promise."

"You think I can sit in a stupid Statistics class right now?" Jordan's voice cracks.

"You have to," Natalie gives him a little shove. "Go. I'll page you if I get any news. Otherwise we'll talk tonight."

But at dinner Natalie has little to report. She's spent half her day waiting to talk to Ms. Saunders, heard "a bunch of mumbo-jumbo" about why the wrong grades were sent out, and extracted a promise from Ms. Saunders to call all the colleges on Jordan's list and explain that his GPA is really 3.1, not the 2.5 his mid-semester grades would indicate.

She's also spoken to Joanne, Jordan's private college counselor, who pronounced this "the worst screw-up I've ever heard of in all my years in this business." For all the money Jordan and Natalie have paid Joanne, for all the certainty her expertise was supposed to provide, there isn't much that she can do now. "I know he's got his heart set on Bard," Joanne tells Natalie. "But we'd better start making a list of safety schools. When Skidmore and his other top choices see those grades, they're likely to reject him too."

Jordan's phone rings off the hook all night as word spreads among his friends. "Looks like it's junior college for Jordan," he mumbles to Finnegan.

"This is scandalous," says Finnegan. "We're gonna hand out flyers tomorrow asking kids who've been screwed by Mitchell to let us print their stories in the *Jacket*. Maybe that'll help."

"It's too late, Finny," Jordan says dully. "Even if they fire Mitchell, Harvard doesn't want you. Bard doesn't want me. Face it, man. We're hosed."

"We need to get started, people," says Theresa Saunders, stylishly dressed as usual in an oversized mustard sweater and form-fitting black slacks, to the 150 chitchatting teachers of Berkeley High who are assembled in the school library for a Wednesday afternoon staff meeting. Saunders' hair, last seen in a neatly trimmed Afro, is now locked into what she jokingly referred to earlier as "treads": "that stage between twisties and dreads."

But Saunders isn't joking now. "First item of business," she says above the continuing buzz in the room. "Dr. Hayes and Dr. James, our 'critical friends' from the WASC Commission, are here to help us with our accreditation process." Two white-haired men—the only ones in the room wearing ties—stride to the front.

"As you make changes in a school, it's like turning the *Exxon Valdez*," Dr. James begins. "It takes a long time. You have to change the people in a school to make it happen."

"We do *that* every year," Amy Crawford whispers sarcastically to Dana Richards. The turnover at Berkeley High is even worse than the recently announced state figures. Half of California's new teachers now quit within five years; at Berkeley High, new teachers currently constitute more than half of the teaching staff.

"WASC puts a stamp of approval or disapproval on a program," Dr. James continues. "But whatever happens with your accreditation, the bottom line question is this: are the students at Berkeley High learning? Can you honestly say, 'We're serving all the needs of all the students and this is how we can prove it'?"

Annie Johnston, Keith's history teacher, raises her hand. "We've been given forty-five minutes a week in which to decide how this school is going to close the achievement gap between students of color and white students—which is an *American* problem. And we have no money to solve it. So all our best ideas, like supporting the Student Learning Center, improving access to students without resources—come to nothing. Everything we can propose simply fits into the structure we've got. Which doesn't work."

The teachers applaud enthusiastically.

"Anyone who serves in a public school district and thinks they're going to get everything they want is living in a fantasy land," Dr. James responds.

"There have to be other schools this size that've gone through this process and found a model that works," Amy Crawford protests.

"There are as many ways to do this as there are schools," says Dr. James. "Sometimes teachers volunteer to come in early in the morning."

A groan arises from the group. "You people have a lot going for you," Dr. Hayes says. "All of us who observed classes here said we'd never witnessed such a high level of discussion, the exchange of ideas, the willingness of students to take part in conversation. On the other side of it, I've never seen such emotion about the disenfranchisement of some groups. We spoke to kids who described themselves as representing a large group, and they said they didn't feel a part of this place. They said 'We can't get access to this program.' They said it in different language but that's what they said. That's got to change."

"We don't have time to work on that problem, and that problem will take a lot of time to solve," a teacher says. "Can you help us with that?"

"Somehow you have to get this faculty to come to a single vision for this school: what you want this school to be known for five years from now," Dr. Hayes replies. "If your vision is to concentrate on kids of high achievement and the hell with the rest of them—say that openly and get on with it."

"Did I just hear what I think I heard?" Amy Crawford groans.

Theresa Saunders steps forward. "We've got to wrap up this part of the meeting," she says, turning to the visiting WASC auditors. "Thank you, gentlemen, for your help." The two men smile benignly, shake her hand, and leave. Saunders turns back to the teachers. "I'll ask that the WASC committee chairs and cochairs meet with me on Tuesday at 3:30.

"Next order of business: as mandated by California Assembly Bill 1626, our school board has approved a new promotion-retention policy."

The teachers are still muttering to each other, the energy in the room as jagged as a steak knife as she continues. "Effective September 2000, only students with a grade of C or better will be promoted. The D will no longer be considered a passing grade. Students with Ds or Fs in their core classes must be retained and must repeat those classes."

Instantly Saunders has the full attention of the teachers, many of whom use the D grade regularly in one of two ways: as a warning to normally high-achieving students (as Jordan and Autumn's teachers did, mid-semester), or as a mechanism to make palatable the social promotion of low achievers who actually deserve Fs (as Keith's teachers have done throughout his school career).

"When we took a look at the 2,700 kids currently at Berkeley High who were here last year," Saunders goes on, "we found that 1,900 of them had one or more Ds or Fs in math, science, English, history, and foreign languages. That means that two-thirds of our kids would have to repeat those classes.

"We don't have the human resource, the space resource, the economic resource to retain all those kids in all those classes. So, since state law stipulates this policy through the ninth grade only, I'm proposing to the board that we not apply it to our tenth-, eleventh-, or twelfth-graders for now. That's still 300 kids—one-third of the ninth-grade class—we'll have to recycle next year. But it's a lot more doable than 1,900."

A veteran history teacher raises her hand. "This policy came into being with no input from the teachers!" she says angrily. "All of a sudden it becomes law. Theresa, this is exactly why we have a lot of good people walking around here saying, 'If it continues like this I'm going to find another job.' I don't know where in our schedule we can find time to talk about these big issues, but we have to."

"You're saying you're unilaterally going to shove this policy down our throats," a math teacher adds. "The teachers would like to be part of the process *before* it's a fait accompli."

"Yoo hoo, guys!" Theresa Saunders' voice rings out. "I know this isn't popular, but at some point I have to make decisions with or without staff input. I'm committed to solid communication, but that doesn't mean we all have input about everything. It means that I, Theresa Saunders, make some decisions in the best interest of everyone and *we move on*." She glances up at the clock on the wall. It's two minutes before five—ten hours after she, and many of the people in the room, arrived here today; five or six hours before she and many of the teachers will finish their day's work. "That's it for now, people."

The issues that the Berkeley Unified School District is attempting to address with its retention/promotion policy—academic achievement, academic standards, and that buzz word du jour, *accountability*—dominate the American discourse on education as the millennium turns and an election year begins.

"Our New Year's resolution," President Clinton says, declaring the rebuilding of public schools his top legislative priority, "is to reach across party lines to help our children reach for the sky."

No one in Berkeley, or anywhere else, would oppose such a noble goal; the question, of course, is how it might be achieved. In his "lame duck" State of the Union Address on January 27, Clinton gets specific, proposing the allocation of billions of dollars to teacher recruitment and training, charter schools, and class size reduction. He also suggests that the government do for children everywhere what Jordan and his private college counselor tried to do for Autumn: "offer these kids from disadvantaged backgrounds the same chance to take the same college test-prep courses wealthier students use to boost their test scores."

Just as Berkeley's retention policy holds teachers and students accountable by holding kids back, Clinton gets tough too, vowing to "help states and districts turn around their worst performing schools, or shut them down." Interrupted by thunderous applause, he adds, "All successful schools have followed the same proven formula: higher standards, more accountability, and extra help so children who need it can get it to reach those standards. I have sent Congress a reform plan based on that formula. It holds states and school districts accountable for progress and rewards them for results."

And how might states and districts be held accountable, and their progress be measured? In California, as in states across the nation, lawmakers offer a two-word answer: *standardized testing*. Despite all that is now known about the damaging biases inherent in these tests—their failure to measure any but the most narrow indicators of learning; the dangerous inaccuracies of the data they yield—no one, it seems, has yet devised an alternative gauge. "[Standardized tests] have failed to provide the information we need about students and specific curricular objectives," writes the U.S. Education Department–funded Educational Resources Information Center. "So far, they have not helped us improve our schools."

Nonetheless, on January 26, Governor Gray Davis releases the Academic Performance Index: a ranking of 7,000 California schools derived from a single statewide exam, ironically named STAR (Standardized Testing And Reporting). Next year, Davis says, the STAR test will be re-administered, with rewards for schools that reach their target improvement rates. "Starting today," he proclaims, "teachers and schools can earn financial rewards if they accomplish the only thing that really matters: improved student achievement."

In response, a *San Francisco Chronicle* editorial warns, "The rankings are based on the results of one test taken last spring, and kids who come to school hungry, who have little support at home, whose English is weak . . . will as a group score lower than kids who are well-nourished, whose parents graduated from college and whose native tongue is English. . . . The rankings should not be the determining factor for parents trying to decide where to send their child to school."

However well reasoned, the *Chronicle*'s warning proves naive. The web site listing the Academic Performance Index (API) scores for Bay Area schools records 4,000 hits in its first half-hour as frantic parents scrutinize the scores of their kids' schools—and prospective schools. Realtors report already exorbitant housing prices spiking in districts with good scores, leveling off in districts with schools whose API ratings are low.

A few days later, in a *Chronicle* op-ed, the dean of UC Berkeley's School of Education says the API "seems to be driven by a 'reform by shame' philosophy." "On the basis of this test alone, schools could either be rewarded or dissolved . . . The scores will confuse the students, their parents and the public."

Sadly, though, the API scores are anything but confusing; they are, in fact, painfully predictable. The public high schools in the wealthiest, whitest Bay Area school districts—Piedmont, Marin, San Mateo—all earn the top API ranking of 10. Of the six Oakland public high schools, three are rated 1, two are rated 2; the "best" high school in Oakland scores a 5. Only Berkeley High's score—a 9—is surprising, causing those who know that two-thirds of its students are failing their classes to wonder if the API has any relationship to reality at all.

Not so Principal Saunders. "Our scores are great," she enthuses electronically in her posting on the "Berkeley Parents of Teens" E-newsletter, to which 700 online Berkeley High families subscribe. "We are the largest high school in our county and the most diverse. We have students at all academic achievement levels and still all of them performed well. This is something about which to celebrate . . .

"Yes, we do have a lot of work to do because the disaggregated data is troublesome . . . However, I do believe that it is important to stop and smell the roses and enjoy our success."

The Berkeley High Jacket analyzes the "troublesome" data, countering Saunders' assertion that *all* Berkeley High students performed well. "While Caucasian and Asian students scored very high, African-American and Chicano/Latino students scored much lower." (Eighty-seven percent of white Berkeley High students, 32 percent of Latinos, and 27 percent of African-Americans scored at or above the national average in reading; 91 percent of whites, 50 percent of Latinos, and 43 percent of African-Americans scored at or above the national average in math.)

"However," the *Jacket* concludes, "the highest correlation found to determine a student's score range is family income."

Challenging that correlation—and every other tenet of conventional educational wisdom—is what CAS is all about. And if CAS is to prove that student performance need *not* be inextricably linked to family income; that students of varying backgrounds, languages, and abilities *can* be taught in one classroom with one curriculum; that students learn best when their minds *and* their hearts are open; then CAS must produce results that are, yes, measurable by traditional standards—including college admissions. And so while Jordan, and then one after another of Berkeley High's elite students, become casualties of the school's college counseling department, CAS does an end-run around the system.

"I've got some really good news for you guys. About college," Ms. Crawford announces as the CAS students pour into her room.

Still reeling from his Bard rejection, Jordan wonders momentarily if Ms. Crawford could possibly be talking about something that could possibly help him. "I'll share my news as soon as everyone gets here," Ms. Crawford adds. "In the meantime I'd like a volunteer to lead a two-minute free-write on the subject of your choice."

Rena waves her hand and takes Ms. Crawford's place on the stool in the center of the room. "Write about how much emphasis Americans place on material items," she instructs her classmates. "What do you think can be done to change it, or is it cool?" Two minutes later she checks her watch and says, "Okay—stop writing! So: who wants to share?"

"I do enjoy the TV in my room and the car outside my house. I do not enjoy people judging me by the shoes I wear," says Melania, dressed today as always in defiance of fashion in a floppy, unbranded T-shirt, no-name jeans, beat-up running shoes.

"People gonna talk 'bout you regardless if you got new shoes or not," says Fatima. "People need to just grow up and not care."

Rena says, "I know this is capitalism and all, but as young people isn't it our responsibility to change it?"

Joaquin saunters in late, his arm around his girlfriend, Mia. "What y'all talkin' 'bout?" he asks.

"Materialism," Rena answers.

"It's one thing to have things you like. It's not a right thing to value that over everything else," Autumn says. She stops, pensively chews her gum, blows a bubble, continues. "Sure, we should change it. But this is the capitalistic world. The people who are running everything want it to be like this. And why should teenagers be the ones who have to set the example? Why don't the old people stand up and say materialism is wrong? They created it." She moves her backpack from the chair next to hers to the floor, making room for the latecomers trickling into the room.

"The civil rights movement was so successful because everyone in it was against what was happening," Jordan says. "It would be impossible to get the teenagers of America together like that. They're too happy with their Hilfiger, their Nikes. Remember—we're in Berkeley. We're two steps ahead of everybody else. Go out to San Ramon. The people out there aren't even thinking about these things."

"That's really the problem," Autumn replies. "People think materialism doesn't affect them. But it does. It affects your morality, your spirituality. I do it myself. I sit up here and say it's wrong to care about a pair of shoes but I don't do anything about it. It's my responsibility to show a better way to my brothers, my friends, at least. To be a good example."

"I don't really believe this," Jordan counters. "But just for the sake of argument: can anyone name a culture that's survived without exploiting others for the sake of materialism?"

"Define 'survive,' " Autumn challenges him.

"I guess I mean 'thrive,' " Jordan replies.

"This is a great discussion. But I'm going to interrupt it for just a minute," Ms. Crawford interjects. "Most everyone's here now, and I can't wait to tell you this good news. You guys: it looks like all CAS students who applied to UC Santa Cruz are basically guaranteed to get in."

Autumn's jaw drops. She gapes at Ms. Crawford.

"A friend of Mr. Ayers' works there," Ms. Crawford explains. "He's a big fan of CAS, and he's been working with the admissions office to cut us a special deal—the kind of thing colleges do for athletes they're trying to recruit. Yesterday UCSC agreed to create some special slots for CAS students."

"Why they doin' that?" Joaquin asks.

"A few reasons. UCSC wants a better connection with Berkeley High and with CAS. They want a more diverse student body. It's a pretty white campus . . ."

The kids snort and laugh. "*Pretty* white?" Jordan says.

"Very white," Ms. Crawford acknowledges. "Anyway, this man is really interested in integrating the school. And you can thank yourselves, too. When we went to UCSC on our retreat last year, you guys made a great impression."

"Is this for real?" Autumn asks hoarsely. "For sure?"

"Let me be clear," Ms. Crawford answers. "This doesn't mean that if you have a 1.0 GPA you're going to UCSC. And if you're lacking a UC-required class you'll have to take care of it before September. But . . . yes. If you have your ducks in a row you can pretty much know you're going. Good deal, huh?"

"Did you hear *that*?" Autumn exclaims. She hugs the girls on either side of her, high-fives the boys around her. "I've got a 3.1 GPA! And my college essay is the bomb! So I'm cool for sure! I don't even have to apply anywhere else!"

Normally Autumn dawdles after CAS lets out, talking to her CAS friends or to Ms. Crawford. But today she flies down the hall, her black backpack thumping against her shoulder blades, her Gap nylon purse bobbing against her hip, rushing to get to Lillian and Lauren. *This is the best birthday present of all,* she thinks. Autumn turned eighteen last week, and her girls treated her like a queen. They took her out to dinner not one but two nights in a row, before and after a sleepover at Lillian's. They gave her a tape recorder to help with her Youth Radio interviews and a pair of Lillian's shoes that Autumn had been admiring, wrapped in bigger and bigger boxes that took Autumn forever to open while the two of them (and the waiter) watched, laughing. Even Autumn's mom gave her a present, and a generous one at that: a really nice black leather coat.

Love is the greatest gift I've got, Autumn reminds herself as she runs from the B building to the C building, where Lillian's next class is. *But getting into UCSC—that's about to change my life!*

The parents and teachers of Berkeley do not take well to their school board's new retention policy. A flyer circulates throughout the schools, headlined:

> COMMUNITY FORUM TO ADDRESS THE EDUCA-
> TIONAL CRISIS WITHIN THE BERKELEY UNIFIED
> SCHOOL DISTRICT
>
> Over 3,000 students of color are scheduled to
> be retained. Is your child one of them?

Held on Martin Luther King Day at a senior center in the mostly black neighborhood of South Berkeley, the forum draws about two hundred teachers, parents, and grandparents of elementary, middle, and high school students. Most of them are African-American; most of them have been notified that their children are at risk of being held back; all of them are angry. Facing them from behind a table embellished by a framed portrait of Martin Luther King is a high-powered panel: all five members of the Berkeley School Board (four of them white; none of them African-American), the county and district school superintendents and assistant superintendent, two Berkeley City Council members, a representative of the teachers union, and Theresa Saunders.

"We have an opportunity here, not a problem," one of the board members opens the meeting. "We've talked a long time about the achievement gap in our high school. Now we have an opportunity to do something about it. We need to work together—home, school, community—to see *all* our students successful. The law requires us to go with this policy now, but we do want to hear your thoughts."

"Society doesn't accept a D or an F in life," adds another board member, explaining that the decision to retain or promote each student will be based on two factors: his or her grades and his or her STAR test results. "We don't want to continue failing our students by passing them on to grade after grade when they're earning Ds and Fs."

As she passes out copies of Berkeley's STAR test results, Theresa Saunders summarizes the data's most salient and distressing finding. "It's really clear that students from economically disadvantaged homes don't come to school with the same readiness as kids from non-disadvantaged homes." Indeed, in the starkest of visuals, the bar graphs reveal that the scores of African-American and Latino students are one-third to one-half as high as the scores of white kids; "disadvantaged" kids' scores are one-third to one-half as high as those of "non-disadvantaged" students.

"This is extremely painful," Superintendent of Schools Jack McLaughlin acknowledges. "But this is a *national* challenge. We've joined a national network to address minority achievement, and I can tell you: Berkeley is the only district that's put the issue on the table."

The parents' hands are waving. "What will the district do to help disadvantaged families that don't have computers in their homes?" a mother asks.

"The school does what it can do; the parents do what they can do," a school board member responds.

"You're not answering my question!" the mother says angrily. "The bigger question is, how did we get here? Why don't you put some money toward understanding this disparity and solving it?"

"Putting standards in place without the programs to back them up is criminal!" says a father. "There needs to be a moratorium on this policy until we have some dialogue on the issue."

"You're going to retain *three thousand* students of color?" A grand-mother stands up in the middle of the room. People call out from the crowd: "Tell it, Elsie!" "Go on!"

"I got a letter telling me my grandson is going to be retained. He didn't sleep that night, and neither did I. I am *not* supposed to get that kind of letter because I've been reading to that boy every day. We need to do something to give these kids self-esteem, to bring these kids up—not down."

"That's right!" The crowd applauds and cheers.

"We know the implications of holding kids back," says Annie John-ston, Keith's history teacher. "When kids fail, you can't just do it *again*. You have to do it better. There's something wrong with the system when it only works for one-third of the students!"

"Teachers know this law will not help students," adds the union rep. "We need to put programs in place that will really address the problems before we implement this law. Where would we be in this country if Martin Luther King had shrugged his shoulders and said, 'It's the law; what can we do?' "

As the parents applaud, the union rep passes out copies of a union resolution that enumerates the reasons for its opposition. "Students are less likely to graduate if they have been retained . . . the policy dispro-portionately affects poor children and children of color . . . teachers can potentially be held personally liable for making the 'wrong' decision regarding retention . . . no plan has been agreed upon for compensating teachers for the huge number of required hours in conference with par-ents of failing students."

"The standards they are using do not include us!" cries a teacher in the Healthy Start program at Malcolm X Elementary School. "Our kids do *not* get snow trips to Lake Tahoe. They do *not* know what a yacht is. Now you're going to keep these children another year in a system that's already failed them!"

The meeting is adjourned four hours after it began, the administrators still asserting that the retention policy, combined with well-funded sup-port programs, will eventually improve achievement; the parents and teachers still arguing that another, less damaging solution must be found.

In the weeks after the meeting the controversy continues: in the pages of the Berkeley High PTSA newsletter ("without social promotion and without an adequate system in place to deal with failing students, many will simply give up and drop out"), the *Berkeley High Jacket* ("At this point, no programs are in place to help [failing students]"); and among the mostly affluent parents of mostly high-achieving students who debate the issue on the Berkeley High E-tree.

"I agree with the school district on this," writes a father. "Kids are moved through the system without learning the material. Somehow the district needs to get the attention of the students and parents, and just passing them through does not send the message that education is important."

"I wonder if this is going to hurt the very kids it's meant to help?" writes Anonymous. "My son squeaks by with Cs and Ds . . . now we have the prospect that he will be held back. My only option seems to be to change him to a smaller private school. I can't help thinking there must be other kids at BHS like my kid, who do not have private school as an option. What is going to happen to them?"

What happens to Keith, as the fall semester draws to an end, is a major reality check. When he picks up his schedule for spring semester—the last semester of his high school career—he finds a sticker on the printout that says, "Please bring this schedule to Flora Russ—Computer Academy." Ms. Russ tells him she wants him to take two more English classes next semester in case he flunks Giglio's. Otherwise, she says, he might not graduate.

Not graduate! How could he be about to get recruited by a four-year college, and Ms. Russ be thinking he might not graduate?

Keith has come this far still believing he's going to make it: ignoring the mounting evidence to the contrary, shrugging off one bad report card after another, promising himself and everyone else the next one will be better. But finals are next week; grades will be entered the week after that, and Keith knows that even if he does better on his finals than he's ever done on a test in his life, he's still going to get Ds or Fs in most or all of his classes.

Of course he's going to graduate! But that's not all Keith has to worry about. This semester was his last chance to pull his GPA up to the 2.5 required by the NCAA—the National College Athletic Association, which makes and monitors the eligibility rules for athletic scholarships and student athletes. Even if his mediocre football season doesn't keep the college recruiters away, his grades make Keith ineligible for a four-year college, ineligible to play on a college team. It's time to face facts. The clock has run out on Keith's football dream.

The hardest part is gonna be telling Moms, Keith thinks. He puts it off as long as he can. But then the Friday night before finals begin, Keith gets home from his five-to-twelve-thirty shift at Mel's Diner and finds his mom still awake. He settles in next to her on the couch. "Nice and quiet around here for once," Patricia murmurs, her eyes on the big-screen TV. Keith's dad is in the bedroom, watching TV by himself; Keith's sister Yolanda, who just moved back home, is trying to get Alonzo, their older sister's four-year-old, back to bed. Even Yolanda's two pit bull puppies are curled up asleep at Patricia's feet.

Keith and his mom watch an *Oprah* rerun together till the commercial comes on. Then Keith clears his throat. "We need to talk, Mom."

"You better not be in trouble again," Patricia warns him. Keith got into a fight at school last week with the cousin of an ex-friend of his. Even though the other kid needed stitches in his head and Keith only had a few scratches, the other kid was suspended and Keith wasn't. Since the other kid threw the first punch, Keith argued self-defense and won. Still, Patricia knows how dangerous a seemingly stupid feud can be. "That boy's friends ain't after you, are they?"

Keith shakes his head. "Dude apologized to me today. He know he shouldn't have sucker-punched me in the hall like that." Nervously his fingers work his twisties, quick and nimble as a spider weaving its web. He decides to start with the easier subject first.

"I found a car, Mom. An '85 Camaro. You *know* how long I been wantin' a Camaro."

"I know how long you been wanting one. I also know how long your money's got to be before you 'bout to buy one."

"The guy's only askin' a thousand dollars. I got that much saved from my jobs."

Patricia gives Keith the look he calls "the evil eye." "What you gon' do with a Camaro when you go away to college?" she asks.

Keith fiddles with the remote, swipes at a smudge on his white leather Jordans. "Keith!" Patricia barks. "I asked you a question."

"I been thinkin', Mom," Keith answers slowly. "About college. Just in case football don't work out—I mean, it still might, but just in case it don't—I might want to go to a junior college. Instead of a four-year."

Keith winces, expecting an explosion. When none comes, he adds, "My season wasn't that great, Mom. You saw how they wouldn't never give me the ball. And anyway . . ." He can't meet his mother's eyes. "I might not make it at a university. If I'm gon' flunk out of a four-year and end up in a J.C., I'd rather just start out at a J.C. in the first place."

"I guess you gon' do what you need to do," Patricia says calmly.

Keith stares at her disbelievingly.

"Did you really think you were gonna surprise me?" she asks. "You been hinting around about this for days."

Encouraged, Keith continues. "There was a fire at Berkeley High on Monday and we all had to go outside. I was talkin' to a hella nice fireman out there. He was tellin' me 'bout the job, tellin' me I should talk to his boss. He even gave me the number. I think I lost it, but I'm gon' call Information and get it again.

"I still plan on playing football at a state college or a junior college. But in case that don't work out, I'm plannin' on bein' a fireman."

"A fireman," Patricia repeats.

Keith nods eagerly. "If I go to a J.C. around here, Dr. Ed said he could hook me up with a job." Dr. Ed, the football team doctor, has always been good to Keith, hiring him to do yard work around his house way up in the hills, driving him home after games. He even had Keith and a few other players over to his house for dinner to teach them how to eat properly—"so you'll know which fork to use when college recruiters take you out to nice restaurants." On New Year's Eve Dr. Ed got a friend of his to hire Keith to work a Millennium party at his mansion in Piedmont. Keith made a hundred and ten dollars in four hours just for taking coats, making conversation, and serving champagne. He was "the only color there," but he had fun anyway, drinking champagne until one in the morning, when Dr. Ed drove him down to his grandma's house in the flats.

"I think you're making a very logical decision," Patricia tells him. "For some kids it's better this way: start off at a J.C., see where it takes you."

"You ain't mad?" Keith's been putting off this conversation for so long, he can hardly believe how smoothly it's going now.

"You know I wanted you to go to a four-year college. But I'm not gonna push you. If you fail you'll be looking at me like, 'Mom, you made me go.' Anyhow," Patricia says, taking the remote from Keith, turning the volume up as the *Oprah* theme song plays, "it ain't me you got to worry about. Or your dad. We'll go along with your decision. But you know what your sisters gonna say."

"You the baby of the family. You gon' be the first one to go to a university," Keith sing-songs the words he's heard a thousand times. "I'll just tell 'em I'm still goin' to college. I know Latisha gon' go off on me. But Yolanda—she'll understand."

"Understand what?" Yolanda asks from the top of the stairs, with still-awake Alonzo fidgeting in her arms. Keith shoots his mom a "help me" look. Patricia shrugs. "You're eighteen now, Keith," she says, her eyes fixed on the screen. "If you grown enough to make your own decisions, you grown enough to stand by them. Now you two take that conversation somewhere else and let me watch *Oprah* in peace."

Jordan's mom Natalie used to come to every PTSA meeting, every Back to School Night. She's still on the Berkeley High Crew team board, although Jordan has stopped rowing, and she's been a mainstay of the

CAS parent support system. Lately, though, her frequent business trips to Japan and Europe have kept her away from nighttime meetings. Until now that hasn't been a problem; Jordan has managed well on his own.

Until now. Sitting in the Berkeley High library at 7:30 p.m., waiting for the PTSA meeting to start, Natalie feels bone-tired. She was on the Internet till three this morning visiting college Web sites, pulling together a list of safety schools as Jordan's private counselor advised her to do. She was up again at seven, calling admissions directors, trying to get Ms. Saunders to write the letter she'd promised to write for Jordan, arranging next week's business trip to Paris.

"Natalie!" She looks up and sees Laura, the mother of Jordan's friend Suzanna, standing beside her. "I heard about Jordan and Bard. I'm so sorry. It's *outrageous,* what happened."

Natalie nods wearily. "I heard Suzanna got into Harvard on early decision. Congratulations."

"Only because she avoided the Berkeley High college counseling process like the plague," Laura says vehemently. "Suzanna collected every transcript, every signature, every piece of paper by herself. She stood there and made sure the packet was sent out. And now the Berkeley High administration is using Suzanna's acceptance to Harvard to prove that the school's college counseling process is working! It makes me furious!"

The meeting is called to order. Laura gives Natalie a quick hug and goes back to her seat. The meeting begins with a report on Berkeley High's "adopt-a-plot" parent gardening program. "We've got several families weeding and watering fifteen plots on the campus already," a mother with a British accent reports. "Pretty soon you should see Berkeley High looking like Versailles." The fifty or so white parents, two Asian parents, and one African-American parent (who's copresident of the PTSA) chuckle politely.

"When do you plan to start the adopt-a-bathroom program?" another mother asks, to more laughter.

"People in the child adoption movement are quite disturbed by the use of the word 'adoption' to talk about plants," a woman with long, salt-and-pepper hair complains.

"Let's call it the scorched earth program," the first speaker replies smoothly.

Theresa Saunders introduces Beth, a volunteer at Berkeley High's new Parent Resource Center. "The PRC was created by the Diversity Project to serve traditionally disadvantaged kids and their parents," Beth tells the audience, which is nearly devoid of such parents. "It's amazing how quickly kids' track records change when their parents get a call from school from someone speaking their own language."

The parents do not respond. Finally a father raises his hand. "How many families have made use of the Parent Resource Center?" he asks politely. "It's gone from three to eighteen contacts a day," Beth answers eagerly. "What else can I tell you?" After another awkward silence Theresa Saunders takes the floor. In a striking deviation from her usual style—making authoritative speeches, ticking off agenda items, leaving little time for questions—tonight she asks simply, "Are there any rumors out there you'd like to have me address?"

The parents in the audience, most of whom are regulars at these meetings, exchange surprised looks. "The pressure must be getting to her," one mother whispers to another. And well it might be. Besides dealing with the college counseling disaster-in-progress, figuring out where to put three hundred "retained" ninth-graders next year, and keeping the WASC process moving toward accreditation, Saunders is also facing increasing hostility from the staff (the teachers have vowed to boycott staff meetings starting in February and continuing until the still-broken clocks and copy machines are fixed) and the students (the *Jacket,* word has it, is preparing an exposé that will call for her resignation).

On top of that there were two arson fires at Berkeley High in the past two weeks, evoking unpleasant memories of last year's rash of fires. In both cases locked doors—to which only staff members had keys—were unlocked, the fires set, and the rooms locked again. In both cases no fire alarm sounded because the system had been disarmed. Only the keen noses and quick actions of teachers prevented tragedy. The police investigation has yet to yield arrests; inspections of the alarm system have yet to explain how it was rendered useless.

And then there was the paddy wagon incident. While Saunders was in Washington at an education conference last week, Barry Wiggan convinced the Berkeley Police to escalate Operation Stay in School, their daily truancy sweep through downtown Berkeley. Instead of the usual routine—police and school safety officers on foot, on bikes, and in patrol cars urging late and loitering students back to school—on two occasions paddy wagons were sent around the neighborhood, just after the lunch period ended, to pick up anyone who seemed to "fit the description" of a Berkeley High student, including some who weren't students at all. "Some have charged that the manner in which students were picked up was racially biased," the *Jacket* reported. "When Saunders was asked about the issue, she said repeatedly, 'Go into the halls of the C building and see who is out there. That's all I have to say.'" The *Jacket* quoted one of the two students who were forced into paddy wagons even after proving that they had no class that period. "Nearly all [the students in the paddy wagon] were black. They think African-American students are more trouble than white students. They never do anything about the park, which is mostly white kids smoking weed."

Days after they occurred, the paddy wagon sweeps sparked an exceptionally unified burst of outrage. The Black Student Union and the student government cosponsored a lunchtime student rights rally in the Berkeley High courtyard, and it was well attended by the press. "Don't just complain—*do* something," BSU president Josh Gray urged the two hundred students gathered around the theater steps. "We shouldn't feel like convicts when we're tardy." Captain Will Pittman of the Berkeley Police Department took the mike. "I'm here to publicly apologize for that, and I hope you will accept my apology. This is what I guarantee: it will never happen again."

Even Barry Wiggan was forced to stand right there on the steps and read from the same script, while students smirked and reporters' cameras whirred. "Police Apologize to BHS Students," announced the front-page story in the next day's *Berkeley Daily Planet.* The whole mess hadn't made *anyone* look good—except the kids, who'd somehow turned cutting class into a cause and themselves into victims of police repression.

Sure enough, the first topic of questioning by the parents is the sweeps. "My guess is that the kids most likely to be picked up are kids of color, kids who dress in a certain way," says the mother who objected to the use of the word "adoption," "because those are the kids who get picked on."

"We pick them all up, even if they're not ours," Saunders says. "In the park we mostly pick up white students. On Shattuck we mostly pick up African-American and Latino/Chicano students. On Telegraph we pick up all kinds. The owner of Barnes & Noble on Shattuck called us and said, 'We have seventy of your kids.' I'm told that when the paddy wagon took the kids away, the store employees cheered."

"At least they're around books," a mother quips, and everyone laughs. Everyone, that is, except Theresa Saunders. "They shouldn't have been there," she says grimly. "They need to be in school."

"My daughter told me some of the kids had handcuffs slapped on them," a father says.

"There were no handcuffs used," Saunders retorts. "The police got them back here and we sifted and sorted who belonged here and who didn't. Any other rumors you'd like me to speak to?"

"I've heard there are problems with transcripts getting out to colleges," a mother says, jolting Natalie out of her sleep-deprived trance.

"I've heard that too," Saunders answers. "I'm not saying people are lying, but I've called every college myself and the colleges are telling me they're getting the stuff they need. If you're having a problem, call me." She glances at the clock on the wall. "Anything else before we adjourn?"

Natalie raises her hand. "I came to this meeting to give a heads-up. My son is in two AP classes. At midterm he was getting Ds in both. He's made up the work, he's doing okay, but his failing grades were released to every college he's applying to. He's already been denied by his top-choice school. My son is devastated by this. It's his fault the grades were bad, but it's the school's fault the grades went out.

"Our kids are smart," Natalie continues, "but they check out in the middle of senior year. If you're at all concerned about your child's mid-term grades, find out if they were released to colleges. My son is going to have to do some serious damage control to climb out of this. Theresa's helping me, but I'm not sure we can fix it."

"It's a work in progress," Saunders says. "Because of her son's grades it may be problematic."

"It may be problematic for a lot of people," a mother says to scattered, ironic laughter.

"Check your child's grades," Saunders advises. "If they're problematic, call us and we'll pull the grades from the transcripts."

"It's too late now," a father says. "The damage has been done."

"To protect our students, to give them the best opportunity to go to the best schools they can get into, we need a policy to withhold their mid-semester grades," Natalie says. "I'd really like some support for that." She gets it, in the form of ringing applause.

"Agreed," Theresa Saunders says. "The meeting is adjourned. Thank you very much for coming."

February 2000: Breakdown

"Mr. Stephens! You will sit here, please." Mr. McKnight, Keith's African-American Literature teacher for his last semester of high school, points to the chipped desk closest to his lectern. In this and all of the H building classrooms, only the furniture is old. Renovated with bond-initiative funds three years ago, the G–H building is the school's only modernized one, with gleaming white tile walls, working blinds and windows, automatic-flush toilets. Home to the African-American Studies department, this corner of the H building also happens to be as far as you can get from the B building, the hub of the school.

"What's wrong with where I'm sitting?" Keith protests from the back of the room.

"We have assigned seats in this class," Mr. McKnight answers briskly. He proceeds through the roster in his hand until everyone in his new crop of students—fourteen of them black, one Latino, three whites—has been assigned a seat. Chairman of the African-American Studies department, a Berkeley High graduate and forty-year veteran of the school, Mr. McKnight exudes the dignity and formality of a prep school professor. He dresses formally, too, as few Berkeley High teachers do. Today he wears a starched white dress shirt, elegant silk tie, navy blue blazer, and gabardine slacks.

"Most of you have been in African-American Studies classes before, so you're aware of our department rules," Mr. McKnight says, methodically enunciating each word. "But I am going to review them nonetheless. There will be no eating, drinking, chewing, or sleeping. I'm going to close my eyes for a moment now to give you the opportunity to throw away any gum you may be chewing." As he does so, two girls tiptoe across the room, delicately remove the gum from their mouths with brightly painted press-on nails, and deposit their gum in the trash can beneath the sign printed in red, green, and black ink.

> ### AFRICAN-AMERICAN STUDIES
>
> PLEASE, be prepared: book-paper-pencil-pen-homework
> PLEASE, be respectful of self and others
> PLEASE, refrain from disruptive behavior!

"Any Walkman I see in your possession becomes mine," Mr. McKnight continues. He strides over to a cabinet, throws open the door. The kids gawk at the sight: a floor-to-ceiling closet overflowing with confiscated Walkmans. "I allow nothing on your head unless it's part of your spiritual or religious belief, with one exception: I'm extremely sexist, so I allow girls one bad hair day a month. Gentlemen! Remove your hats, please!" Four boys pull off their knit caps.

"You'll need a notebook exclusively for this class. And unless I notify you otherwise, you are to bring this with you each day." Mr. McKnight passes out dog-eared paperback copies of a novel called *The Nubian*. "Please open to the foreword. If we miss anything at all in a book, we might miss some of the meaning. Now: Mr. Stephens will read for us."

Keith glances around wildly, then sinks into his seat. The girl beside him scoots her desk closer to his, opens his book, points to the first line, nudges him encouragingly.

"There is an . . . expression in the . . ." Keith begins.

"tradition," the girl whispers, and Keith continues.

". . . tradition of the . . ." he stops again.

"the Wolof of Senegal," Mr. McKnight says.

"The Wolof of Senegal that says, 'Wood may remain in water for ten years, but it will never become a . . .' "

". . . crocodile," another girl says.

Keith stumbles through the paragraph, his classmates calling out the words when he falters. Instead of mocking his mistakes or distracting him from his efforts, as many of these same kids did in Mr. Giglio's room last semester, here the atmosphere is one of seriousness and shared purpose. Instead of making jokes to cover up his lack of preparation, sauntering around the room, ignoring the lesson entirely as he did in Mr. Giglio's class, here Keith is a portrait of studiousness, *The Nubian* positioned an inch from his nose, upon which is perched a pair of the non-prescription granny glasses he and many other boys have taken to wearing as a fashion accessory.

Slowly Keith comes to the end of the first paragraph; the girl next to him starts reading the next one. "Succumb? Is that how you say that?" she queries Mr. McKnight, who is standing at the window, his neatly trimmed receding Afro backlit by a halo of winter sun. "Yes ma'am," he answers. "Now let us discuss the quote of the day. 'Wood may remain in water for ten years, but it will never become a crocodile.' What does that mean? Ms. Calhoun?"

"It means if you ghetto, even if you go be with white people in the hills you ain't gonna eat caviar," the girl says. "You still be eatin' chitlins."

"Yes. Good. Ms. Brown?"

"She said what I was gonna say."

"We learn by repetition. Put it in your own words."

"I don't know . . ."

"Don't ever start a sentence with 'I don't know.' "

"It's like . . . when we were in slavery the white people wouldn't let us learn to read." The words burst from the girl's mouth. "Now African-American people at Berkeley High are failing. We can stay here five years, we still don't graduate."

"You always gonna be who you are," Keith offers. "Even though some people do change up."

"That's a good analogy, Mr. Stephens." Keith ducks his head, this time with pride.

When the bell rings a few minutes later Keith stops at the lectern on his way out. "Awwight then, Mr. McKnight," he says, hoisting his back-pack onto his shoulders. "Have a good day, Mr. Stephens," Mr. Mc-Knight answers.

"I'll do that," Keith says, and he means it. Finally, he's top of the heap: last semester, senior year. Since he's only trying to earn the credits required for graduation, not the heavier load he'd need to be eligible for a four-year college, Keith only has to take three classes: African-American Literature, World History (since he flunked it last semester), and English (since he flunked Mr. Giglio's class, too). He gets out for the day at lunchtime now. *Made in the shade,* Keith thinks, sauntering down the hall, accepting hugs from the girls, palm-slaps and "What's up"s from the boys, reveling in the attention of his many admirers.

"Welcome to your last semester at Berkeley High!" Amy Crawford greets the CAS seniors. She looks around the room. "Anyone seen Darnell? Or Lynndra? Or Jordan?"

"They're probably on line at their counselors' offices, like half the rest of the school," Sarah says.

"Before we throw ourselves into the new semester," Mr. Richards says, "we wanted to hear your reflections on the last one. The idea behind CAS is to have some connection between students and teachers. To treat you guys like change agents, leaders in community organizing . . ."

"The retreat was a real bonding thang," Catherine says.

"I've been in CAS since it started, so I feel really comfortable," says Autumn. "I'm an outgoing person. It's easy for me to talk in the big group. But I like it when we break into small groups too."

"We're going to be doing more of that," Ms. Crawford says. "One of our goals for next semester is to transcend cliques, get you to hang out with people you wouldn't otherwise get to know."

"Oh, did you feel like there were cliques in here last semester?" Melania asks sarcastically. All of the forty-five students present burst into laughter—the Latinas clustered in their usual corner, the white girls sitting front and center, the white boys behind them, the African-American girls sitting and leaning against the counter in their back corner, the biracial girls sitting between them and the African-American boys, who are perched as if for flight near the front door.

"One clique right here!" Shakila calls out.

"Mr. Richards," Luis says urgently. "Sorry to interrupt the discussion, but next period—"

"We know. There's gonna be a walkout," Mr. Richards says.

"What do you think about it?" Luis asks. All eyes are on Mr. Richards; all chitchat stops as he considers his answers. "Did you see the new *Jacket?*" Luis presses him.

A special edition of the *Jacket,* "Berkeley High in Turmoil," greeted students, teachers, and a shocked administration when they arrived at school for the new semester. In an editorial blaming the school's crisis squarely on Theresa Saunders, the *Jacket* staff wrote, "Students aren't trying to get the 'A,' they're trying to make sure that they actually get credit for classes taken, and that their transcripts actually get sent to colleges. Teachers aren't focusing on their lesson plans; they're debating tactics, planning boycotts and discussing the possibility of a strike . . . Our school is falling apart."

"If the walkout's for something positive I'm all for it," Mr. Richards answers. "If it's just a bunch of kids skipping class, I'm against it."

"How many of you are thinking of walking out?" Ms. Crawford asks. About one-third of the students raise their hands, most of them hesitantly.

"It's for a good cause," Joaquin says. "They ain't organized it very well, but they know what they wanna do."

Autumn reads from the flyer that was circulated early this morning. " 'Clean up Berkeley High. College Advisor. A time for change.' " She shakes her head. "Sounds heck of vague to me."

"Yeah, they're not totally together," Rena argues. "But how many seventeen-year-olds are?"

"When my brother went to Berkeley High they had big walkouts all the time," Lacy says. "It would be great if the students pulled together and *did* something."

"If anyone's out there making good points it should be us—this group," Luis says with quiet fervor. "I don't want to sound self-absorbed, but—"

"But what CAS does, the world follows," Steve says. " 'Cause we're the bomb!"

"We should go get the other CAS classes," David proposes. "A lotta people are like, I don't want to walk out. But if we're apathetic, nothing's ever gonna change."

"Last week someone was passing around a petition in a Black Student Union meeting," Autumn says slowly. "Mr. McKnight wouldn't let any of us sign it unless we *all* did. If we all walk out, and we get all of CAS to go too, that's acting collectively. It says a lot more if we all do it together."

"The walkout is a way to get attention," Mr. Richards says. "But what are you gonna do when you *get* the attention? Don't get all focused on Theresa Saunders and her foibles. If you get interviewed on camera, it's all about saying something intelligent and thoughtful. Here's my suggestion: go get ninth-grade CAS, make some posters with them, show some leadership."

"Do it in a smart way," adds Ms. Crawford. "Don't upset people. Don't make noise in the halls."

Some of the students rush out of the room. Others linger uncertainly. Autumn considers her options. *I don't want to get all caught up in something stupid and end up in some kind of trouble. But if this really is for the good, I should be there.* She decides to meet Lillian, Emily, and Lauren outside their second-period classes and see what they have to say.

"What do we want?" Joaquin yells into the bullhorn.

"A decent school!" the four hundred Berkeley High students marching behind him yell back.

"When do we want it?"

"Now!"

"This isn't a walkout," says one CAS senior to another as the demonstrators—the Berkeley High house blend of black, white, Latino, Asian, and biracial kids—are led from their brief rally in the park across the street to the sidewalks encircling Berkeley High, then back through the school gates they'd marched out of a half hour before. "It's a walk-in."

"We want change! We want change!" Their chants echoing off the B building walls, the students mass outside Theresa Saunders' office, shouting at her as she stares back at them through the metal mesh guards on her windows.

"Do you want to walk through the hallways? Go to the courtyard?" the march organizers—some of them CAS students, some off-duty *Jacket* reporters, some student government leaders—call into the bullhorns.

"Yeah!" "No!" "Power to the people!"

"Who's got the weed?" a boy asks a girl.

"How many of you are mad about Proposition 21!" Joaquin's amplified voice rings out.

"Yeaaahh!" the kids scream.

"What's that?" a girl asks no one in particular. It seems surprising that she could not know. The classrooms and hallways of Berkeley High, like the windows of many houses and stores around town, have been plastered for weeks with bright red-and-yellow "NO ON 21" placards. Flyers announcing anti–Proposition 21 rallies, sit-ins, and hip hop concerts circulate daily—like the one that came out today.

The 411 on Prop 21

This Initiative (appearing on the March 7 ballot)

- Lowers the age for juveniles to be eligible to be tried in the Adult courts from 16 to 14
- Allows for juvenile's confidential records to be released to jobs and college admissions
- Expands 3 strikes and the death penalty

- Expands mandatory sentencing and limits alternative methods of juvenile rehabilitation

California spends each year . . .

- $60,000 per inmate
- $6,000 per student
- $51,000 per correctional officer
- $28,000 per teacher (first year)

For every:

- 1 Black male that goes to a UC or CSU (California State University), there are 5 in Prison.
- 1 Latino male that goes to a UC or CSU there are 3 in prison

A recent *Oakland Tribune* op-ed headline commented, "Prop 21 Is So Bad It's Started a Youth Movement," and indeed, the threat of the measure's passage has clearly helped spark today's protest.

After confronting their principal the students walk out again, this time trailed by an entourage of markedly restrained Berkeley motorcycle cops, TV news trucks, and newspaper reporters jotting notes as they run to keep up. Through the streets of downtown Berkeley the teenagers march, stopping the lunchtime traffic on Shattuck, waving to the EZ Stop clerks watching from the doorway. And then suddenly, without discussion or premeditation, they turn onto the UC Berkeley campus, heading for Sproul Plaza like next-generation homing pigeons returning, thirty-five years later, to the roost.

"We want change! We want change!" the students roar as they are photographed and filmed on the steps of Sproul Hall, where some of their parents once shouted out their own nonnegotiable demands. "For a five or a ten?" a UC Berkeley student quips, but quickly a crowd of university students gathers around in a show of spontaneous support. The People's Park and Affirmative Action wars were fought on this hallowed ground, both of them failed attempts to convince this university to better serve its community; and to this day much pontificating transpires in Berkeley about how the university might share its rich resources with local youth. But here, today, the elite students of UC Berkeley share what they have with these emissaries of the town's only public high school, offering their younger counterparts cardboard and markers, extra bullhorns, bottles of water, a bigger crowd for the news cameras' narrow eyes.

Half watching and half listening as his fellow students chant "Schools Not Jails! No On 21!" Keith, here out of curiosity more than conviction, stands with some friends at the outskirts of the crowd, his head nodding to the rap music playing on the boom box one of the guys carried on the mile-long march. When his friends go off in search of a blunt to smoke, Keith stays behind—he tried marijuana a few times, didn't like feeling out of control of his body, prefers "the natural high of just bein' Keith." *This is just a bunch of people who got together to do somethin' and ain't doin' nothin',* he decides. After a few minutes he wanders off campus and onto Telegraph Avenue for a slice of Blondie's pepperoni pizza.

Meanwhile the reporters are jostling for position on the Sproul Hall steps, anointing "leaders" with their microphones. When they try to interview the white Berkeley High students only, the white kids step aside and defer to kids of color. When the reporters ask what they're marching for, the students talk about the shortage of counselors, their overworked, underpaid teachers, the threat and the message of Prop 21.

After dispersing for a lunch break on Telegraph, the protesters march back to Berkeley High through the Milvia gate, black, white, and brown hands clasped and waving. As they chant "The Youth United Will Never Be Divided," the TV videocams record this moving multicultural moment, the cops and school safety officers stationed at the gate part like the Red Sea waters, and an unusually affable Theresa Saunders, media microphones jabbing at her mouth, wades into the crowd of demonstrators and asks, "Would you like to go somewhere and talk?" A triumphant cheer arises. Saunders leads the students to the steps of the

Community Theater for an impromptu question-and-answer session that is punctuated by the students' shouts of anger, tears of frustration, and derisive laughter. To their questions about the clocks, the copy machines, the counselors, the safety officers' insensitivity, Saunders offers variations of the same answer: "I want to fix it. But if I don't have the money, I don't have the money."

"You had the money to hire more security guards," a boy calls out.

"You can buy a clock at Walgreen's for ten bucks," offers another.

"It's not that simple. How do you think the system operates?" Saunders asks, finally, pleadingly.

"It doesn't," another boy answers in disgust.

By the end of this week Theresa Saunders will have replaced the school's incompetent college counselor, reinstating her popular predecessor; established a new, stricter tardy policy; laid plans for implementing the new, stricter retention policy; and distributed the first issue of *The Student Buzz,* in which she reports all of this news to the student body. Via the parent E-tree she calls a Saturday community forum to "discuss the recent Special Edition of The Jacket, laws regarding slander and libel in student papers, the Promotion and Retention Policy, and Team Building between BHS and our Community."

Among the mostly white parents on the E-tree, the responses fly. "Why is she holding a school meeting at a Baptist church in South Berkeley?" a father asks, an oblique reference to the racial-turf implications of Saunders' invitation. "Is she threatening to sue the *Jacket* for libel or slander?" the mother of a *Jacket* staffer wonders.

"Theresa Saunders is the best thing to happen to BHS in a long, long time," another father writes. "Ultimately the budget, the bureaucracy and the physical plant are the School Board's responsibility, not the principal's."

"If her critics think the best thing to do is hound her out of her job and look for a replacement—who will have to possess the wisdom of Solomon, the charisma of John Kennedy, and the patience of a dozen saints—they'd better be ready for a long recruitment process," argues another.

"Many many parents are being missed in this dialogue who are not connected and do not have access to E-mail," "Anonymous" reminds the E-tree subscribers.

To avoid a showdown with the boycotting teachers, Saunders cancels the first staff meeting of the semester; the teachers hold a union meeting in the school library instead. "I just saw Theresa," a stunned art teacher whispers, sitting down again beside Amy Crawford after a quick trip to the bathroom. "She's in the hall. And she's crying."

The next day Amy Crawford's fourth-period students tell her that Ms. Saunders came into their first-period class, sat down, and told them that she really wants to listen, is really sorry that the school isn't working better, and that she really wants their feedback. By the end of that day the teachers are buzzing: the famously aloof Saunders has been seen walking the halls, talking to students, asking the staff how it's going.

But too late. The private crisis at Berkeley High has gone public. Throughout the week, in the pages of the *San Francisco Chronicle,* the *San Francisco Examiner,* the *Berkeley Voice,* the *Berkeley Daily Planet,* and the *East Bay Express,* and on several TV news shows, the *Jacket's* accusations are reported, the students' complaints aired.

An alarmed Mayor of Berkeley, herself a Berkeley High graduate, jumps into the fray. Citing the unflattering media coverage, the *Jacket* editorial and the student walkout, the school's probationary WASC accreditation, mishandling of college applications, and lack of teacher resources, as well as "complaints of downtown merchants about the lack of supervision over the 3,000 plus Berkeley High students who enter the downtown during the lunch time and the number of students found roaming throughout the downtown during school hours . . . gambling, smoking pot, painting graffiti, and etching windows," Mayor Dean calls for a special meeting between the city council and the school board "to discuss the serious problems at Berkeley High School."

And so, in the first days of the spring semester—while kids are still lined up in the counseling department at all hours of the day, trying to get their new schedules fixed; and the teachers are vowing to continue boycotting staff meetings, even those required for WASC recertification, until their demands are met; and the arson investigation that began last month continues—the whole world, or so it seems, is watching Berkeley High.

Sitting in her African-American History class on the first floor of the H building three hours after she decided not to participate in the walkout, Autumn hears the shouting from the theater steps. "Maybe we should've gone after all," she mutters to Lauren. Lauren shrugs. When the walkout was getting underway, Autumn, Lauren, and Lillian went looking for their friend Jamilah, vice-president of the Black Student Union and co-founder of Youth Together, to get her "professional opinion."

"YT's not supporting the walkout," Jamilah told them. "Neither is BSU. It's too disorganized, too spontaneous. They don't even know what their demands are." Autumn and her friends decided to go with Jamilah's advice. But their classes have been emptier than usual today, even for the first week of a new semester, and Autumn wonders now if they've been short-sighted or selfish—and, in the process, missed a memorable Berkeley High event. "They're just out there yelling at Ms. Saunders," Lauren whispers back as their teacher starts talking about the abolitionist movement. "Like *that's* about to do any good."

While Keith wanders through the record stores and head shops of Telegraph Avenue, and Autumn sits in African-American History, hoping that Berkeley High will keep it together long enough for her to get her diploma and get out, Jordan is at home, staring at the walls in his basement room. He hasn't been to school yet this semester, so he doesn't know about the walkout, or the special issue of the *Jacket,* or the media coverage of Berkeley High's public nervous breakdown. Jordan has been otherwise engaged, having a very private breakdown of his own.

It kicked in between finals last week and the start of the new semester while his mom was in Paris on a business trip. Jordan can't even say what the "it" is, although since his mom got back and found out how much school he'd missed (Jordan figured Ms. Crawford might call her, and sure enough, she did) Natalie's been asking him like a million times a day. All Jordan knows is, he doesn't have the energy to do anything. Doesn't care about anything, or anyone. Wants to quit everything in his life that's quittable: the crew team, CAS, his girlfriend. Today is his eighteenth birthday, and he doesn't even care about that.

"Is it because of Bard?" his mom keeps asking him. "Are you worried about getting into college?" Jordan just shrugs. He knows the Bard rejection is a factor, but that's not the only explanation for how he feels— or rather, doesn't feel. "I don't even feel numb. I just feel 'a-feeling'— like amoral."

Jordan has been trying to get his mom to chill out. "I've gone through stuff like this before. I'll get over it faster if she'll just get off my case." But Natalie's not hearing it. She insists on asking Dr. Walrod, the therapist Jordan's been seeing off and on since eighth grade, about referring Jordan to a psychiatrist, maybe putting him on Prozac. "She says I *should* quit CAS, take regular classes instead. She thinks I need more structure in my life." Jordan's small, satisfied grin belies his protests about his mom's overprotectiveness. "She's really worried."

"I was really pissed and worried to find out he blew off school while I was away," Natalie confirms. "He's eighteen today and yet he still seems to need parenting. I don't want to keep babysitting him, but he doesn't seem ready to let me go. I feel like the message of last week was 'Don't go away.' In six months he'll be on his own. I can't keep being the cop, making him do his homework, making him go to school . . .

"I have a lot of friends who are mental health professionals. They're all saying he's probably still reacting to his dad's death. I know he'll be fine in the long run, but if he doesn't get back to school and soon, he's not going to graduate."

"Through all the shit with my dad," Jordan says, "it wasn't like I was happy, then he died, then I was depressed. It was like I was depressed about him, then he died, then I was even more depressed. I've been depressed all through high school."

Jordan is not alone. According to *Time* Magazine's October 1999 Special Report, "A Week in the Life of a High School: What It's Really Like

Since Columbine": "Nationally, an estimated 1 in 20 children and adolescents suffers from depression. While doctors have long dispensed
drugs like Ritalin to children and adolescents, teen prescriptions for
antidepressants such as Prozac, Zoloft and Paxil have grown rapidly in
recent years."

"The Littleton rampage led to a national paroxysm of hand-wringing
and urgent calls for intervention with troubled youth," reports "Dying
Young," the cover story that appears in Sunday's *San Francisco Examiner*
during Jordan's current episode of depression. The *Examiner* reports that
suicide is the third leading cause of death nationally among youths fifteen to twenty-four years old, and that the country's suicide rate among
the young has nearly tripled since 1952. "Among adolescents, the ratio
of attempted suicides is estimated to be between 100 and 200 to one
completed suicide," adds the executive director of San Francisco Suicide
Prevention. "That is mayhem. It means there is real chaos in homes and
schools everywhere."

"If any good can come of Littleton," *Surviving High School* author Dr.
Michael Riera tells the *Examiner,* "it might be for us to wake up and look
in our own backyard. We need to learn how we can recognize kids that
are in trouble, and what to do for them, as well as providing more
resources for parents."

"The jump from being a child to being a young adult is much bigger
now," adds a San Francisco juvenile hearing officer. "Kids are inundated
with things they can't handle . . . and adults are failing their children—
they are not giving them safe environments to go to school, they are not
showing them [proper] ways to entertain themselves. What are we doing
to our young people? They are dying."

The things kids must handle and the ways in which they handle them
vary—as do so many other factors in their lives—not only with each
teenager's unique psychological constitution and family background,
but also along lines of race and class. In his private practice, Oakland
psychologist Dr. John Nickens sees many Berkeley High students, about
half of them white and half of them black, about half of them affluent
and half of them poor. Most of his adolescent patients are boys; 25

percent are involved in the juvenile justice system. "The thing that brings them is almost always a problem at school. They're getting bad grades, they're getting in fights, they're getting suspended, they're getting arrested. A counselor tells the parents their kid should be in therapy and they call me." African-American and married to a white woman, Dr. Nickens is fascinated by the racial and social identity challenges posed to Berkeley High students.

"The black kids I've seen from Oakland high schools have mostly or all black friends. The white kids I've seen from private schools have mostly or all white friends. The kids from Berkeley High—especially the middle-class white kids—tend to have black, white, Asian, Latino friends. They go to parties together. Their get-high group, which can be 75 percent of their socializing, will be very mixed. Consequently they have this awareness of racial and ethnic issues, of how their personal issues relate to issues in society—unlike kids from private schools, who don't see their school environment as having anything to do with anything.

"Berkeley High kids are more likely to see racial differences as irrelevant than the general population. They know people from each racial group who are smart, stupid, good athletes . . . they don't draw the hard boundaries that have gotten this country into so much trouble. At the same time, this intermingling creates a particular issue for the white kids. They need to prove to their friends that they're not stuck up, even if they live in a big house with all the amenities. Their behavior takes on a feeling of trying to erase the advantage."

The psychological differences between white and black kids, Dr. Nickens says, stem directly from this "advantage" and the lack thereof. "The most significant difference I see between the affluent kids, who tend to be white, and the disadvantaged kids, who tend to be black, is that the more affluent kids have a more internalized locus of control. That is, they can accept and acknowledge their own role in their own lives more easily. The notion of self-responsibility is not foreign to them. They feel more empowered; they believe that if their behavior becomes different, different things will happen to them.

"The disadvantaged kids have a more externalized locus of control. They tend to see themselves as victims of the world. They believe that what happens to them has more to do with their race than with their individual behavior. 'I got suspended because the school's racist.' 'I got arrested because they always see the black kids first.' They relate to authority figures very differently. They see teachers, police officers, even their therapist as being able to give and take away everything—including positive change in their lives."

Different ethnic groups, Dr. Nickens says, have different relationships to therapy. Economics is one reason. Although he says that "managed care is the great equalizer; I see truck drivers and physicians with the same HMO," being able to afford health insurance at all, let alone a plan that covers psychotherapy, remains less common among families of color. Disparate cultural approaches to suffering and to its remedies is another reason Dr. Nickens rarely sees Latino or Asian-American clients: both groups, he says, prefer to keep problems in the family. And "Black families tend to be more involved in religion, to rely on the church and on their spiritual beliefs instead of relying on therapy. Even white kids whose families are involved in religion don't use religion to mediate or explain why things are going on in their lives, the way a black kid might."

Autumn, for one. Being both a black kid *and* a black-and-white kid, she fittingly seems to balance an internal *and* external locus of control, acknowledging both the external power of racism over her life and her own power, which she attributes to God's. She goes to church with her family every Sunday, prays "constantly," and considers her spiritual faith her greatest strength—as she writes in "My Philosophy," her first English paper of the new semester.

> God speaks to you all the time. You just have to be willing to listen. Not with your ears but with your heart. It took me a long time to realize this. Well actually it did not take that long seeing how I am only eighteen years old. He prepares you for things by taking you through something and then

allowing you to realize what to do with that. Never under estimate him. You may not know what he is doing, but you need to allow his will to be done. When you stop trying to control everything and find an answer for everything you will be free and at peace.

Accepting that you can not control everything is the beginning of any type of acceptance. You can, however, control everything that **you** do. You must and inevitably will have to take responsibility for your actions and thoughts. Responsibility and the controlling of self are things that must be dealt with in order to reach any type of peace or self empowerment.

Only time and the will of God can truly turn the lights on in your life. You may keep on going through the same things until you get them right, but in this process there are deep revelations of self. Keep yourself rooted in happiness, control yourself, be responsible for yourself, your happiness and your failures. Keep God close and ask him for the eyes to your own soul.

Although he stopped going to church with his mom as soon as he got old enough to refuse to get in the car, Keith, too, is going through a spiritual resurgence. Soon after he realized that he wasn't going to college on a football scholarship, he started going to church again. "I just felt like I needed to go back. The first time I went the pastor said, 'If you want to redeem yourself come up to the front.' I went up and he gave me a hug. I felt like I was home again." His brown eyes, normally sparkling with wit and mischief, are dark and somber. "I redeemed myself. They wrote me a letter today. It tells the dates of the Bible study and stuff. And it says, 'Thanks for joining the family again.'"

Although Keith says he gets depressed "all the time, over little stupid things I shouldn't even get depressed about," he laughs out loud at the thought of seeing a therapist. "When I feel bad I can talk to my mom about anything." No one in Keith's family, no one he knows, has ever been in therapy—not even when Keith was threatening to kill himself three years ago. "We were havin' a family argument; I don't even remember what about. I ended up getting all upset about something that was not that serious. I took off out the house, ran out onto the railroad tracks. My dad was like, 'What's that fool doin'? Let him do it.' But my mom jumped in the car and chased me down. I didn't really wanna kill myself. I ain't crazy. I just wanted some attention." His eyes dance again. "And I got it."

Keith's mom did suggest, once, that the family go for counseling. "A couple years ago we were having this little family discussion and my mom was like, 'We need help.' I said, 'It ain't that serious, Mom.' We just figured it out ourselves." He laughs again, affects his imitating-white-people face and voice. "This is rich white people in therapy: *'What's wrong with me? Oh, what's wrong with me?'* " Now he's Keith again. "Only *you* know what's wrong with you."

"Therapy is an accepted form of medicine in our household," Jordan says flatly. "My parents sent me to therapy for the first time when they got divorced. I was seven or eight. My mom's really into therapy. So was my dad. Since I plan to be a therapist, I guess you could say I'm into it too.

"I don't know if any of my friends are in therapy. I'm the only one I know who talks about it, but that's just me not giving a fuck. I see it as a helping hand coming through whatever I'm going through. Plus Dr. Walrod is someone to bounce ideas off of. I know a lot of shrinks don't give feedback, but he usually does. I force it when it's not offered. I try talking to my mom sometimes, but that's kind of strange. I need an objective opinion when I feel like shit, the way I do now."

Jordan identifies himself as Jewish, even though he isn't, by Jewish law, since his father and not his mother was a Jew. But he doesn't belong to a synagogue, celebrates only a few Jewish holidays with his Jewish friends, and—unlike Autumn and Keith—draws little emotional or spiritual sustenance from his religion. "I'm a cultural Jew. For me being Jewish is mostly about feeling connected to my dad."

What going to church does for Autumn, going to Dr. Walrod does for Jordan. "I talk to Dr. Walrod about my relationship with Kristen, my relationship with my mother. Being my surviving parent, she gets the brunt of whatever I feel about her *and* my dad." He grins ironically. "The great thing about a therapist is, he only hears your side."

"The developmental task of a teenager," says Jordan's therapist, clinical psychologist Dr. Stephen Walrod, "is to establish a sense of identity: what you believe in, your own sense of values. That's done in large part by differentiating yourself from your parents, defining yourself in relation to them. When a teenager's parent dies or is unavailable because of an addiction, there's a certain level of insecurity because there's not a stable, predictable emotional environment to push up against."

Dr. Walrod is white and so are 70 percent of his patients; 23 percent are African-American, 10 percent Latino or Asian. Most of the high school students he sees are boys; most of them middle or upper-middle class. Unlike Dr. Nickens' patients, none of Dr. Walrod's are involved in the criminal justice system. The reasons they come or are sent to him reflect the differences in the two therapists' client demographics. Most of Dr. Walrod's teenage patients are referred, not because of an arrest or a school suspension, but because of "difficulty performing up to their parents' expectations in school, unsatisfactory social relationships, having hostile, volatile kinds of noncompliant relationships with their parents." Some, like Jordan, come because of "difficulty adjusting" to divorce, or the death of a parent.

"Jordan had already lost his father before his father died. His father wasn't available in the full sense of the word. Nevertheless he filled some sort of psychic space, a certain role in the family, so there was a real shift in the psychic economy when he died. Some teens react to that by acting out, getting into trouble, not maintaining responsibility for themselves as an expression of their grief. Others try and become the thing they want their parent to be: responsible, predictable—filling in the role of the absent father, filling the shoes of Dad.

"The consequences of that aren't going to be known until the teen gets older. They have unmet needs that may catch up with them."

The English teachers at Berkeley High have unmet needs too. And a few hours before the spring Back to School Night a delegation of them, including Amy Crawford, meets with Theresa Saunders to let her know how they're going to attempt to get them met. Instead of adhering to Back to School protocol—meeting parents in their individual classrooms, talking about their individual students—all the English teachers are going to gather all the parents in two rooms and tell them (just in case they haven't read a newspaper or watched TV recently, or have been vacationing on another planet) just how screwed up Berkeley High is.

"We're trying to do something positive for your children," Amy Crawford says earnestly to the fifty parents crowded into an English classroom on the second floor of the C building. "Most of us have 150 students. We're working twelve-hour days; we're paid for six and a half. And we're the lowest paid teachers in the county.

"If we assign three essays per semester in each of our classes—which many of you have said is too few—it takes us 150 hours per semester to read and comment on them. We want to reduce our class load from five to four so we can read every word your kids submit and give them the kind of education they deserve."

Although some parents grumble that they want to talk about their own children with their children's own teachers, most are seasoned veterans of Berkeley and Berkeley High politics; they know how long they could be here tonight if someone doesn't cut to the chase. "What, specifically, do you want us to do?" asks Jordan's mother, Natalie.

"Read this letter." Ms. Crawford passes out copies of a two-page flyer outlining the teachers' situation and demands, signed by all but four of the school's English teachers. "Vote for school board members who support smaller class loads. Let them know that you support that, too."

. . .

Across the campus in the H building, one white couple and one black mother show up to visit Keith's African-American Literature class. "We thought you'd be in that room with all the other English teachers," one of the mothers tells Mr. McKnight. "All the other English teachers are *where?* Doing *what?*" he asks incredulously. "I don't know anything about that."

One floor down, Autumn and Lauren's African-American History teacher, Mr. McKnight's daughter Ivory, sits facing an empty classroom. "I begged my students to bring their parents tonight," Ms. McKnight says, shaking her head. "I guess they don't see the point."

. . .

THE BUZZ

To: BHS Staff
From: Theresa Saunders
Date: Friday, February 11, 2000

I know that the past two weeks have been difficult. And I apologize to you for the frustration, confusion and disruption that have occurred. I want you to know that I am sincere in my desire to work with you to improve BHS. Additionally, I want to apologize for the mistakes, misunderstandings, and missteps on my part that have led to some of the problems experienced by the staff and students at BHS. In my meetings with students, I have listened to their concerns and WE, collectively, have attempted to address them. Thus, the creation of THE STUDENT BUZZ. I am hopeful that WE, the BHS staff and administration, can also work collaboratively to address our mutual concerns in ways that are positive and yield positive results for everyone—students, staff and community.

Have a Great Weekend!

Autumn Davesse Morris. *Photo: Rebecca Weissman, Berkeley High Class of 2000*

Jordan Van Osdol Etra.

Keith Jamell Stephens.

Sixties Day, the highlight of Spirit Week: (left to right) Emily, Lillian, and Autumn at Autumn's locker, where they meet for lunch every day.

Sixties Day: Jordan (on right) and friends in the courtyard in borrowed Polyester.

Sixties Day: Keith and his teammate Ci Ci, the first girl ever to play on the Berkeley High football team.

Spirit Day: Autumn (with Yellowjacket tattoos on her cheeks) and Emily, full of school spirit, on the Community Theater steps.

Spirit Day: Jordan thought he'd have to smuggle Kristen into the gym for the Spirit Rally, but somehow no one noticed she wasn't a Berkeley High student.

Tropical Day: Keith, in the most photographed bikini of the day.

Amy Crawford and her teaching partner Dana Richards, in the portable the CAS class was moved to after the fire destroyed their classroom and everything in it.

Alan Miller, in the "Achievement Is For Everyone" T-shirt the teachers were asked to wear every Friday.

Greg Giglio (second from left) on Spirit Day with Keith and classmates. Taliah, on Keith's left, wrote in his eighteenth-birthday card: "Enjoy life, try being more tactful, & do your work. The world needs more smart, intelligent Black males out here, not just another 'great athlete.'"

African-American Studies Department Chair and the best-dressed teacher at Berkeley High, Robert McKnight.

The CAS retreat at the Headlands youth hostel: Jordan (top right), Autumn (bottom left), Amy Crawford (on left banister).

Principal Theresa Saunders, herding students back to class: "Fourth period! Go to your fourth period class!"

The dread school security supervisor Mr. Wiggan, Vice Principal Doris Wallace-Tanner, and Berkeley Police Captain Bobby Miller, observing the student rally protesting the "Paddy Wagon sweeps."

Principal Saunders talking to the press at the Paddy Wagon protest.

Standard Operating Procedure at every school dance: every student is searched with a metal detector before being let in.

Keith (at right) and friends at Sproul Plaza, UC Berkeley. Thirty years after the Free Speech Movement was born here, Berkeley High students rallied, chanting "We want change!" after walking out of school.

Autumn (bottom center) and fellow poets at the Berkeley High Women's Poetry Slam: "Less testosterone, more metaphors!"

Lauren, Autumn, Lillian, and Emily at Berkeley High's Kwanzaa celebration, sponsored by the African-American Studies Department.

Jordan on the courtyard with CAS director Rick Ayers, who was there for Jordan when his dad died.

Keith's English class: Mr. Giglio in his "Achievement Is For Everyone" T-shirt; the students in their coats and hats (the heater was broken all winter).

Students pour down the C building steps at lunchtime. After the fire, paper posters and banners were banned—but somehow they still appeared. *Photo: Rebecca Weissman*

On Sixties Day there are no cliques at lunchtime.

April 12, 2000: Berkeley High is burning. *Photo © Ian Buchanan, Berkeley High Class of 2001.*
Print by Rebecca Weissman

Michael Morris, Autumn Morris, their stepfather Tony Smith, mom Pamela Smith, and five-year-old RaShawn Smith outside their apartment complex on their way to church.
Photo: Rebecca Weissman

Natalie Van Osdol and Jordan Van Osdol Etra on their deck. Jordan's beard is dyed kelly green for St. Patrick's Day.
Photo: Rebecca Weissman

Three generations of Berkeley High graduates: Patricia Stephens, Keith Stephens, "Mama" Alice Frazier, Kenneth Stephens Jr., and Kenneth Stephens Sr., at Mama's house in West Berkeley. Missing: Keith's sisters Latisha and Yolanda; Latisha's son Alonzo.

Lillian, Jamilah, Autumn (top), Emily, and Jabris at African-American Graduation.

Keith and his beloved Ms. Russ at African-American Graduation.

Jordan (on left), his date Claire (right, listening), and a friend, munching on sushi at their pre-Prom party in the hills.

Autumn (top left) and André, Emily and Josh Gray, Nicole and Dennis at their pre-Prom party in the flats.

Jordan and Claire at the Prom.

André and Autumn at the Prom.

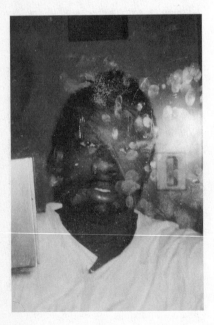

Keith on his Prom night—in the Berkeley city jail.

Keith gets out of jail with his belt missing; his sister Latisha dares him to let go of his pants.

The rally to free Keith: (from left) Yolanda, Latisha, Keith, Mama, Keith's cousin Angel. Behind Angel, rally organizers Josh Gray and Megan Parkinson.

The Greek theater, June 15: Graduation day for the Berkeley High Class of 2000.

Jordan (in beach sandals) and Finnegan in their CAS Graduation scarves, slogan by Autumn: "Consciousness Through Creative Communication."

Best friends, soon to be parted. Lillian, whose mom is Chinese and whose dad is African-American, is wearing her "Asian Pride" and African-American Graduation scarves; Autumn's wearing her African-American and CAS scarves.

Keith, the only graduate in a "Chevy's Fresh Mex" sombrero.

2/16/00

URGENT

message to all BHS teachers: Your Berkeley Federation of
Teachers (BFT) site representatives recommend that we continue to **BOYCOTT** staff meetings by not attending today's
WASC workgroups. It is our position that our requests of
the original petition have not been met.

BFT cannot be certain how the BHS administration will respond to this action, and whether there will be consequences
for temporary, probationary or permanent teachers.

The teachers honor the boycott, as they've been doing all month. And
so the WASC workgroups are not convened, and at 3:30 on Wednesday
afternoon Theresa Saunders sits at a table in the school library with only
five of the hundred and eighty-five Berkeley High teachers, calling the
meeting to order. Without acknowledging the reason for or significance
of the empty room, Saunders does what she's become so good at doing
these past months: going ahead, no matter what.

"This is a list of concerns I've heard," Saunders says, distributing a
pink handout called "Staff Issues," which includes:

- Lack of unity
- Not consulted, included, not told the truth
- Theresa needs to delegate
- Why doesn't the district have money?
- Demoralized; loss of confidence
- Kids not in class
- Need to focus on the classroom craft of teaching

"I'd like you to number your priorities and hand this back to me," Saunders is saying as one of the boycotting teachers appears in the library
doorway.

"Theresa," she calls out in a strangled voice. Saunders rises; they meet halfway. The teacher whispers a few words. She and Saunders embrace. The teacher rushes out of the room, and Saunders returns to the table.

"Marcia Singman died an hour ago," Theresa Saunders says. Every mouth at the table drops open; every face at the table goes pale.

"I thought she was getting better," one woman whispers. Yesterday the fifty-five-year-old Ms. Singman—chair of the Performing Arts department, a thirty-two-year veteran of the school, known as "Mama Siggy" to legions of adoring past and present students—had a stroke following knee surgery. Several students and staff members, including Theresa Saunders and Robert McKnight, returned from their visit to the hospital with a reassuring report. "I thought so too," Theresa Saunders replies, her face as glassy as a frozen lake.

She tries to continue with the meeting. She stops. "This is tough," she says. Her face still expressionless, tears begin coursing down her cheeks. "This is tough," she repeats. The librarian hands Saunders a box of Kleenex. "This is a wonderful, wonderful teacher we have lost today," Saunders says, and then she collapses, sobbing into her hands. Not one of the teachers reaches out to the grieving principal.

"I hope you know," Saunders says, her usual crisp delivery dissolved by her tears, "it's not that I don't want to hear your concerns. But I just can't . . . I can't . . . go on right now."

The school is empty of students at 4:00, but in classrooms and hallways teachers huddle, comforting each other as the news spreads. In the school's health center, volunteers start calling psychology interns to lead grief-counseling sessions tomorrow.

In the *Jacket* office the student reporters sit at their iMacs, crying and writing tributes to Ms. Singman for a memorial section in the issue they'll bring to the printer tonight. Rick Ayers, who, besides being CAS director is also the *Jacket* faculty adviser, is there writing, too. "Marcia was one of those '60s dreamers. She created one of those corners at Berkeley High that is safe, and truly wonderful, for students."

In the B building Phil Halpern, a CAS video teacher, sits composing the poem that will appear anonymously in that memorial edition, surrounded by photographs of Marcia Singman's dancing students. The poem will serve, too, as the announcement of her death, to be read to first- and second-period students when they arrive at school tomorrow.

> *Beloved Marcia Singman died yesterday afternoon.*
> *It feels like the beating heart of the school*
>
> *just stopped beating.*
>
> *Marcia.*
> *Our affirmation of hope.*
> *Our source of strength and serenity . . .*
> *Of hope and the belief that yes we can.*
>
> *Adults and children, far and near:*
> *Tears pool together for the death of Marcia Singman.*

. . .

"In the past, when teenagers dealt with death," says Jordan's therapist, Dr. Walrod, "it was mostly a result of war. Young people today are experiencing death in a far more random and prevalent way. In the African-American community there's been an incredible incidence of death. AIDS has been a powerful circumstance in the lives of many teenagers, as have suicide, substance abuse, and violence. In any case, death poses a particular challenge for young people. Adolescence is a period of identity instability, a time when teens are looking for models to whom they can attach themselves. For someone who's that kind of model to die can be particularly disturbing and disruptive to a teenager."

The students who were attached to Marcia Singman—mostly girls, mostly white, Asian, and African-American—gather all through the next day in the Community Theater's Green Room, the designated grief-counseling space. The girls create an altar on a card table, surrounding a photograph of Ms. Singman with candles, flowers, cards, poems. They sprawl on the floor in a tangle of long dancers' legs, cry in each other's graceful, muscular arms, ignoring the chairs arranged by the grief counselors and their invitation to "sit in a circle and talk about their feelings." "Maybe after a while," a girl responds politely through her tears.

Robert McKnight and two or three other teachers sit upright in chairs against the wall, their own grief contained in being silently, solidly present for their students. When one girl's sobbing turns convulsive Mr. McKnight rises from his chair, walks slowly across the room, bends to be close to her, and stays there without speaking or moving until her choking sobs subside.

Downstairs in Marcia Singman's windowless closet of an office, as dancing students beam down from the hundreds of photos taped to the walls, a girl with blonde hair to her waist and a ballerina's body is crying into Marcia's phone. "She's *dead,* Mommy! She's dead!" the girl wails. "Can you come quick?"

And a few steps from Marcia's office, in the studio where most of her classes were held, Marcia's students dance spontaneously in her honor. As parents and teachers watch, pressing tissues to their tear-slickened faces, black boys and white girls, black girls and white boys weep and laugh as they leap and turn, pirouette and plié across the wooden floor.

Neither Jordan nor Keith knew Ms. Singman. Autumn didn't know her well, although her good friend Emily, a fourth-year dance student, is "*really* sad." "This reminds me of two years ago," Autumn says, "when so many kids died right at the beginning of school. Everyone was sad all the time. Everyone was crying all the time. And it just kept happening."

Marcia Singman's memorial is held in the Berkeley Community Theater. Several hundred teachers, parents, students, and ex-students, many having flown in from foreign countries, sit enthralled by the school's Jazz Ensemble, its Ballet Folklorico and African-Haitian dancers, its orchestra, and the grand finale that brings everyone to tears: a ceremonial dance by all of Marcia's current students, accompanied by the Berkeley High choir director's solo rendition of "Amazing Grace."

In the theater foyer afterward, snacking on the Calistogas and home-

baked cookies provided by the PTSA moms who organized the memorial, red-eyed teenagers and adults of all ages, races, and factions
exchange hugs, Kleenex, and memories. The ever-sanguine Alan Miller,
having "kept it together for the kids," admits to breaking down privately
at home this morning. "Marcia was one of the few teachers at this school
who stayed out of the infighting. This was a particularly cruel time to
lose her." Theresa Saunders circulates through the crowd at the side of
a school board member; Amy Crawford laughs and cries with a group
of CAS students who were students of Ms. Singman's.

"At least this school can pull together when it has to," Autumn's friend
Emily says, surveying the ample spread of food, the elegant sprays of
flowers, the thoughtfully arranged display of Marcia Singman memen-
tos. "Too bad it took this to make it happen."

"I had this zit on my forehead this morning," a girl in a tight black
minidress tells a group of similarly dressed girls. "I popped it. Then I
couldn't believe Ms. Singman just died and I was so upset about a *zit!*"
Her friends laugh and dab at their faces with their sleeves.

"With all the trouble around here," an art teacher says to Robert
McKnight, "all the arguing about how to attract and keep good teachers,
you never realize how many wonderful people we still have at this school
until you lose one."

"Ms. Singman always told us, 'If you can walk, you can dance.' She
taught us to learn from ourselves and from each other," a girl, still wearing her leotard, tells a note-taking *Daily Planet* reporter. "We loved her.
We loved the respect she gave us. She had so much faith in us, she gave
us faith in ourselves."

March 2000: On the Down Low

"We're the Berkeley High peer sex educators. And we're here to drop some info on you." One adult counselor from the school's health center and four students who get class credit for volunteering there are lined up in front of forty gigglingly attentive CAS seniors.

"I got up at 7:30 in the morning for this?" mutters Jordan, back in school and back in CAS after a few extra therapy sessions and some time alone; back to his "normal depressive self, no Prozac required," as he kept telling his mom he would be if she'd just chill out. "I've heard this presentation like fifty times." Each time he's intended to take the health center up on its offer: anyone who shows up at its one-hour safe sex class gets twelve free condoms a month, every month, no questions asked. Jordan hasn't made it to the class yet, so he's still buying his at the drugstore. Or not.

Across the room, Autumn, who's also heard the safe sex rap before, shrugs out of her backpack and sits up expectantly. No one in CAS knows this about her—the CAS "bonding" trip is cool and all; still, there's only so much of her personal business Autumn chooses to share with her classmates—but the subject of sex and love has a very special meaning to her right now.

"I'm Katie," says one of the peer educators, a lesbian who's a member of Berkeley High's Gay-Straight Alliance. "Did you know that two-thirds of teenagers are sexually active by the end of high school? Did you know that only half of those kids use condoms? And that thirteen young people in the U.S. are diagnosed with HIV every five minutes? We're not assuming you're sexually active, but we want to make sure that if you are, you stay safe." Katie turns to Mr. Richards and Ms. Crawford. "I'm gonna ask that you teachers leave the room now so we can talk privately."

As soon as the teachers are gone, a senior with shoulder-length dreadlocks addresses the class. "I'm Monte. We're taking it on faith that you guys are mature enough to handle this. Now—everyone get up and stand on one side of the room. This exercise will be done in silence."

The forty CAS kids crowd together, jostling and laughing. "If you feel like you belong to a group that has a long history of oppression, walk across the room," Monte instructs them. Abruptly the laughter stops. Every girl and every student of color walks across the room. Along with the other white boys, Jordan stays put. "Notice who's next to you," Monte says. "Notice how you feel. Then walk back."

The students are quiet now, and serious. "If you've ever been discriminated against because of your age, race, or sexual orientation, walk across the room." This time every student walks, stops, looks around, walks back.

"If you or anyone you know has ever been pressured into having sex." Half the girls and a few boys walk across the room. Both Autumn and Jordan stand still. *Lamar didn't force me,* Autumn tells herself, as she's told herself many times in the past year. *But this time I'm going to wait . . .*

"If you or anyone you know has had sex while drunk or high." Every one of the students crosses the room.

"If you or anyone you know has had unprotected sex." Again, everyone.

I need to quit doing that, Jordan thinks. When he first got together with Kristen three years ago, Jordan was still a virgin. "We waited more than a year to have sex. We didn't want it to be rushed. We wanted it to be special. I'd had 'the first time' hyped up to me as this big amazing thing, and it was—even though my mom walked in the front door right in the middle of it." In the beginning, he and Kristen used condoms almost every time. But recently—when they weren't in one of their broken-up phases, that is—they'd gotten sloppy.

"If you or anyone you know has ever questioned their sexual orientation," one of the peer sex educators says. Some of the students giggle; fifteen others, including Autumn and Jordan, walk across the room. Jordan is absolutely positive that he's straight, but his female friends sure aren't. Lately it seems like half the girls he knows are experimenting with bisexuality: having sex with each other on Saturday nights, giggling about it with their boyfriends on Senior Step on Monday.

Autumn walks for the same reason: she, too, knows a lot of girls who are "questioning—on the verge of bisexual." Autumn doesn't have a problem with that. Even though homosexuality is against her religion—her stepfather is vocal about his opinion that it's "disgusting"—she believes "God will handle it." What Autumn does have a problem with is her peers' double standards: "Everyone thinks it's okay for girls but not for guys. I hear people saying bad stuff about gay guys all the time. I say, 'If it was two girls you wouldn't say that.' They say, 'Yeah, well, two girls together is okay. Two guys together is scandalous.' "

"Walk across the room if you feel your life has been affected by HIV." As he walks, along with Autumn and half of their classmates, a movie plays in Jordan's head: the day last year when he went to get his HIV test results at the health center. He'd gotten a pass from his history teacher ("One good thing about the health center being right on campus is that the teacher has to let you out of class if you ask to go there"), then ran down the hall and over to the B building, his heart pounding like a conga drum the whole way. "I hadn't had unsafe sex. Not much, anyway. I hadn't used needles. But I'd seen my mom's friends dying of AIDS. Just the thought of that disease, that test is so earthshaking: this is your life—positive or negative—on a piece of paper." When the counselor told Jordan the test was negative, he promised himself to start using condoms every time. *I'm still promising,* he admits to himself now.

How can anyone's life not *be affected by AIDS?* Autumn wonders, shuffling across the classroom with the others. Her mom works at a hotel in San Francisco, so naturally she's known a lot of people with AIDS. Autumn can't imagine a world without the disease, a world in which sex is not linked to death. To Autumn, AIDS is "a big problem for the world, and a serious consequence of something I've done before and will do again. But not anytime soon," she hastens to add.

"Walk across the room if you think you or your partner might be infected with HIV." This time no one moves.

"Thank you guys for participating in this," a Latina on the panel says. "You can sit down. Any questions or comments?"

"It makes me sad," Autumn says, "that every one of us feels we get discriminated against. We all walked on that one!"

"I thought there would be more people who used protection," says Elizabeth, whose identical twin, Jessica, nods in agreement.

"No one in this class thinks they might be HIV positive," says Julia. "That surprised me."

"Was there any time you didn't want to cross the room?" the adult counselor asks.

"Yes!" several kids answer. "The one about anyone you know questioning their sexuality," Raven says. "No one would have crossed if the question was just about *you*." Her classmates nod and laugh.

"For the next exercise, do you guys feel comfortable working as a whole group, or do you need to break into small groups?" the counselor asks.

"Whole group!" the students shout. "This is CAS," adds Sarah, who's sitting on her best friend Julia's lap. "We know each other better than most classes do."

"Okay," the counselor says. "I need a volunteer."

Melania goes to the front. Katie hands her a wooden dildo and a packaged condom. A titter ripples through the room, followed by rapt silence. "Don't open it with your teeth," Monte says as Melania starts to do just that. "And what do you do if there's pre-come on the outside of the condom?" he asks.

"Can you just wipe it off?" asks a girl as Melania unrolls the condom onto the dildo. "No! Take if off and throw it away," Monte answers. "Now—what kind of lube are you going to use?"

"Umm . . . is chocolate syrup okay?" asks another girl. "No. Anything that tastes good has oil in it," Monte answers matter-of-factly. He turns to Melania. "How you gonna remove it?"

"Take ten steps back from your partner . . ." Catherine calls out, and the class bursts into laughter. Melania hands the limp condom and the erect dildo to Katie and returns to her seat. "Comments? Questions?" the counselor asks.

"Most teenagers are nervous the first time they have sex," Lacy says. "They don't feel comfortable bringing up the subject of protection."

I would have felt a whole lot less comfortable getting pregnant, Autumn thinks. Even though she went on the pill as soon as she and Lamar started having sex, for the whole seven months of their relationship she insisted that he use a condom every time too. "Do I look like I want a baby?" she snapped when Lamar questioned her. "I'm not about to be one of those Berkeley High teenage mothers, carryin' their babies to the child care center across the street on their way to class. I'm 'bout to *graduate!*"

"If you can't talk to your partner, should you be having sex with your partner?" Monte asks.

"*No!*" several students say. "I know people who got pregnant like that," Rena says. "They knew all that stuff but they didn't use their knowledge when the time came."

Hands are waving now. "I heard you have the day-after pill in the health center," Catherine says. The counselor nods and explains, "It's a very concentrated form of the birth control pill."

"Doesn't it make you really sick?" asks Elena.

"Some people get nauseous," the counselor answers. "The sooner you take it, the better."

"Do you guys know the other risk factors for HIV?" Katie asks. The bell rings before anyone can answer. "Listen up, you-all!" Katie shouts over the hubbub of the students gathering up their jackets, orange juice bottles, backpacks. "Even though you're graduating, you can still get services at the health center till the end of the summer. HIV tests, STD tests, pregnancy tests, counseling, condoms. It's right across the hall, it's all free, and it's all confidential!"

I won't be needing any of that, Autumn responds silently. *Not this time around.* She thinks now of her brand-new boyfriend, Jareem. *Even his name is heck of cool,* she muses dreamily. Jareem, whose brothers' names all start with a "J," was named after Kareem Abdul-Jabbar. Like his name-sake he's tall (six feet, taller than Autumn), dark, and handsome. Autumn's full lips, shining with clear gloss, curve into a satisfied smile. *Jareem.*

Last year when Autumn went to the health center for a pregnancy test, she was really glad the center was free, and really glad their services were confidential, and *really* glad her test was negative. Despite the pill and the condoms, every time she and Lamar made love she'd felt worried afterwards—and guilty. "Part of my religion is that you don't have sex till you get married. When I did it I felt I wasn't being true to what I believed in. I know a lot of people don't feel like this, but to me sex is a sacred thing.

"I'm not a saint. Obviously I've messed up. But I learned a lot from my experience, and now I have to make decisions based on what I learned. My decision is, I want to try to wait till I get married before I do it again."

Lamar. Even though it was more than a year ago when he broke up with her, even though Autumn is in love, now, for the first time since then, the memory still hurts. "I thought everything was good with us. I was happy. Everyone knew it was Autumn and Lamar, Lamar and Autumn. Then one day he told me he wanted to separate. He said he needed to focus on basketball and his grades, and he couldn't do that with me in his life. Just like that—he turned around and stopped talking to me.

"One day I saw him in the halls and I was like, 'Why are you doing this? You said you loved me. I gave you my virginity.' He just kept walking like I was nobody. I was thrashed like my insides had been taken out and put over there and I was looking at them."

Since the endless nights she spent "crying over Lamar so much I felt like I was crying blood," Autumn hasn't needed to be tested for HIV or pregnancy—because she hasn't let another boy into her life. Her plan for senior year was to keep it that way: focus on her grades, on the friendships she neglected when she made Lamar her whole world last year, throw herself into her last year of high school. She kept to that plan until the first Saturday night in March, when she met Jareem at a party she went to with Lillian, Lauren, Emily, and Jamilah.

"We started talking that night and we haven't stopped talking since. He lives in Antioch, forty minutes away, so we only get to see each other on weekends—always with a whole bunch of people at a basketball game or a party. We haven't been alone together yet. We haven't even kissed. But he already invited me to come to church with his family. And we talk on the phone every night."

Autumn's brown eyes gleam. "His phone bill was a hundred dollars. We were like, 'This can't happen.' So now we take turns calling each other. We try not to talk so often. We try to write letters instead. We have one of those New Age type of relationships: we're friends, we care about each other, we choose to have a relationship that requires intimacy we can't have right now.

"The good thing is, we still know how we feel when we're apart. His nickname at school is 'Sexy' and I can see why. But I don't worry about that, and he doesn't worry about me. Later on it'll come in handy that we don't have to be all up under each other for us to have a solid, trusting relationship."

Autumn heads over to the C building for her AP World Lit class, gliding down the hall, her platform sandals seeming to be floating on air. "I was just so attracted when I met him—and not physically. That's how I know I love him." A frown flits across her face. "When I told Emily I'd invited Jareem to the Prom she said, 'Are you sure you're not moving too fast?' I was *heck* of insulted. Even though later I realized that she probably said that because she finally broke up with *her* boyfriend.

I told her, 'After everything I've been through in my life, do you really think I'm going to say I feel deeply about someone and not mean it?' "

Emily is waiting for Autumn now outside Ms. Anderson's class, along with Lillian and Jamilah. The girls meet at the start of fourth period every day; after it, every day, they drift down the hall to Autumn's locker where they hook up with Lauren for lunch. Autumn's beatific smile returns as she walks into the classroom with her friends. "I love him. I do!"

"I have an announcement to make," Emily says as the students are taking their seats. "My good friend Autumn is in love!"

"I don't know how I can hold class after such an important announcement!" Ms. Anderson smiles from her stool in the front of the room. "But unless you've got more to say on that subject, Autumn . . ." Autumn shakes her head, grinning. "Then let's get started on *Madame Bovary*."

Autumn is keeping up with the reading—she ended up with a C in Mr. Miller's class last semester and won't let herself fall behind again. But she hasn't been able to get into the novel, mostly because she can't relate to the main character. "Emma Bovary *says* she's in love, but she's always whining about her problems. She doesn't understand love! She doesn't know how to count her blessings. And that is *so* annoying to me right now!"

"I don't believe this is happening," Autumn whispers to Emily as Ms. Anderson starts recounting Flaubert's life story.

"What?"

"It's like if you always wanted to go to Cal or Yale and you just found out you got in." Autumn can't keep her face from twisting into that silly grin.

"You got it ba-a-ad, girl," Emily whispers.

"And that gots to be good," Autumn replies happily.

A few doors down the hall, they're talking about sex in Keith's English class too. Keith took Ms. Theodore's Poetry class because he needs the credit to graduate, and because Ms. Theodore told him he'd get a B, minimum, if he did. "I've had a soft spot in my heart for you since I had you as a freshman, Keith," Ms. Theodore told him, giving him one of her famous hugs. "You're a diamond in the rough."

Ms. Theodore is hella tight, and her class is, too, Keith thinks. Unlike his Computer Academy and African-American Studies classes, there are all kinds of people in it—about the same number of white kids as black, plus a few Latinos and Asians. A couple of guys from Giglio's class are the only people Keith has met before. Keith's never seen anything like it at Berkeley High. So many kids come to class every day, they have to go out in the hall and look for chairs.

A white girl reads a poem about having sex in a car. "That was *good!*" Keith shouts when she finishes. He applauds wildly.

"That could go in the literary magazine, Cassandra," Ms. Theodore agrees. "Cars are painfully sexual, don't you think? Lube job! I need to get my valves oiled—"

"The stick! Get a tune-up!" Keith adds.

"That's a metaphor for a relationship," Ms. Theodore says. "When cars are new they smell good, they look good. When the relationship gets old, it gets rusty, broken down—"

"You gotta replace it with a new one!" Keith yells, laughing.

The class is getting rowdy now, as it often does; about every fifth word Ms. Theodore says is "Shh." "You guys are getting the metaphor concept. Shh! Any other metaphors?" She shouts to be heard over the side jokes and titters.

"Never buy a used car when you know it's been in a wreck," Keith says. The boys in the class hoot and howl.

"Good!" Ms. Theodore says. "Shh! I'm going to read you a kind of a trippy poem by the former Poet Laureate of the United States, Rita Dove. I hope no one gets freaked out. Let's try and be mature about this, okay?" But as she reads the lines about a woman washing her daughter's hairless vagina, several of the boys sitting around Keith do indeed freak out. "Oh *no!*" they groan in a chorus.

"Guys, come on," Ms. Theodore implores them.

"That would be a good poem if *I* wrote it?" Keith asks incredulously.

"If that was about someone's toe there wouldn't be all this nervous laughter," a girl says.

"What was that wrinkled string between the mother's legs?" a friend of Keith's asks. The class explodes with laughter. "That's her Tampax, fool!" a girl informs him haughtily.

"Well, excuse *me* for not bein' up on *that!*" the boy defends himself.

"Hel-lo!" Ms. Theodore shouts, shaking her head in affectionate disgust. "Anyone in here ever take Social Living?"

Indeed they did, every one of them. Since the mid-seventies the one-semester Social Living course has been a graduation requirement for every Berkeley High student. The only exemptions are granted to the few whose parents refuse to let them take the class—those who object on moral or religious grounds to their children's participation in graphic discussions of sex, drugs, homosexuality, child abuse, eating disorders, suicide, and all the permutations and consequences thereof.

Most students take Social Living as freshmen. Keith didn't get around to it until his senior year, and he says he might as well have skipped it. "It was just a class I had to take. I listened to all that talk about condoms and AIDS, but it's not nothin' I didn't know before. It hasn't affected what I do. I use condoms when I do somethin.' But I don't hardly do nothin'."

Keith lost his virginity when he was sixteen in what he calls "an experimental situation." "The first time I had sex I didn't use a condom. I didn't really know what I was doing. Ever since then I try to use one. I always look at the girl first to see if she's clean. I just go with girls I've been knowing for a long time. You got to know the person. You can't just get anybody." He reconsiders what he's just said. "Man, I know I should think about that. But a lot of times I don't. I don't know what's wrong with me."

Keith's been in two long relationships: one from eighth to tenth grade—"she was hecka cool, but she hella hurt my feelings. I ain't never really trusted any girl since"—and one from the end of tenth grade through eleventh grade. "I had kind of deep feelings for Jasmine. It wasn't like we just got together—I had knew her family and everything. Then all of a sudden she tells me her grandma thinks we shouldn't go together anymore, that she needs to concentrate on her school. I never let *her* interfere with my school. And I had football to deal with too."

Since he got over Jasmine, Keith has been happily single and happily near-celibate. "Now I'm just a player. I don't go with no girl. You can't get lonely when you a player."

Player or not, Keith says there is one girl who holds a special place in his heart. He and Tandeeka are close—"I can talk to her hecka good, and her mom likes me more than any other boy"—but Tandeeka isn't sure she wants more than a friendship with Keith. "I'm always, like, 'What you mean, you ain't ready?'"

He lowers his voice confidentially. "But if she was ready, I wouldn't be. I like people feeling sorry for me so I throw it in her face. It's part of the role, part of the shield I wear. I be like, 'No one likes me, why don't you like me?' And Tandeeka be like, 'Keith, you know I love your black ass.'

"The thing about Tandeeka is, she's confused. She don't know what she wants: a boy or a girl. There's a lot of girls like that at Berkeley High: tryin' boys, tryin' girls. I don't care as long as they let me be part of the party!" Keith laughs mischievously, then tugs thoughtfully at one of the diamond studs in his ear. "But two guys together—that's terrible. God made women to be with men. Two women—God will probably let you get away with that. It ain't too much they can do. But with two guys? That's a lot of damage."

"At most high schools you see very strong gender roles: girls are passive, boys are macho. Girls wear tight, form-fitting tops and have high rates of anorexia. Berkeley High has less of that," says Dr. Lynn Ponton, author of *The Sex Lives of Teenagers* and professor of psychiatry at UC San Francisco. Dr. Ponton has seen many Berkeley High students in her twenty years of private practice. "At Berkeley High the boys and girls both wear baggy pants, baggy sweatshirts. The gender and sexual margins are more blurred. I think that's good."

Also good, says Ponton, are the exceptional sexual support systems Berkeley High offers its students: the mandatory Social Living classes, whose teachers often become de facto confidantes and counselors; the school-sanctioned Gay-Straight Alliance, mentored by out lesbian teacher Annie Johnston; the on-site health center, where kids get free, confidential mental, physical, and sexual counseling and health services; and the Berkeley High child care center across the street, where teen parents get free child care and parenting classes. "I've had Berkeley High teen moms who actually see the school as protective and helpful to them. *That's* unusual," Dr. Ponton says. "And although it's never easy for a gay or bisexual teenager to come out—fifty percent of the runaway kids I see got kicked out of their homes because their parents found out they're gay—the Gay-Straight Alliance helps set a good tone."

But even with these supports in place, Dr. Ponton says, Berkeley High students face the same daunting, and often life-threatening, sexual challenges as teenagers everywhere. "Twenty-five percent of HIV cases nationwide are transmitted in adolescence. Adolescent girls are at greatest risk because their cervices are still developing and because they don't, as a rule, have good negotiation skills. Many of them cannot tell boys to use condoms.

"Parents have shied away from this whole arena. They don't realize that fifty percent of sixteen-year-olds nationwide are having intercourse. They don't realize that one birds-and-bees conversation is not enough, and that abstinence-only sex education is not effective. The right wing is adamant about abstinence-only sex ed programs. They get Congress to pay millions of dollars to school districts that offer them—even though they've been shown to be less effective in reducing HIV rates and all risky behaviors. It's very scary."

"Parents don't understand the world their teenagers live in," agrees Dr. Anthony Santangelo, Director of Berkeley High's health center. "Our peer educators tell us that young people really want to protect their parents. They'll lie as much as they have to out of a sense that if they told their parents the truth, there's no way their parents could handle it."

Last year Dr. Santangelo's staff served nearly half of the students at Berkeley High, administering eighty-seven HIV tests, 185 pregnancy tests, and more than 600 tests for sexually transmitted diseases—or STDs—to a diverse clientele that closely mirrors the school's demographics. "Students come in because they have no one to talk to, because they don't have correct information," Dr. Santangelo says. "Our peer health educators go into the classrooms, talk about how STDs get transmitted, how people become pregnant—and all of a sudden we get an influx of students who need to talk about their particular circumstances."

More than one-third of the students seen by the health center come for counseling, often to talk about troubled love relationships. A March *Jacket* story headlined "Keep It on the Down Low: Relationships That Students Don't Want to Talk About" includes several anonymous first-person accounts—all of them by girls—of being mentally, financially, and physically abused by their boyfriends. "Perhaps, if BHS weren't so indifferent (if I were a little smarter) I would not have been taken advantage of," writes a sixteen-year-old junior whose boyfriend stole her money, dumped her, then screamed "slut" at her in the halls. "But all I can do now is share my story, hoping it will help someone else figure out what type of relationship is best for them." In the accompanying poem, "The Womb of Desolate," fifteen-year-old Chinaka Hodge writes, ". . . I will follow you/footsteps behind/Your untouching/Lust . . . I'm tripping over/Your half truths/And my forgotten virginity."

Dr. Santangelo moved to Berkeley High three years ago from nearby Oakland Tech. "The diversity of class and ethnicity is striking at Berkeley High, and the poverty is less striking than it is in Oakland. But despite these differences, I don't think that being a student of color and gay is any easier at Berkeley High. At Oakland Tech the gay students, especially kids of color, were very, very cautious about who knew. That's true here also."

A *Jacket* story on gay teachers and students at Berkeley High confirms Santangelo's observation. "The Bay Area is famous for its positive attitude toward gays and lesbians," the article begins, "but not a day passes when I don't hear, 'Blood, that's hella gay,' or 'Man, what a faggot!' " And the article ends: "I leave you with this question: if love conquers all—religious barriers, racial barriers, distance barriers, and all other kinds of barriers—why should it not conquer gender barriers as well?"

Dr. Santangelo offers one reason. "For teenagers, issues of sexual orientation are very difficult to deal with. Period. This is particularly true in the black community. It's closer-knit; there's a sense of people knowing your business, of having no other community to go to. White kids have more opportunity to move between groups. They go off to college. They have mobility. Kids of color are not afforded that sort of anonymity."

Although Berkeley High's sex education program doesn't confine itself to promoting abstinence—"We'd miss the half of our kids who are already sexually active"—Dr. Santangelo says abstinence is always presented as an option, and to an increasingly receptive student population. "If you go to any movie, watch any TV show, you see that teenagers are being conditioned to be sexually active. If you watch MTV it looks like everyone's doing it. Yes, teens are sexually active. But we've seen that teens are reflecting a bit more on abstinence as a viable option."

Only 900 of the 80,000 public high schools in America have health centers like Berkeley High's—in part because they are so controversial. "It's a no-win situation," Dr. Santangelo says. "If we say we reduce the number of teen births, we're accused of advocating abortion. If we say we change kids' risk-taking behaviors, we're accused of infringing on parents' rights to raise their kids. But if we don't accomplish those goals, we're accused of being ineffective."

Nonetheless, Dr. Santangelo believes that every school should have a health center like Berkeley High's. "Children do not go from childhood to adolescence with the blink of an eye. It takes a lot of people in a child's life for them to navigate all the challenges and pitfalls of adolescence. Some parents are very grateful for the help we offer with that. Others are terrified, which gets translated into, 'I don't want anybody talking to my child about these things.'

"Those who say we're trying to take the place of parents are partly right. We do take their place when parents aren't doing their jobs, when their relationships with their children are abusive, when their children have run away or just need someone to talk to.

"We keep students in school. We give them alternatives to life-threatening behaviors. We prevent suicide. We absolutely feel that we save lives."

. . .

"I can tell you this 'cause this is truth
The state of California just declared war on youth!"

Niles Xi'an-Lichtenstein, a leader of Youth Together, cofounder of Berkeley High's Hapa (biracial Asian) Club, and first-prize winner in a recent statewide poetry slam, yells into the mike in his hand, then passes it to fellow YT leader Pam Pradachith.

"Who's mad that Prop 21 passed?" Pam shouts at the crowd: 150 mostly African-American Berkeley High students, who are crammed into the Student Learning Center the day after California voters passed the Juvenile Justice Initiative by a margin of 62 to 38 percent.

"WE ARE!" the crowd roars back.

In San Francisco at this moment, 500 teenage protesters are marching through the streets chanting, "Ain't no power like the power of the youth!" A student group called the Third Eye Movement is calling for a statewide conference, "Upset the Set-Up." This morning's *San Francisco Chronicle* editorial, "Hard Time for Young Offenders," called Proposition 21 "California's new child-rearing manual": "If Your Kids Misbehave, Lock Them Down with Hardened Adult Criminals and Then Watch Them Grow."

"Proposition 21 also expands the definition and penalties for gang members," the *Chronicle* editorialized, "a disturbing development considering the past biases against young people of color who are sweepingly—often erroneously—assumed to have gang affiliations . . . If we really think children as young as 14 have the same reasoning and judgment as adults, then maybe they should be allowed to buy liquor and drive automobiles—and, for goodness sake, vote."

Here in Berkeley High's Student Learning Center, hip-hop blasts from a boom box; a DJ stands ready to scratch some tunes; potato chips, cookies, and juice boxes are laid out on a table in the resource room, and freshly painted signs hang on the walls:

EDUCATE YOURSELF/PROTECT YOURSELF!

CALIFORNIA IS #1 IN PRISONS, #41 IN EDUCATION

WHAT SHOULD WE DEMAND?

"You-all should have some ideas about how to stop this thing!" Pam walks around the crowded room, handing the mike to one student after another.

"Whether you go to jail or not, this is gonna affect you," says a sophomore named Ayoka. "Girls, you think you can't find a good man *now*—in three years they're gonna all be behind bars. We're gonna lose our African-American brothers over this!"

"We can't go kick it on a corner with three of our friends anymore," says a boy. "They're gonna jack us up for bein' a gang. We need to take this seriously, you guys, and figure out what to do!"

"It's so unfair!" exclaims a black-and-white biracial girl. "They can arrest me for hanging out with my *softball* team. And I'm not even black—it's just that my skin is brown!"

"We should have a walkout," suggests another boy. "Not get out of class and go kick it, but hook up with the Oakland schools. We could all wear white and black—"

"When we walk out we be missing our education," Pam argues. "We should walk *in* to a school board meeting. We should make them say the Berkeley Police Department won't enforce this, that Berkeley believes in educating our kids, not incarcerating them." She looks around the room. "Did anyone write anything they want to share?"

Hands wave, and the young people who are the target of Prop 21—

the African-American teenagers who have been labeled "super-predators" in the campaign to pass it—do in fact take up a weapon: *poetry*, to express their outrage. Once again Ayoka asks for the mike.

> *"This is no proposition*
> *This is the vision*
> *Fuck the manufactured education*
> *We done sat for a lifetime in these steel seats*
> *Till we got hemorrhoids*
> *So we could be made into working androids*
> *The real education*
> *Begins within*
> *Knowing and cultivating yourself*
> *Is where true knowledge begins*
> *Cause the only thing for us and by us*
> *Is who and what we decide to be . . . "*

Keith's classmate and chronic sparring partner Josh Gray reads:

> *"Ask me, don't stereotype me!*
> *Is it because I wear baggy clothes, black puff*
> *   jacket and a baseball hat you categorize*
> *   me as a thug?*
> *Ask me if I am the president of the Black*
> *   Student Union*
> *Ask me if I am going to a four-year college*
> *   after high school.*
> *Ask me if I am on the City of Berkeley*
> *   Youth Commission board.*
> *Just because one young black brother did*
> *   something bad to you, doesn't mean I am*
> *   going to do the same thing.*

You want to lock me up in chains, but where is my
  chance to change?
Ask me if I am going to overcome any challenges
  America gives me. The only person can stop me
  is God.
So ask me, don't stereotype me!"

The poetic revolt continues that night at the March poetry slam, held in a biology lab in the G building, cosponsored by CAS and the Computer Academy and attended by the usual standing-room-only crowd. "Welcome to the slam," Rick Ayers opens the event. "I just wish the ignorant people who voted for Prop 21—"

"Would get shot!" someone calls out from the audience.

"—I just wish the people who think teenagers are career criminals and predators could be here tonight. Because this is how *real* teenagers are," Ayers continues. "Our M.C. for tonight is the one, the only, the incomparable Lauren Chambers!"

Autumn leads the audience in a rousing cheer for her girl, who's wearing a bright yellow Old Navy fleece sweatshirt inside out over baggy denim Gap painter's pants. "The poets will be judged on three qualities," Lauren announces, writing them on the board. "Performance, writing, audience hype factor.

"Everybody have fun. Don't get sad about your scores. It's not about winning—it's about telling everybody what's up." Lauren chooses five judges from the audience, equips them with paper and markers for scoring, and kicks off the event with her own poem:

"My class
Everyday where I am supposed to come sit on my ass
Everyone becomes a part of the system
Where all we do all day is listen
It would be cool if my teacher knew my name
And not just my face

For a whole 45 minutes I must sit in one place
Don't be inquisitive and ask questions
Because your classmates place you in sections
"They" have it just the way "They" want it
I know you're asking who "They" is
"They" is the people who knew you wouldn't make it
"They" is the people who create this system just so you fail
I hate to say it but for some of us "They" win everyday
And a lot of us have not yet realized there is a "They"
So before you start to place people in sections by what they do
Sit back and say, "IT'S A STRUGGLE AND HE'S TRYING TO
    MAKE IT TOO"*

Reading from journals decorated with happy faces, skulls and cross-bones, fluffy kittens, and Pokémon; reading from crumpled pieces of binder paper and performing from memory, twenty teenage girls and boys of various races, body types, and sexual orientations raise their voices and their arms before an appreciative, boisterous crowd that includes a few teachers and parents—Pedro Noguera, Amy Crawford, and Lauren's mom among them.

Reggie, a football player and the only African-American boy in Autumn's AP English class, reads:

"Yes it hurts when we let ourselves be called bitch and nigga
the words sting like a Teflon trigger
The inhabitants of this plantation
live in incarceration
bathing in self-degradation
Like the 21st Proposition
I serve the absurd with words of rendition
As long as they imprison the masses
I'll continue to kick asses.
Revolution! Revolution! Revolution!"

A white boy wearing a torn T-shirt and frayed jeans recites from memory:

> *"Arrested for being downtown*
> *Penalizing me for being free*
> *Ignore the problem it'll go away*
> *But people are dying everyday*
> *My grades ain't high enough*
> *Sorry kid, life is tough . . ."*

A heavy-set African-American girl with cherry-red press-on nails keeps her eyes locked on the piece of binder paper gripped in her hands as she reads:

> *"Boys are not reliable*
> *your whole sky will darken as he creeps away*
> *The rising is always fast and brilliant*
> *the setting bloody and violent*
> *Why not try a woman instead?*
> *Her fingers are wise*
> *they make your womb rise . . ."*

Another black girl punches the air with clenched fists, punctuating the anger of her verse:

> *"They're killing our brothers.*
> *They took them all: Tupac, Martin, Malcolm*
> *Don't worry, Maya, we will rise.*
> *Don't worry, brother, I'll be here when you get out . . ."*

Cassandra, a red-haired white girl who's Keith's classmate in Ms. Theodore's poetry class and a frequent slam finalist, twists a braided plait between her fingers as she reads from her journal:

"Chilling with the girls and guys,
smiling high,
someone says "Do you wanna try?"
But I don't fly
So I lie.
She asks, "Why don't you drink?"
I say, "because I like to think . . .
For myself,"
See, people can do what they want to do,
It's okay to be an addict,
I just don't want to be part of the clique,
That's begging for money on Shattuck."

And then, pacing across the room in her baggy gray cargo pants and oversized white T-shirt, fingers splayed across her chest, a glowingly in-love Autumn performs "I Am a Woman":

"I am hope personified
I am the tear drop come alive
I am the sound of footsteps that run and hide
I am the struggle you battle inside

"I am love, true love
unconditional giver
Never ceasing river
I am the stars you see from afar
what you can't hold
but what you can feel
everything that's real

"I am as cool as water
and I burn like fire
I am strong, bold
what you can see

and invisible still
an optical illusion
at will

"Woman
wo-from the womb
the womb which gives
life to the man
Woman"

In acknowledgment of the recently implemented new Tardy Policy (brainchild of the WASC Committee on Safety and Discipline, it requires students who are more than five minutes late to class to report first to the attendance office. There they must stand on line to receive a time-dated pass, which must then be checked by a gauntlet of teachers serving hall duty in each successive building. The outcome, often, is that tardy students miss most or all of their classes instead of just the first few minutes), a science teacher, Lee Amosslee, is granted special permission to perform his poem, "Hall Duty Time," to an appreciative crowd composed largely of the students who are its targets.

" 'Scuse me young
lady
'scuse me young man
did you hear the bell
the one that just rang?

"Your education
it's waiting for you
but you will not get it
unless you will move.

"Hall duty time
is it a crime?

"Excuse me young lady
where is your class?
Now why did you tell me
to kiss your sweet ass?

"Excuse me young man
I know lunch is short
But that's no excuse
The rules to abort.

"Hall duty time
can feel like a crime . . .

"Then she yells at him
and he cusses out her.
In the halls there's commotion
everyone's in a stir.

"I push him aside
and into a class
and keep him in there
until the rest pass.

" 'Off to class you go now'
I say to the fighter
'Thanks for your respect.'
We leave feeling lighter.

"Hall duty time
don't feel like a crime . . . "

As the laughter and applause subside Lauren says quietly, "Our principal is sitting on the floor." All eyes search the room. And so she is— scrunched up against the wall in blue jeans and a Berkeley High T-shirt, making a rare nighttime appearance at a student event. After a boy insists that she take his seat, the kids turn their attention away from Theresa Saunders, who stays until the slam ends at ten, then slips without fanfare out the side door.

The new Tardy Policy and its adjunct program, Operation Stay in School—roving sweeps of downtown Berkeley stores and streets conducted by teams of Berkeley High administrators and Berkeley police officers rounding up truant students—sparks the predictable response from the student body: they hate it. The front page of the *Jacket*'s April Fool's issue features a full-sized photo of "Warden Saunders—Operation ALWAYS-IN-SCHOOL," and the banner headline, "Theresa Saunders' Reforms Fix Berkeley High School/Brilliant Use of Prop. 21 Will Turn School into Jail; Everyone Happy."

"In perhaps the finest tactical move of her career," the caustic article begins, "Saunders has implemented a new program that will solve nearly all the school's problems at once. The Plan, dubbed 'Operation Always in School,' will convert Berkeley High into a prison. 'We realized after California passed Prop. 21 that the proposition classified three or more teenagers wearing the same type of clothing as a gang,' said an elated Saunders. 'So, we decided we could just arrest all the students for gang activity.'

"Merchants from Shattuck Avenue have praised Saunders' new plan. The teachers are also excited about the new plan. They will now be employed as prison guards and, as such, will make a lot more money and have a much stronger union. 'I used to be an advocate for the students,' said English teacher Rick Ayers, 'but when they showed me my first paycheck I said, "Lock em up!" '

"In related news, the WASC Committee has announced that they will grant Berkeley High School a six-year accreditation at the end of the year, citing the school as a model for all academic institutions throughout the country." '

The staff, in fact, is divided on the Tardy Policy. Some see the crackdown as a necessary evil, a kind of behavior modification exercise they hope will yield an unprecedentedly present, punctual student body. Some support the new policy out of sheer desperation. Over the years, endless schemes have failed to get the huge numbers of chronically tardy and absent Berkeley High students—disproportionately the same students who rack up Ds and Fs—to class on time. Other teachers resent the role it assigns them. "I didn't go to college to be a cop," AP English teacher David Bye mutters, returning to his post after chasing a pair of wayward students down the hall of the C building. "I just want to teach the literature. But I guess this is part of the package, being a public high school teacher."

And some find the "tardy line" that now winds through the counseling department for most of each day too much of an embarrassment to bear. "Have you looked at the *line?*" an incredulous rookie counselor asks Vice Principal Doris Wallace-Tanner. *"They're all black kids!"*

But despite the debates and disruption, it seems that Marcia Singman's death, and the school community's tender response to it, has engendered a new spirit of unity. The teachers stop boycotting WASC meetings and staff meetings; instead, they elect a Shared Governance Committee designed to "allow all the various interest groups in the school to have some input into decision-making." At a well-attended staff meeting in early March, Theresa Saunders sits among the rank-and-file; the teachers elected to the committee take her place at the front of the room. "No one will be able to hijack the staff meetings anymore," a committee member explains. "The administration will become an interest group itself. They'll have to go around lobbying for their proposals, same as us. Comments? Questions?"

"I'd rather the administration administer," Rick Ayers says. "But if this is how it has to be . . . Will people be paid for their time, sitting on the Shared Governance Committee? Who's got the time and the energy for this?"

"At least it gives us some control over the agenda," a science teacher says.

"Maybe we could get time off to do it," another teacher suggests.

"We're going to hear an important update on contract negotiations before we break into WASC work groups," a committee member says. She introduces Alan Miller, vice president of the Berkeley Federation of Teachers.

"The BFT has declared an impasse in our negotiations with the Berkeley Unified School District," Miller says. "We've also filed an Unfair Labor Practices grievance. So far the only commitment the district has made is to keep us the lowest paid teachers in the Bay Area. So, in case you haven't heard, there's a protest rally tomorrow after school in front of the school district offices. Teachers are coming from all the schools, from all over town. We have no excuse not to be there. It's right across the street. See you there tomorrow!"

"The kids have no clue about the relationship between attendance and achievement," says a math teacher, sitting in the reconvened WASC Committee on Achievement Disparity. "When I flunk kids they are genuinely shocked: 'But I was here every day!' They honestly believe if they come to school that should be enough."

"I don't see the connection between achievement disparity and attendance," says the mother of a ninth-grader, in attendance "to find out what's going on at Berkeley High." "It's about citizenship," a teacher explains. "If they don't learn to show up in high school, how will they learn it?"

"The school is losing $20,000 a month because of kids being absent," an English teacher says.

"Also, kids who aren't attending school often get into trouble," adds another teacher. "They're not getting appropriate adult supervision. They're getting unwholesome peer supervision. With Prop 21 on the books, that's dangerous."

"I'm not servicing my students to the best of my ability," a history teacher says, "because every day I'm catching up so many students who weren't there the day before."

An English Language Learner (ELL) teacher says, "Every year in mid-December we lose twenty-five students from the ELL classes because their parents take them back to their home countries. Since we have no attendance policy, the parents don't understand why their kids drop from a B to a D. Plus, I have parents who keep their high school students home to baby-sit when a younger child is sick. And we wonder why we have an achievement gap . . ."

"If we're serious about closing the gap, we need an official attendance policy," a history teacher says, "some clear understanding of the consequences of student absence." There are nods of agreement around the room.

"I'll tell Theresa we want a policy from the board," the committee chair says, glancing at the clock on the wall. The teachers pack up the papers they've been grading during the meeting and toss their Starbucks cups into the trash. The forty-five minutes allotted for this discussion of the achievement disparity at Berkeley High have elapsed.

.   .   .

"Two/Four/Six/Eight—The District must negotiate!
Three/Five/Seven/Nine—Pay us for our overtime!"

Several hundred teachers and students, many of them from Berkeley High, chant slogans in the bright springtime sun. As passing cars honk in support, the teachers wave their homemade picket signs: "Will Teach for Food." "We know how to use the California surplus!" "Professional pay for professional work." "To maintain high standards in my classroom I work 15–20 hours of unpaid time each week." "Show us the money!"

"Teaching is a profession. It should not be confused with martyrdom!" Alan Miller shouts into the bullhorn from the steps of Berkeley City Hall. "Berkeley Unified: listen up! If you value your children, you will value your teachers!"

The teachers from Willard Middle School, an uphill mile away, march in from Milvia Street singing their adaptation of "Solidarity Forever":

"To teach it is an honor and a privilege yes it's true
But the landlord don't take nothin but that hard cash when it's due

206

In these parts to be a teacher is to be homeless and blue
But the union makes us strong.

"If you can throw a baseball you can buy a midsized town
And if you can tell a joke on TV you could wear a crown
Yet those who teach our children hunt for pennies on the ground
But the union makes us strong."

"After reporting that teachers worked 30,000 unpaid hours in February," the *Jacket* says, "BFT President Barry Fike commented, 'There are ways that we can shut down parts of this district without going on strike' . . ."

"The same week the stock market had its busiest day ever and California anticipated a budget surplus of at least $4.2 billion," the *San Francisco Chronicle* story on the rally comments, "400 Berkeley teachers sang protest songs on the district office steps to deplore their $29,000 starting salaries."

April 2000: Feelin' the Heat

"Your mom called," Lillian's brother tells Autumn as the two girls walk into Lillian's house after school on a Thursday afternoon. "She wants you to call her back."

Autumn nods, follows Lil to the kitchen, and decides to ignore her mother's message till later. *She's probably just mad at me about something. Whatever it is, I don't need to hear about it right now.* Autumn's sleepovers at Lillian's big, peaceful house in Concord—fifteen miles from Berkeley, twenty miles and a world apart from her own family's apartment in Alameda—are like little peaceful vacations. And Autumn could really use one of those right now.

Much as she hates to admit it, all the college news that's been flying around Berkeley High this week has been getting to her. Kids from her AP classes are running around waving their acceptance letters from Vassar and Yale and Princeton, getting hugs and congratulations from teachers. In CAS, where Mr. Richards greets every college acceptance announcement with a reminder that "what counts is who you're becoming, not what college you're going to," just about every day, someone announces that they got into Stanford or Harvard or Brown, most of them rich white kids, most of them with scholarships they probably don't really need. Reggie, Autumn's AP English classmate, got a full scholarship to the University of Southern California, where Autumn applied, too, after their recruiter sent her an application. Autumn hasn't heard back from USC and she isn't really expecting to. *Not that it matters,* she reminds herself. *Not that UC Santa Cruz isn't a perfectly good college.*

And then there are her girls. No big surprise: Emily got into every single school she applied to, including Swarthmore and UCLA. *That's what happens when you have your own room and your own computer and you study all the time and you don't have a life,* Autumn thinks, then hates herself for thinking, when Emily tells her the news.

And Lillian. Lillian! Occidental College is begging her to go there, flying her down to L.A. this weekend, all expenses paid. Lil's also been accepted by the only black college she applied to, Xavier in New Orleans—her top pick, since she's planning to go to medical school and theirs is one of the best. And yesterday Lillian got her fat acceptance packet from "Cal," as everyone calls UC Berkeley. True, Lil's mom works in the Cal admissions office; and Lil's parents paid for her to take SAT classes; and all her life, they've given her exactly the kind of financial, emotional, and academic support that Autumn could only dream of. But it's also true that Lillian worked hard for those acceptances, earned every one of them. Autumn couldn't be prouder of her, or happier for her.

Still . . .

Now that it's time to let go of the fantasy that Autumn and Lil dreamed up when they became best friends four years ago—the two of them sharing a dorm room at Cal, the best public university in the country—Autumn can't help feeling just a little sadness, too.

"Fix me a plate," Autumn commands her best friend as Lillian stands peering into the open refrigerator. Lillian snorts, as she always does when Autumn tries to boss her around. "I don't think so, Smarty Arty," Lillian snaps back, using the nickname they took from a Chris Rock comedy routine, "The Smarty Arty Negro." Lil carries her plate down the hall to the bedroom she shares with no one. Autumn shrugs, takes a plate from the cabinet, pulls open the refrigerator door, and starts rummaging through its contents. As usual, Lillian's family's fridge is overflowing with all kinds of good food.

Autumn doesn't think about her mother's call again until the next morning. "You just now calling me back?" her mom scolds when she hears her daughter's voice. "No matter how grown you think you are, when I call you, you need to call me back!"

"All right, Mom. I'm sorry," Autumn says wearily. *I will be so glad when Mom and I can just be friends,* she thinks. Autumn knows for sure that's going to happen someday. She can see her mother's good qualities and feel the love between them, even now. But sometimes it's hard, waiting for that day to come. "Why'd you call me, anyway?" she asks.

"You got into Cal," her mom answers flatly.

"What?"

"You got into Cal."

"Mom! You opened the letter?" *I can't believe that's the first thing I said!* Autumn thinks. "Are you sure? Read it to me! Was it a big fat package or a letter?"

"A big old envelope full of all kinds of paperwork. You think I'd be telling you this if I wasn't—"

"Oh . . . my . . . God . . ." Autumn breathes. Then shouts. *"Oh! My! God!* I got into Cal! I can't believe it! I gotta tell Lillian! Bye!" Autumn slams down the phone, flies down the hall, bursts into Lillian's bedroom.

"I heard!" Lillian whispers. The two girls look at each other wide-eyed. Then they fall into each other's arms, sobbing. "It worked!" Autumn says, and Lillian knows what she means. A month ago Autumn got a questionnaire from Cal, asking for more information about the hardships she'd faced during her school career. "They want hardships? I'll give 'em hardships," Autumn decided, and she wrote sixteen typed pages, every word true and heartfelt. "We need to call Lauren," Autumn gasps.

"Let's . . . not . . . do . . . that . . . just yet," Lillian says slowly. She blows her nose delicately, a mischievous grin spreading across the wide planes of her face. "I have a better idea."

That day at lunch when Lauren comes looking for her two friends, she finds Lillian comforting a distraught Autumn in their fourth-period English classroom—a discarded, distinctly skinny UC Berkeley envelope on the desk in front of her. *"Bump* Cal. I didn't want to go there anyway,"

Autumn is muttering. "I'll just go to a junior college and transfer in two years." Lauren sits down, hard, beside Autumn. Tears well in her eyes. She puts her hand on Autumn's back, exchanges a worried look with Lillian. "You can still go to Santa Cruz, can't you?" she asks softly.

Suddenly Autumn and Lillian jump up and rip off their jackets, exposing the Cal sweatshirts they're wearing underneath. They stick matching Cal visors onto their heads, wave little Cal pennants at a bewildered Lauren. "We got in!" they shout, laughing uproariously.

"You both got into Cal?" Lauren demands. "You did? Why'd you make me almost cry? You guys are so mean!" Then Lauren is crying. "I'm so proud of you guys! I can't believe you're going to Cal!"

"We'll wait for you. In two years you'll be there with us," Lillian tells Lauren, who's still a sophomore. With Lauren shaking her head in disbelief, the three of them head out of the C building into the bright April day, squinting beneath their Cal visors, sweating in their Cal sweatshirts as they cross the crowded courtyard. "What's up, Cal Berkeley," Keith Stephens calls out as the girls pass the Slopes. "What's up, Keith," Autumn answers, and she and her friends continue on to EZ Stop for a celebratory lunch of turkey croissant sandwiches, Smokey Red BBQ Doritos, and orange juice.

Five minutes later Keith is on his way up Milvia to his job at Mel's Diner when he's stopped by his least favorite school safety officer, a guy Keith's known since junior high. "You got two choices, Keith: get suspended right now, or let me check your backpack." The safety officer glowers at Keith, blocks his path across Milvia.

"You ain't got no reason to be messin' with me like this." Keith glares back. "I ain't done nothin'."

"I saw you throw a water balloon across the street on your way in this morning," the officer says. "That's a minimum three-day suspension." This being the first hot-weather week of the year, the water balloons have been flying at Berkeley High, as they do during the first hot-weather week every year—despite the stern warnings being issued daily in the student bulletin.

"I ain't done nothin'," Keith repeats, and walks away. The next day the same safety officer comes to get Keith out of class and marches him down to Doris Wallace-Tanner's office, where Keith receives a three-day suspension for throwing water balloons and for "defiance." "He just decided to pick me out," Keith tells his mom that night. "I didn't *even* throw no water balloon. He made the whole story up."

With Keith in tow, Patricia shows up at Ms. Wallace-Tanner's office the following morning. After a half-hour conference, Keith's suspension is reduced to one day. "I wasn't about to let them mess with you like that," Patricia tells Keith as they cross the campus on their way back to her Saturn. "Not with you about to go to college."

San Francisco City College is not quite the Division One, four-year university Keith and his mom had been planning on. But still, when the City College football coach started calling to see if Keith wanted to play for his team next year, Patricia started campaigning to convince Keith to go. "You can always be a fireman later," she's been telling him. "This is your chance for a college education."

Keith talked to the coach on the phone; he even took BART and two buses into the city to meet him and check out the campus. The coach said Keith had to take a placement test to register, and he scheduled Keith to take it. When Patricia started getting letters from the coach, asking why Keith had missed the test, Keith told his mom he needed to ask Ms. Russ to tell him what was on that kind of test and help him get ready before he took it. Plus, since football season ended, Keith's been concentrating on all the things he was too busy to take care of before: making money at Mel's and doing yard work at Dr. Ed's up in the hills, getting his Camaro fixed up, trying to pass his driving test (which he's already flunked twice), and doing enough schoolwork to make sure he graduates. Now that he's this close to getting out of school, Keith's not so sure he wants to sign up for another two years of it—even to play college ball.

"Soon as we get home," Patricia says as she turns onto the freeway for the twenty-minute drive home to Richmond, "I want you to call and make a date to take that test. Then we can talk to Ms. Russ about helping you out."

"Awwight, Mom," Keith agrees distractedly. *Maybe the coach could hook me up with an apartment,* he thinks. A couple of Keith's friends play junior college basketball, and their coaches got them places to stay. San Francisco's too far to go from Richmond every day, but having his own place—*that could be hella cool,* Keith thinks.

"Nice to see you, Jordan," Jordan's AP Statistics teacher says sarcastically, glancing at the absence note Jordan typed onto his mom's letterhead this morning. Mr. Jegers squints at the forged signature, hands it back to Jordan. "Take this to the attendance office after class."

Jordan sinks into his seat and nods a greeting to his friend Zack, who raises his eyebrows questioningly in return. Jordan hasn't been to school since his mom left for Japan on a business trip ten days ago. It's hard to say why, exactly. First one of their cats got sick and had to be put down—that took several trips back and forth to the vet, and it was pretty upsetting, too. Then their other cat got diagnosed with diabetes. After that the familiar inertia set in, and Jordan found himself sleeping away most of every day, unable to drag himself out of bed. His mom has been calling every night; luckily she hasn't asked any direct questions so he hasn't had to lie. Not exactly, anyway.

"Any questions about the test tomorrow?" Mr. Jegers asks the class. Jordan listens to the ensuing exchange, his binder still zipped inside the backpack on the floor beside him. He quickly determines that he's fallen too far behind to catch up. He'll have to cut class tomorrow too; there's no way he can pass the test. *I'll just bust my butt cramming for the final,* he tells himself.

Incredible as it seems (to Jordan, since he's the only one who knows it), eight weeks before the end of his senior year, Jordan is at risk of flunking out of high school. *I know I need to graduate in order to go to college. And I know if I flunk any of my classes I won't graduate. I just can't put those two pieces of information together and do something about it.*

"You going back East next year, man?" whispers Zack, who just got his acceptance packet from Vassar. Jordan shakes his head, his eyes downcast. Everyone knows that Jordan got screwed out of going to Bard. Everyone also knows he applied to a bunch of other colleges. "What about Skidmore?" Zack asks.

"I'm wait-listed," Jordan mutters. "But I don't think I'll get in."

"So where you going?" Zack asks.

"UCSC." *If they'll still let me in,* Jordan thinks. He and his mom took the hour-and-a-half drive to visit UC Santa Cruz the weekend before she left for Japan. Natalie was super-positive all day, saying how beautiful the woodsy campus was, what a terrific education Jordan would get there, how happy she'd be to have Jordan close to home. *Mom's fine with me going to UCSC. At least she says she is. I'm fine with going to UCSC. At least I think I am. But I know if I'd gotten into Bard or Skidmore I wouldn't be screwing up like this.*

I'll talk to Mr. Ayers, Jordan decides. It was Mr. Ayers' friend who hooked up the CAS students to go to Santa Cruz in the first place. Maybe that same guy would understand Jordan's situation, fix it so he can go there in the fall, even if he flunks a couple of classes this semester. *Or maybe not,* Jordan thinks with a sinking feeling. A couple of CAS kids have already had their UCSC admissions revoked because of low first-semester grades. *There's always summer school,* Jordan tells himself. The thought depresses him even more. Who goes to summer school after senior year? *Nothing's turning out the way I thought it would,* he thinks numbly. *So what else is new?*

"We've had lots of Berkeley High kids accepted to their top-choice schools this year, as we always do," says Rory Bled, the popular Berkeley High college adviser who was replaced by Barbara Mitchell, then frantically rehired in February—too late for Jordan and many others—after Mitchell botched the job.

"Admissions officers love Berkeley High kids," Bled says. "They're engaged. They're inquisitive. Whether they're A students or D students, they're asking questions. Where else do students interrupt a college recruiter who says, 'We have 35 percent kids of color' to ask, 'But how many of them are African-American?' The diversity at this school produces kids who are passionate and compassionate. Berkeley High isn't a perfect place, but college admissions folks know it's a very special place."

This year, though, being a Berkeley High kid wasn't always enough. "We've also had some very disappointed students and parents. A number of good schools rejected some of our kids who would never have been rejected two years ago—and that's not just because of the problems with Barbara Mitchell. This has been the most competitive year ever. I'm hearing the same thing from college counselors across the country. Most of the elite schools are rejecting 80 percent of their applicants. UC Berkeley admitted only 25 percent for the fall of 2000. That's their lowest rate ever.

"One reason is the baby boomlet. When I started at Berkeley High in '94, there were 420 students in the senior class. This year we have 720. The other reason is, there are a lot more kids being encouraged to apply to college for whom that wouldn't have been a choice even one generation ago. We have kids of color applying to the Ivies now. They wouldn't have considered that before."

Bled says that since 1998, when affirmative action was abolished and minority admissions plummeted in the UC system—especially at its premiere school, UC Berkeley—the same students being turned away from the UCs are being heavily recruited by other prestigious schools. "Private colleges have been swooping down quite aggressively and taking underrepresented kids. I'm not talking about kids who are underqualified. We have some extraordinary students of color in this school. There are a lot of colleges trying to encourage students that they might not have thought of before."

However special Berkeley High may be, it exists in a society and an era in which the issue of college admissions criteria—always a hot button in a country that has yet to deliver on its founding promise of equal opportunity—is more controversial than ever. Race, as it so often is in America, is the hottest button of all.

Even here in the "People's Republic of Berkeley," Bled is disturbed to hear affluent white parents grumbling about "less qualified" students of color "taking precedence" over their children. She hears no such complaints, though, from the students themselves. "Our society is not going to be dominated by one ethnicity any more," she says. "That's great, and Berkeley High kids know from personal experience how great that is. Yes, we have issues of race and parity at this school. Yes, there are places on the school grounds that are segregated. But the kids get past race more than we give them credit for—certainly more than we adults do."

In the pressure cooker of college admissions, Bled says, it's parents who feel the heat most. That's why she wrote in a letter to parents in the April issue of the PTSA newsletter:

> While I wish that all your children could get into their first-choice college, I know that there will be some disappointments and many tears. Just keep in mind that your children will recover from rejection much more quickly than you will. At some point, they will look at you with astonishment when they find that you continue to seek revenge on the colleges which didn't accept them, and they'll tell you to get over it. Please listen to them.

"It's a huge mistake," Bled says, "to assume that going to an Ivy League college is an entrée to a fulfilling life. There are lots of miserable human beings out there who have had wonderful, expensive educations. I have two white male sons, and neither of them went to Ivy League colleges, and that was just fine. Sure, it's easier to get a great first job out of Harvard—but once you're looking for your second job it becomes less important where you went to college.

"The importance of the Ivies is greater for students of color. Their futures are affected a lot more because of networking opportunities that wouldn't normally open up to them. Plus, they tend to give back to their communities.

"Whether they go to college or not, my goal is for students to leave

Berkeley High with really good choices," says Bled, whose workdays start before dawn ("I'll see kids at 6 a.m. if they'll bring me a latté") and never truly end ("I can't leave the house in sweats; parents follow me around in grocery stores"). "College is only a stepping stone to make young people feel they can be successful—in the true, not the financial meaning of the word—as individuals.

"Berkeley High students develop a sensitivity that helps them become finer human beings. If there's any hope for positive change, it's through that human being."

"The college admissions process shapes the future of our country. And there's an emerging national crisis in that process."

So says Bob Laird, newly retired admissions director of the University of California at Berkeley. Laird is an outspoken advocate of greater investment in public education—by parents *and* by government. "I've been saying publicly for some time that the single most important thing liberal parents can do is send their kids to public school." Laird puts his offspring where his mouth is; his son is currently a freshman at Berkeley High.

Chagrined by white flight from the public schools, Laird is even more concerned about what he sees as a dangerous paradigm shift in the government's approach to education. "The federal government is shifting financial aid programs from grants to loans, putting the burden of education on the individual rather than on society. In California's budget this year, an alleged Democratic governor is proposing scholarships based solely on what he defines as 'merit'—which means taking scholarship money from poor kids and giving it to kids with high test scores, most of whom who don't need it. And measures like Prop 209, which dismantled affirmative action in the UC system, are being replicated in Washington, Florida, Michigan.

"All of this magnifies the already growing gap between the wealthy and the poor. We have a two-tiered, separate and unequal society, with a few folks left in the middle. How can we change this? In part, by changing who goes to UC Berkeley."

Although Laird agrees with Rory Bled that "you don't need to go to Berkeley to have a successful life," he also acknowledges the many ways in which it can help. "Graduating from UC Berkeley means greater access to the best jobs, greater access to the best professional schools and graduate schools. If you are one of the five leading companies in your field and you are hiring college seniors, Berkeley will be one of them you'll visit. UC Santa Cruz probably won't be.

"It's all about who writes your letters of recommendation; who picks up the phone for you. There's an elite point in the academic pyramid, and UC Berkeley is on it. The faculty at Berkeley know the faculty at Harvard, Yale . . . That's why, in the admissions process in a public university, you have such great responsibility to find those individuals who might make a difference in their own lives, in their communities, in the state, in the country."

And that's why, Laird says, it's not just minority students who are injured by blows to affirmative action. "Given the achievement gap between white students and students of color, which is not going away any time soon, and absent the ability to consider race and ethnicity, the more competitive admissions becomes, the less able a campus will be to admit African-American, Latino, and Native American students. This hurts *all* students, because who's in the classroom has a lot to do with what students learn from each other, the range of viewpoints and experiences to which they're exposed."

Laird chuckles ironically. "Some kids come here from homogenous suburbs with the notion that 'I'm going to UC Berkeley to get diversified.' Then they get here and complain that they don't have contact with minority students. Well, we don't assign white students African-American roommates! Diversity is more difficult and uncomfortable than people expect it to be. We're undoing the effects of three hundred fifty years. It doesn't happen easily."

As challenging as achieving—and living with—diversity may be, Laird believes that the struggle to meet the challenge is worth the effort. "Given the demographics of this state and this country, I don't see how someone could be considered educated unless they've had deep exposure to all cultures and backgrounds. And in terms of public policy, what would it mean if California's flagship public university were 97 percent white and Asian, in a state where whites don't even make up a plurality in the public schools? That's a kind of apartheid. I don't see how a society that describes itself as equal can hold to that value."

Laird asserts that "despite public impressions, the university is deeply committed to ethnic diversity." The post–affirmative action drop in minority admissions, he says, has only sharpened that commitment. Renewed outreach and recruitment efforts are being directed at students of color, and admissions policies are being re-examined "to identify students who have done remarkably well under extraordinary circumstances: low family income, single-parent or no-parent family, disability, homelessness, abuse, an hour-long bus ride to get to school each day . . ."

Students thus identified in the initial reading of the 33,000 applications submitted to UC Berkeley last fall were referred to a program called "Admission By Exception"—"A By E" in Cal parlance. A By E allows each UC campus to reserve 6 percent of freshman slots for students who would not otherwise be eligible. In March, UC Berkeley's top A By E candidates were sent a pre-admissions questionnaire—the "PAQ"— soliciting more information for the final selection.

The PAQ is the document that inspired Autumn to write sixteen pages about the hardships she's faced. And A By E, Bob Laird says, is the process by which Autumn became one of the 301 African-American students—out of an entering class of 8,300—admitted to UC Berkeley for the fall of 2000.

To some extent, the UC system's stepped-up recruitment efforts were successful. "Minority Admissions Up for UC," local newspaper headlines announced jubilantly in April. But the headlines were somewhat deceiving, as the *Berkeley Daily Planet* explained in its April cover story. "Much of the recovery in black and Hispanic admissions comes from more of those students being admitted to lesser-known campuses. Flagship Berkeley is still well below 1997 totals as is UCLA . . . black students accounted for about 3 percent of admissions offers. By comparison, blacks make up about 7 percent of California's population."

"An admissions process is supposed to uncover excellence," says Bob Laird. "You have to look at the whole file, the whole person, to find the kids who've pushed themselves the furthest, done the most with what they had; the ones who are the most thoughtful with the most grit and focus and purpose.

"These are the future leaders of our country we're looking for."

An admirable 85 percent of Berkeley High graduates go to college—60 percent to four-year colleges, 25 percent to two-year junior colleges. Yet, only 14 percent of the students who graduate with enough credits to qualify for four-year colleges are African-Americans—although those students comprise 36 percent of the student body and 31.7 percent of the school's graduates. These numbers notwithstanding, it is the mission of Berkeley High School, and every high school, and every dedicated high school teacher, to produce the best outcome possible—for each student; for society; for the world these teenagers will inherit tomorrow from those who make policy today.

But how is it to be determined what, exactly, constitutes the best possible outcome for any given student, or group of students? And what should be the role of public schools in producing that outcome? Should schools function as the social butter churn that Thomas Jefferson first envisioned them to be: skimming off the cream, "and the residue dismissed"? Should schools and schoolteachers educate our young in ways that meet the needs of society as it now exists, or in ways that encourage them to challenge and change it? Should society be responsible for providing education at all?

These questions, and the wide range of answers to them, drive and divide the national movement for school reform—a movement that has yielded such disparate "solutions" as private-school vouchers and the small-school model, embodied at Berkeley High by the Computer Academy and CAS.

These questions also spark conflict—not only in the national discourse, but between small schools and the larger ones within which they exist, and within the normally close-knit staffs of the small schools themselves. Striving to teach with the big questions in mind can even cause strife between team teachers who used to agree on the answers; who used to be best friends; whose once shared, now divergent beliefs about what is best for students threaten their very ability to teach together effectively.

"Your grades will not necessarily be the same from both of us. For me your grades are about coming prepared, turning in homework," Amy Crawford tells the CAS students on a warm April Friday, the one day each week when the whole class meets together. Normally, she and Dana Richards stand shoulder-to-shoulder in front of their class; today, they are back-to-back.

"From me you're all getting good grades, 'cause I think grades are ridiculous," Dana Richards says.

The students shift in their seats. "So . . . we're all getting As from you?" one girl asks Mr. Richards. "And bad grades from you?" she asks, turning to Ms. Crawford.

"I'll put it this way: you'll have to go out of your way to get a bad grade from me," Mr. Richards answers. "I don't want you guys focused on grades when you should be focused on the real work of this class: your internships, your presentations."

"And I'm the bad guy who thinks grades actually have some meaning," Ms. Crawford says.

The students look from one teacher to the other. "Oh. I just remembered," Mr. Richards says. "Sometime this period there's gonna be a 'surprise' emergency drill."

"Are they doing that 'cause of that fire in the C building last week?" Leila asks. "I heard it was arson."

"It's believed that it was, yes," Ms. Crawford answers carefully. "The rumor is, it was an adult. It happened in a locked bookroom. Only teachers have the key to that room."

"Was it you, Ms. Crawford?" Elena teases. "We saw you jumping up and down when we all got sent home."

"We don't know much about it," Mr. Richards interjects. "Ms. Crawford and I both blew off the meeting."

A flush pinkens Ms. Crawford's porcelain skin. "No," she says through clenched teeth. "I went."

She whispers a few words to her partner, then turns to the class. "I want you guys to get into your internship groups, talk about where you're going with them. We'll be right back." She and Mr. Richards leave the room.

"Lately there's been so much tension between the two of them," Catherine says aloud as soon as the door closes.

"I think Ms. Crawford's feelings are hurt because everyone likes Mr. Richards better," Steve says.

"Personally, I can't get anything done with Mr. Richards," Melania says.

"You can't have a serious conversation with him," Jamilah agrees.

"We shouldn't even be talking about this shit," Joaquin says.

"They should make a curriculum and rules and stick to them," Catherine says. "They're the teachers, not us."

"That's not what CAS is all about," argues Jordan, here for the first time in two weeks. "It's supposed to be a community. We're all supposed to be responsible for keeping it together."

The two teachers come back into the room. "You guys want to debrief us?" Ms. Crawford asks. "What did you get done while we were gone?"

"All we did is argue," Melania reports.

Ms. Crawford shakes her head. "You guys are seniors. You shouldn't need your teachers in the room in order to get your work done. Well, we're here now. Let's get serious. We've only got twenty minutes till the fire drill."

Amy Crawford is sad, and angry, and most of all disappointed about what's happening between her and Dana Richards. "We were really good friends, and we're not now. That's hard on us and hard on the kids. We have the obligation to maintain a level of professionalism, but his idea of professionalism and mine are very different."

Ironically, the discord between the two teachers is about the very challenge that gets both of them up in the morning: how to turn an academically, racially, economically, and psychologically diverse group of eighteen-year-olds into an activist community of self-motivated, inquisitive lifelong learners. They still share the goal, but the once-slight variations in their approaches to reaching it have evolved, over the year, into seemingly irreconcilable differences. "Some kids can work without structure, but most kids need a lot of it," Amy Crawford says. "That's not Dana's style. He thinks if you can blow kids' minds, the protocol of how you do it isn't important. We disagree.

"When we started working together I thought we'd complement each other, that we'd both learn and grow. And I have grown a lot through the process. I've learned to be more relaxed about certain things. I've also learned that team teaching is a huge undertaking."

The conflict with Dana is only part of the reason that Amy recently told Rick Ayers that she won't be teaching in CAS next year. "I think CAS has the potential to be a great program. Parts of it have been the most rewarding teaching I've done. The sense of community is like nothing I've been able to achieve anywhere else.

"But it's been really frustrating to see this great mix of kids and not have the time and the resources to spend with the neediest ones—to write up a contract with each of them and follow through. It's been frustrating knowing that some kids aren't doing much with their internships, not having the structure in place to check in with them in an effective way, not having a teaching partner who supports that kind of structure.

"I've been pretty depressed this year, feeling like I wasn't having a life. So I started thinking about what I could pull back on. It can't be the amount of prep I do. It can't be the time I spend reading and grading papers. The only thing I could cut was the five extra hours a month I spend in CAS meetings."

Shortly after Amy's announcement, Dana Richards also told Rick that this will be his last semester in CAS. Starting next year he'll be running the new Environmental Studies Institute at Berkeley High, for which he invented the concept, created the curriculum, recruited the staff, and wrote the grants that will fund it. Amy respects and admires Dana's passion, and intends to follow her own.

"When Rick started CAS he wanted it to be a viable program for kids of color to get empowered, get an education. My dream now is to work on that same goal with the most at-risk kids in the school, to be more focused on teaching and on being a role model—but with lots of structure and clear expectations and checkpoints. That's what I need. And that's what I think kids need, too."

The contrast between Keith's behavior and his classmates' behavior in Mr. Giglio's laid-back, often chaotic Computer Academy class, and the same kids' behavior in Mr. McKnight's tightly run African-American Studies class, would seem to support Amy Crawford's argument. Why, then, doesn't Greg Giglio—and every other teacher at Berkeley High—run his classroom with the strict rules and immediate consequences enforced by Mr. McKnight?

"Mr. McKnight can get away with that. I can't," Greg Giglio says. And why not? "Fear," he says simply. "The kids are afraid of him. I don't have that persona."

Learning to deal with up to eight different personas and teaching styles each day, eight different sets of rules, eight different sets of expectations—this is one of the many inadvertent lessons offered to today's high school student. In one teacher's class he or she may eat a Happy Meal, or play a boom box, or stroll in and out of the room at will. Next period, he or she might be punished for taking a sip from a water bottle, or speaking out of turn, or wearing a hat.

"All right! Hats off! Let's get started. Mr. Stephens! Quiet down, please."

Keith is back from his suspension, cracking up the boys around him in the back corner of Mr. McKnight's room. "We are going to begin our presentations on Chapter Five of *The Nubian*," Mr. McKnight says. "Ms. Calhoun, please . . ."

As one student after another presents from the lectern, the buzz from the back of the room continues. "I want you to know that while I'm grading the presenter I'm also grading *you*," Mr. McKnight says, frowning at Keith and his friends.

Two minutes later: "Mr. Stephens. See that seat by the door? Take it."

And two minutes after that Mr. McKnight's meticulous enunciation and professorial manner bite the dust as he faces the boys in the back, hands on his hips, eyes flashing, neck rigid. "You guys got about five seconds to be quiet or leave. You got asthma? I'll give you a pass to the health center. Otherwise I don't wanna hear you *breathe*. I'll give you an F for the last nine weeks of this class! You hear me? *You on my last nerve.*"

There's the faintest of giggles from the back. "Mr. Hamilton—hit that door. I don't care *where* you go. Come back tomorrow." Mr. McKnight strides over to a girl who's rubbing lotion on her arms. "Go to the principal's office! 'Bye." He grabs the lotion bottle as the girl is gathering her things, pitches it across the room into the metal trash can by the door. It lands with a crashing thunk. The kids near the door jump in their seats.

"Now we can get on with our discussion," Mr. McKnight says calmly, and turns to the student at the lectern.

"Is a warrior *prepared* to die, or *ready* to die?" Mr. McKnight asks.

"Nobody ready to die unless you crazy!" Keith calls out.

"That's good," Mr. McKnight says, turning to Keith. "And what are the weapons of a true warrior?"

"Knowledge. Your mind," Keith answers.

"Anything else?"

"Creativity," Keith says.

"Self-determination!" "Self-esteem!" "Discipline!" other students throw in.

"A soldier's shield is his mind," says Josh, lisping around his new tongue stud. The students turn to Keith expectantly. They are not disappointed.

"I agree with the guy with the tongue ring," Keith says. He is rewarded by an outburst of laughter.

"I must be your girlfriend, 'cause you always talkin' about me," Josh says.

"But I disagree that a soldier and a warrior are the same thing," Keith continues. "The soldier fights for the white man's laws."

"What does white have to do with it?" Josh shoots back. "Every time you see a white boy saggin', talkin' Ebonics, you say he's acting black. But why is that acting black?"

"To be a warrior you have to be free. To be a soldier you followin' orders," Keith contends. His friend Dominic applauds.

"What is this, Batman and Robin?" Josh asks sarcastically.

"Think for yourself, soldier," Keith replies.

"We only have thirty-five seconds left," Mr. McKnight interrupts. "I want you to write out your thoughts and bring them tomorrow. I will collect them and I will grade you on them." The buzzer sounds. "Until tomorrow, ladies and gentlemen."

"Josh is still wrong," Keith gets in the last word. He walks across the room, throws his arm around Josh. "Awwwight, Batwoman," he says, and then continues on his way.

Although African-American Studies is a department with open enrollment, not a small school with screened admissions and membership criteria, Mr. McKnight and his colleagues work closely with the Computer Academy, in which many of the students who take African-American Studies are enrolled. "Bob McKnight and I have a very good rapport," says Computer Academy founder Flora Russ. "He takes the kids where they are and doesn't make comparisons with others. That's what we do, too."

The Computer Academy brochure describes the ten-year-old program as "a dynamic school-within-a-school designed for students who have not realized their full potential." Nearly 80 percent of the 190 current Computer Academy enrollees are African-American; about 60 percent are male. "Our close-knit environment allows students to thrive," the brochure promises, "an outcome evidenced by our 95+ percent graduation rate."

How this success is achieved is a matter of some controversy. Flora Russ bridles at accusations of "social promotion." "Computer Academy teachers will fail their students if they're not doing the work that needs to be done. They'll support their students, they'll be there for them, but they will not give them grades they don't deserve. And our classes are absolutely not dumbed down. When WASC came to one of our English classes last year, they asked if it was an AP class.

"Sometimes we get really tough mixtures of kids. That's what happened in Keith's English class with Greg Giglio, for example. But those situations are the exception, as our success stories prove." Enthusiastically Russ recounts story after story of Computer Academy graduates who transcended their parents' drug addictions, abuse, and poverty to become stockbrokers and Ph.D.s, landscapers and Web designers.

"We take a student population that's very diverse—not ethnically, but academically—and we move them forward. We have kids who barely graduate and kids who get a free ride to UC Berkeley working together in the same class. They support each other."

Just as Keith did, three years ago, applicants to the Computer Academy must sign a contract that includes the following vows:

> I agree to comply with the following as it is essential to my success as a student. (Read each item carefully and initial each to which you agree.)
>
> - To attend all classes, all periods, with no cuts.
> - To perform at a C level or above. If my performance falls below a C level, I will get help from my teachers outside of class time.
> - To positively represent my family, myself and the Computer Academy by following all rules and regulations established by the school concerning conduct between periods, during the lunch hour, and after school while on school grounds.
> - To not use illegal substances during school hours.
> - To take advantage of the opportunities the Computer

Academy offers such as mentors, internships, field trips, performances, dinners, community projects, etc.

Academy students must also complete the Prioritizing Grid early in their high school careers. Keith's reveals some surprising priorities: "To get out of B.H.S. To go to college. To buy my mom and dad a house" all rank higher than "To go play with the pros," "To win a Super Bowl," and even "To have a nice life."

"There's something about graduating," Flora Russ says. "It makes them walk taller. And if they don't graduate there will be years of trauma, years of society looking down on them. That's what scares me about standardized tests. I'm not saying to give them grades they don't deserve. I'm saying don't expect our kids to know the same things that kids who've spent time in Europe know.

"Outside the Academy, Berkeley High has lots of kids who get to their senior year and then totally screw up. If our kids make it to their senior year we're usually able to get them through."

Keith, for example. "Keith is a Computer Academy success story in that he's going to graduate on time. But he hasn't taken full advantage of the program. Keith got through by going to summer school, by taking less demanding courses.

"I like Keith. He's very funny, very popular, very personable, with very deep feelings and sensitivities. He has a lot of charisma, a lot of potential. But it's not going to be realized unless he puts in the work. If he puts the same energy into his education that he's put into football, he'll be more than he thinks he can be."

Keith is on Shattuck, on his way to his job at Mel's Diner after lunch, when he hears the sirens, sees the fire trucks speeding toward Berkeley High. *Another fire*, he thinks nonchalantly, idly wondering if this one will be big enough to make them send everyone home, like they did for last week's fire in the C building.

Autumn is in African-American History, Jordan in AP Biology five minutes into fifth period, when yes, the school *is* evacuated. And as the teachers herd the kids to the football field they see that yes, it is a big fire—the biggest one ever. Usually when there's a fire at Berkeley High (there have been ten so far this year) the alarms go off and there's smoke in the halls of the C building (where all the past fires have been set), and a fire truck or two shows up.

But this fire is different. Serious. It's in the B building, for one thing, where the principal's office and all the counselors' offices are, and the library and the health center and the records office. And this isn't a quick-to-be-extinguished trash can fire. Soon it is apparent: *the building is burning.* Flames shoot out the first- and second-story windows. The smoke is so thick, so pervasive, it quickly turns the sunny springtime day gray.

As they are rushed past the B building, Autumn, then Jordan stop short, gaping at what they see: *the CAS room is on fire.* Their journals, their artwork, the framed photographs and posters and artifacts that Mr. Richards collected and cherished and displayed from every possible surface of the room; the garden where they'd had some of their most heated seminar discussions; the wooden computer table Mr. Richards built and painted with his own hands . . . *burning.* Even as they watch, the firemen hack away at the CAS classroom walls, trampling the artichoke plants with their heavy boots and hoses.

At 1:00 the fire is still burning and the students are sent home. The last WASC meeting of the year, scheduled for 3:30 in the library, is cancelled. At 4:00 Lillian and Lauren are wandering through the courtyard, asking every adult they see if tonight's poetry slam is still happening. A dazed English teacher directs them to the scribbled note Amy Crawford taped to the locked doors of the C building before she left. "Slam cancelled due to fire. Sorry!" "How does *that* make sense?" Lauren asks Lillian angrily. "The slam wasn't even in the B building!"

But the cancelled meeting, the cancelled slam are only the beginning. The next morning during second period, the B building, suddenly, is on fire again. The 400 staff members and students in the building—including several wheelchair-bound special ed students whose classroom is ten feet from a gas main—are evacuated in the record time of two minutes. This time the firemen take no chances: they cut holes in the roof, flood the building with water, demolish everything that might possibly catch fire again. The students are sent home, instructed not to return until after the week-long Spring Break that wasn't supposed to start till next Monday.

"This is the most depressing thing to happen to me since my divorce," Greg Giglio says, standing in a group of teachers on the C building steps, watching as the firemen hose down the principal's office and the school safety officers sweep the last students off campus. "Two days ago they didn't have money for copy machines or phones or raises. How are they going to pay for *this?*"

"Whoever's doing this is *ill*," says Alan Miller. "The special ed kids could've been killed." A student runs up to him, hands him a homework assignment. "Sorry it's late, Mr. Miller," the boy says, and sprints toward the gate, a school safety officer in hot pursuit.

"We should be processing this with the kids," Rick Ayers frets aloud. "Not chasing them away. Some of them are happy to have a longer break, sure. But a lot of them are crying, too. This is sad."

In the extensive media coverage of the Berkeley High fires—that night, the next day, throughout the next weeks—it is rumored and then confirmed that the cause of the fire is arson. It is rumored, but unconfirmed, that the arsonist is a teacher. The damage to the school is estimated at a quarter million, then a million, then two million dollars.

In the weeks and months to come it will become painfully clear that the damage to the school—and the people and the community whose well-being depend upon it—is far greater, even, than that.

May 2000: Ready or Not

On their first day back after Spring Break—after the fire—the students and teachers of Berkeley High return to a very different school from the one they left ten days ago.

What hits them first are the physical changes. The main entrance isn't on Milvia Street any more; it's across the campus on Martin Luther King Jr. Way. The courtyard looks a bit like an upscale trailer park now, with rows of gleaming new portables, stand-ins for classrooms and offices lost to the fire, spilling over onto the concrete pad beside the theater, where the teachers' parking lot used to be. Signs designating each portable's function are taped to the doors—"Administration," "B205, Ayers," "B207, Giglio." Electricians who are frantically trying to finish wiring them scramble around, hammering and drilling. And the singed, still-stinking B building hulks in the midst of the campus like a beached whale, corralled inside a chain-link fence, surrounded by Port-O-Potties and Dumpsters, the cavities in its carcass patched with sheets of plywood. Trucks marked "Blue Water Environmental Services" and "Four Star Cleaning and Restoration" are parked on top of the map of Africa on the Slopes, each truck discharging teams of workers who zip themselves into white plastic bubble suits before they enter the building.

The biggest difference, though, is in the mood of the place; "the vibe," as the kids say. There are so many *strangers* here now, all of whom, the students are told, must be obeyed. Besides the usual school safety officers—suddenly even Wiggins and Billy Keys seem relatively benign, or at least, *familiar*—the campus is crawling with uniformed and plainclothes policemen; rent-a-cops with billy clubs strapped to their sides; tall, ominous-looking men in suits and dark glasses; and, in odd juxtaposition, mothers. There are dozens of them here, recruited via the exclusive but efficient parent E-tree, the only communication channel the fire didn't destroy. The mothers wear tense looks on their faces and white plastic "Visitor" badges pinned to the red jackets they were issued in rushed training sessions at 7:00 this morning. They roam the campus and the halls, sniffing for smoke, guiding students to their relocated classrooms, keeping time for the teachers now that, once again, Berkeley High's clocks and bells are not functioning. Most of them are white, an expanded circle of the "Mothers of Excellence," the "Moms Who Rule the School"—the parents who have Internet access and use it, who fill the classrooms on Back to School nights, who buy books and minifridges and Appreciation Lunches for the teachers, who organized and catered the Marcia Singman memorial and staffed the now-demolished information booth.

The halls themselves look different, too: strangely naked, stripped of the artwork—now ruled dangerously flammable, and banned by order of the fire marshall—that used to festoon every surface. No more canary-yellow flyers advertising dances and summer jobs and poetry slams. No more brightly hand-painted signs announcing last-chance deadlines for buying yearbooks and Prom tickets. No more posters featuring the seductive photos and campaign promises of candidates for Prom queen and student body president. The school's personality, the students' creativity, is gone from the halls, leaving only headless thumbtacks and dingy brown paint behind.

Each set of doors that connects the C building to the B building is padlocked shut now, draped in thick link chains, sealed with silver duct tape and hung with signs, inexplicably in Spanish:

PELIGRO

ASBESTO

Peligro de Cáncer y Enfermedad de Pulmón

PROHIBIDO PASAR

There are all kinds of strange new rules, too. "Administration is tightening security like never before," reports the *Berkeley High Jacket,* produced during Spring Break and distributed today. "Students can only be on campus between the hours of 7:45 and 4:00. A staff member must supervise students at all times. It is now mandatory for students to carry their ID and class schedule with them continually, and there will be no tolerance for kids walking the hallways. A new omnilock system is in place [to] record who enters and leaves which room and when. Surveillance cameras are being installed . . ."

And then, of course, there is the lingering stench of smoke—and, it seems, of toxic chemicals—that permeates the halls and classrooms of the C building, where Amy Crawford greets her CAS seminar at 8:50 on this warm spring morning.

"Welcome back, everyone," Ms. Crawford says with her usual hearty good cheer. "Can we start by talking about the break? What'd you guys do? People who went to the National Poetry Slam in San Francisco— can you tell us about it?"

The students peer curiously at Ms. Crawford, at each other. A question hangs in the room, as palpable as the burned-cork smell of smoke: *Is she really going to ignore what's happening here?*

"Rena?" Ms. Crawford prompts. "You were at the slam."

"There were poets from Bosnia, from Europe," Rena responds, slowly at first, then with mounting enthusiasm. "There were teams from the Navajo Nation and the Hopi Nation. After each team read their poems, their friends ran up and hugged them. The Berkeley High team— Chinaka, little Eli, Niles, and Daniel—won the whole slam."

"Let's give a hand to Daniel," Ms. Crawford says, and the class applauds a boy who rarely speaks, who usually sits silently in the corner, his furrowed face shadowed by the brim of his ever-present baseball cap. "Anyone else have a Spring Break story?"

"I went to look at colleges in New York," says Joaquin.

"I went to DC to visit schools," adds Elena.

Silence again.

"Anyone want to talk about the Elian thing?" Ms. Crawford asks. Last week the image of a soldier in riot gear pointing a firearm at the terrified six-year-old Cuban boy was emblazoned on front pages everywhere.

"If that little boy was American and he was being held in Cuba, we would've bombed them by now," Ameya answers. Ms. Crawford nods encouragingly. But the discussion falls flat.

The morning sun is rising, streaming onto the backs of the students whose desks line the room's south-facing windows. Malik twists in his seat, pushes open the window nearest him.

"Shut that window!" Ms. Crawford barks. The kids stare, open-mouthed, at their teacher again. Ms. Crawford *never* yells. Normally, the madder she gets the more quietly she speaks. "That's where all the toxic stuff is." She gestures at the boarded-up windows of the B building, ten feet away. Wordlessly Malik shuts the window.

"How can they say this building is okay when there's all this stuff flying around?" Elena asks.

"The fire marshal says the C building has been tested and it's safe," Ms. Crawford answers, "but they can't guarantee anything."

"I heard if there's another fire they'll close the school for the year," Rena offers.

"Tight!" says Joaquin.

"*Not* tight!" counters Autumn, who just got here, her usual twenty minutes late. "I want to go to college."

"Just so you know—there are cameras all over the place," Ms. Crawford says, surrendering, finally, to the conversation she's been trying so hard to avoid.

"We should protest the cameras," Joaquin declares.

"Why?" Ms. Crawford challenges him. "I don't like to be watched either. But I want them to catch the person who did this. The fire was set really close to a gas main. The fire chief said we were really lucky no one died. Personally, I don't want to die at work."

"Personally, I want to live to go to college," Autumn reiterates.

Mike Hassett, chair of the English department, leans around the desk that's propping the classroom door open and sticks his head into the room. "Sorry," he tells Ms. Crawford. "You have to keep the door closed. Police orders."

"But we can't open the windows," Ms. Crawford protests. "And it's sweltering in here. Can we go outside, at least?"

Hassett shakes his head. "Sorry," he says again. He drags the desk out of the doorway. As the door closes behind him, Amy Crawford stares at it as if in a trance. Then she goes to her desk, opens a drawer, and pulls out two scented candles. "Anyone have a lighter or some matches?" she asks.

"Not me!" "He-e-e-ll no!" "That's heck of cold, Ms. Crawford!" students call out. A burst of nervous giggles ripples through the room.

Ms. Crawford doesn't even crack a smile. "I promise not to tell," she says flatly. Joaquin digs a disposable lighter out of his pocket. Ms. Crawford lights the two candles, places them carefully on a table in the center of the room. She inhales deeply, then frowns. The faint lavender fragrance is no competition for the acrid fumes.

"We can't even go to the bathroom without being escorted by someone in a red coat," Elena says. "Do we not have bells?"

"No bells," Ms. Crawford replies.

"No phones?"

"No phones."

"No fire alarms?"

"It depends which building you're in."

"They tryin' to kill us!" exclaims Raven.

"How did the fire get so big?" Elena asks.

"They won't talk about specifics," Ms. Crawford answers. "It's under investigation."

"I'm on it," Daniel pipes up suddenly from the corner. "I'm on the case." He pulls a rumpled piece of binder paper from his pocket, glances meaningfully at Ms. Crawford.

"Do you have a poem you want to share, Daniel?" she asks. He nods, then shuffles to the front of the room. Facing his audience, the shy boy in the baseball cap becomes a commanding, confident performer.

" . . . *and in local news today fire fighters were called in to Berkeley*
  High School on what is believed to be yet another arson fire.
    They were unable to squelch the
raging inferno of academic apathy
and circular inadequacy
the school is burning
the school is burning . . .
I make my way into
campus, scope the scene.
For towering flames
I hope and dream . . .
The school is burning!
The school is burning!
While this dude is turning to me
saying something through lips moving I discern it to be
"I heard the arsonist was a teacher"
I nod and move on with a grin—
it all seems so logical
since it's now practically commonplace from students to deposit
  full clips
and with no quips
rip and shatter innocence.
In a sense, faculty lighting up books
like incense should be expected.
Let's consider this a science experiment,
though not curriculum directed,
since the book room was
specifically selected.

The text is gone now
so to hell with the lesson plan
Though crudely delivered
I feel the sentiment
of this maniacal messageman:
School was turned into an
assembly line. No longer can
we let it stand . . .
The school is burning
The school is burning
The school has burned
And from the classes' ashes
I await the phoenix to emerge
The school is burning
The school still burns
The school is burning
Tides are turning
soot is churning
producing smoke signals which paint the sky . . .
Atmospheric text births new verses
as old ones die."

The CAS students burst into cheers and applause. Ms. Crawford says quietly, "*Wow,* Daniel," then bends her head once again toward the candles' flickering flames.

"I'm not gonna sit cooped up in this room for the rest of the year!" she blurts, jumping to her feet. "I hate this." Her blue eyes fill with tears; her red-lipsticked mouth quivers. "I'll be right back," she says, and runs out of the room.

"They got my teacher *crying,*" Elena says.

"This is hecka wack," Autumn adds.

Ms. Crawford bursts back into the room, her eyes red-rimmed, a crumpled Kleenex clutched in her hand. "Okay, you guys. I got special permission to hold class on the Steps. But listen: they're watching things really carefully right now. If you need to go to the bathroom, tell me so I can go with you. If you get caught walking around, there *will* be consequences. Even if you're willing to take them, I'm not. So play by the rules. Deal?"

"Deal!" her students agree, and follow her like ducklings in a row out of the classroom, down the steps to the courtyard. As they're on their way out, they run into Jordan on his way in.

"I need to talk to you," Ms. Crawford tells him. Jordan nods grimly. He knows what she's going to say. He's failing CAS, and with five weeks left it may be too late to fix it. Ms. Crawford has already made herself clear. She will *not* pass seniors who don't deserve the grade—even if it means their college acceptances will be rescinded. Even if it means they might not graduate.

Mr. McKnight takes attendance with his usual deliberation, calling out each student's name, looking around to confirm each one's presence or absence, accepting information from the present about the absent. "He's sick." "I saw her on the bus." "She's not here today."

"Mr. Stephens! Quiet, please. I have some announcements to make," Mr. McKnight says when the roll call is complete. "Those of you who had a locker in the B building: they do not have a date yet when you will be able to retrieve your property. As soon as they take the possessions out of the lockers you will be notified as to the condition of the contents."

"Awww . . ." "What about my bus pass?" "I had my leather coat in there!" the students complain. The door opens, and Ms. Calhoun, the ever-punctual star student, stomps into the room, her long extensions angrily slapping her back. "This guy in a red coat sent me and my brother to OCS," she fumes. "My brother's still in there, but I just walked out. I am *so* sick of high school!"

"They haven't said what they're planning for students who are tardy, now that the attendance office is closed," Mr. McKnight says slowly. He shakes his head. "Regardless . . . we have work to do, ladies and gentlemen. I'm going to give you an assignment, and I am going to want it tomorrow, and I am going to want it neatly typed."

A girl raises her hand. "How I'm gonna type my homework? The computers are in the library."

Mr. McKnight frowns, considers this for a moment. "You raise an excellent point, Ms. Davis. All right, then. For those of you who do not have a computer at home, I will speak to Ms. Russ about allowing you to use a computer in her room. You'll need special permission, because the doors now have locks on them that are coded."

"Or you can just get Josh Gray to pick the locks," Keith suggests.

"That is *not* funny, Mr. Stephens." Mr. McKnight glowers at him from the lectern. "Not funny at all."

Beginning on the April 20 anniversary of the Columbine massacre and continuing into May, the media turns the nation's attention to that tragedy once again, with live reports from Littleton and endless replaying of year-old videotape. "Do Our Kids Feel Safe?" asks a special issue of *USA Weekend,* its cover photo depicting a boy writing over and over on a classroom blackboard: "Please don't let me get hurt in school today." On May 6 there is more bad news from Littleton about a boy who *did* get hurt in school: a Columbine basketball star, whose best friend died in the massacre, sets up a CD player so it endlessly replays the lyrics, "I'm too depressed to go on/I never thought I'd die alone," and hangs himself in his family's garage.

In the Bay Area, headlines about the Berkeley High fires compete with headlines about Columbine and threats of copycat crimes at two local high schools. On April 19 at Alameda High—where Autumn's brothers will go—a "hit list" is written on a bathroom wall and graffiti warns, "Asians Die 4-20. All of them." At nearby Encinal High, two fifteen-year-old boys are charged with five felony counts of terrorism after hate messages are spray-painted on the school walls, a flyer listing the names of more than 100 students who "will die on 4-20" is distributed at school, and a letter addressed to the Encinal principal is found in one of the boys' homes, warning, "I have a gun and I'm gonna go on a rampage."

It is against this backdrop that worried Berkeley High parents pour into the Community Theater for a post-fire emergency meeting on the evening of the first day of school. On their way in they pass through a media gauntlet in the courtyard, which is crowded with TV vans topped by whirling dishes and illuminated by floodlights hoisted high into the purple-streaked sunset sky. Reporters jostling for position on the Steps thrust microphones at each passing adult. "Are you a parent? Can I talk to you? What do you want for your child?"

The mayor of Berkeley opens the meeting. "I assure you that the City, and I personally, will do everything to ensure your children are safe at school," she tells the several hundred assembled parents. "We'll find a way to resolve this crisis, and maybe find better ways of doing things in the process."

"This case is the number-one priority of the Berkeley Police Department," says BPD Captain Bobby Miller. "First, we have to make the school safe. Second, we need to catch whoever's setting the fires. Someone did it, and someone knows who did it. To solve this crime will take all of us. Anyone who knows an arsonist, or someone who has a propensity to set fires, please, call the hotline we've set up for that purpose. I have to plead with you to help us make this campus safe and keep it that way."

"I want to be straight up about this," Berkeley's assistant fire chief says. "We were very, very fortunate that no one died in this fire. The students and teachers could have been trapped in that building. The potential for firefighters to die was very high. This was not paper towels in a sink. This arsonist took out a whole building and did tremendous damage to the infrastructure of this school. We're hoping there won't be any more fires, but we can't say there won't be. *Tell your kids tonight:* setting even a little fire is *serious.*"

Matthew Mock, a therapist with Berkeley Mental Health Services, gets the first and only laugh of the evening. "Our observation is that the students are calm, and annoyed that there are more adults who look like parents on campus." When the laughter subsides he refers to the flyer "Helping Your Teen Cope with School Crises," included in tonight's handout.

As a parent you can support your son/daughter by:

- Being available to listen to his/her feelings and concerns (at times he/she is ready to talk about them)
- Sharing your own feelings in an appropriate manner
- Providing structure and encouraging your teen to maintain a stable routine
- Showing confidence in your teen's competency and coping skills
- Modeling a calm, positive outlook
- Being concerned but not overprotective

Remember that:

- Teens have a normal desire to handle things themselves and may have mixed feelings about sharing with parents.
- As a parent try to be aware that you will also be having reactions to the anxiety around issues of school safety and that this may affect your communication with your son/daughter.

"If your teenager has concerns that need to be addressed," Mock urges, "please use our services or the school health center. We're all focused on the emotional needs of your children."

"Our new motto is, 'It's Not Business as Usual,'" declares the associate school superintendent. "We have been *busy* at Berkeley High School over Spring Break. We had to set up a new entrance to the school and relocate fourteen classrooms. Double our security staff. Hire twenty-four-hour security personnel. We've imported fifty radios and twenty-five mobile phones, trained sixty volunteers, and brought in a hundred red coats for high visibility. We have new practices—name tags, ID cards—and we are going to stick with them. Everyone who's here has to belong here."

Theresa Saunders, characteristically elegant in a navy blue tailored pants suit, tells the parents how she got the news. "I was at a meeting off campus when the school secretary paged me. He said, 'Theresa, sit down. There's been a fire.' I can't tell you how devastating it was. *I can't.* The thing you care most about as an administrator, besides that students are learning, is that they're safe . . .

"We've had to make some changes. Hall passes—no more. Students with gaps in their schedules—no more. They can't go off campus except at lunch. Students must be with us all day, every day. They must be under the watchful eye of some adult on campus. *Always.*"

Rory Bled, the college adviser, speaks last. "As you know, our database was affected by the fire. But we will be able to get transcripts out to colleges by the May deadline . . .

"I went to Berkeley High," Bled adds. "My sons went to Berkeley High. And I've never seen this community work together as hard as they did to get this school open today. We had a wonderful crew of people here all through the break—including Easter Sunday. They were all here for one reason only: to make sure the students feel safe about being in their school."

The parents are asked to submit their questions and comments on index cards. The first one is, "I hope the district will raise teacher salaries." This reference to the stalled contract negotiations (which have sparked a teacher slowdown and the formation of PIST—Parents In Support of Teachers, now threatening a one-day school boycott), is greeted by wild, unanimous applause.

The questions that follow—varied in detail, but consistent in focus—reflect the parents' two worst fears. The first is that there will be another fire, possibly a lethal one next time. "We had a good first day. And there are still some security issues to work out," Theresa Saunders says. "We have a gate the kids call the A-Hole . . ."

"The teachers call it that too," a teacher calls out from the audience.

"We've had it fixed several times, but it keeps getting torn open. Otherwise we've got things pretty well under control."

"Every area of this campus is subject to surveillance," the assistant fire chief adds. "Everyone's being watched on this campus—*everyone.*"

The second big fear the parents express is that their children's health will suffer, now or in the future, from exposure to toxins.

"The B building was built in the 1950s," the assistant fire chief explains. "There's asbestos in the roof, and there were holes cut in the roof to ventilate the building. Asbestos does cause problems when it's inhaled. The B building is *not* safe. In the C building, every time someone opens a cabinet for the first time they're going to smell smoke. People with asthma, with compromised respiratory systems, need to know it may impact on them."

A woman in the audience bypasses the index card protocol, speaking directly to the administrators on the stage. "I'm Berkeley High, class of '93. And Harvard/Radcliffe, class of '97—thanks to the fantastic education I got here. I thank you for that. But I'm concerned about the health center. How will it function? How will you access the medical records of ill children?"

Anthony Santangelo, director of the health center, the most severely fire-damaged area of all, responds from the audience. "We're displaced. Our equipment, our medications, our records are gone. We're hoping to get a special portable with exam rooms by the end of the week. In the meantime we're asking folks to sign parental consent forms so we can still treat your children."

The next question silences the room. "I heard a rumor that it's an employee setting the fires." It would have been impossible *not* to hear this rumor. Since the fire, it has been circulating widely among students, parents, and staff. In his letter to CAS parents on April 13, Rick Ayers wrote, "It has seemed quite likely to many that these fires are being set by a staff member. Not just set by a staff member, but a staff member who is begging to be caught . . ."

And in a moving editorial, "Let's Take Back Our School," the *Jacket* editors wrote: "Everyone complains about having to go to school. But think about it: do we want it gone? Do we want it destroyed? Of course not . . . There is something to the sanctity of school, to protecting the 'innocence' of youth . . . it is here, in these drab Berkeley High halls, that we are expected to make the transition between child and adult, to find ourselves and build our own identities . . . it is a tragedy that someone cares so little about this process that they are willing to disturb it, even knowing lives may be lost. It is all the more tragic, however, to know that this firebug is, authorities are now suggesting, a staff member . . ."

"It could be an adult, a student, a nonemployee," BPD Captain Miller responds. "Even *you* are a suspect at this point. We're looking at everyone to learn who's setting these fires."

"Dr. Mock will now meet in the foyer with anyone who needs counseling," the superintendent of schools announces. With this the meeting ends, and once again the parents face the reporters. "Are you satisfied that your child will be safe here?" a reporter asks a mother, who shakes her head emphatically. "The meeting left me with more questions than answers," she says.

Cinco de Mayo has always been a big day at Berkeley High. In years past there have been red-green-and-white posters plastered throughout the halls for weeks in advance, all-school assemblies featuring spirited performances by the school's Ballet Folklorico dancers, and a home-cooked Mexican feast served in the courtyard by Chicano/Latino club members. This year a simple black-and-white flyer is circulated on May 3, advertising a "Cinco de Mayo/B Building Survivors/Break-In the Portables Party," to be held on the cement "patio" around which the portables are clustered like a circled wagon train.

Although the district agrees to provide the food—1,500 cardboard trays dispensed from the snack bar, each bearing one bottle of Gatorade, one corn dog or one barbecued chicken leg, one apple, and one small bag of chili-flavored Fritos, the closest thing to Mexican food on the menu—it's clear from the get-go that no one's *corazón* is truly in it. Rick Ayers, the event's unofficial ringleader, distributes colored chalk to the CAS and Computer Academy classes now relocated to the portables, and in the hour before lunchtime a few students kneel on the ground, drawing psychedelic Quetzalcoatls and writing Cinco de Mayo messages across the cracked cement. Special ed students in wheelchairs watch, a few of them having been lifted to the ground to participate, as Mr. Ayers exhorts the CAS and Computer Academy students to stop drawing separately and "Bring it all together!" Greg Giglio monitors his students' artwork closely, reminding them frequently of the difference between drawing and "tagging." "No gang signs," he warns, squinting suspiciously at a tangled logo.

A boom box blasts mariachi music, a lone Latino student shows up wrapped in a Mexican flag, Mr. Ayers whirls a CAS teacher around in a spirited if not particularly Mexican dance, and kids of all races watch from the portables' steps, trading corn dogs for chicken legs, impossibly blue Gatorades for impossibly red ones. But even before the lunch period ends they drift away dispiritedly, shaking their heads, dropping their grease-stained trays into overflowing trash cans. Nothing is the same at Berkeley High since the fire. Not even Cinco de Mayo.

"These kids are *scared*," says Susan, an English teacher and a thirty-year veteran of Berkeley High. "Every time there's a strange sound they jump."

Six teachers and a therapist are gathered in a portable on the first Wednesday afternoon—the regular staff meeting time—since the fire. Other teachers sit with other therapists in other portables for the same reason. As the Berkeley Mental Health director said, when he invited the teachers to break up into small support groups, "The last thing that gets taken care of at a school site is the teachers. This is a chance to take care of yourselves." Although one teacher objected—"We're so fragmented in this community; we should be talking as a whole group"—most teachers welcomed the offer.

"It's post-traumatic stress syndrome," the therapist nods. "Hearing a fire truck, a scream—it'll set them off. And it'll be like that for a long time. Especially those who were in the B building."

Kiko, a young English teacher, says, "This situation makes it hard to work, to focus. I've relaxed the deadlines a lot. I can't keep track anyway. My grade book is in my classroom. And my classroom is in the B building. Or was."

"Were any of the rest of you in the B building when the fires broke out?" the therapist asks.

"I'm glad I wasn't," a math teacher answers. "I've talked to the people who were and it sounds *terrifying*—teachers frantically trying to get their kids out before the building burned down around them, the librarian running around closing all the windows to try and save the books . . ."

"And now we've got this work-to-rule thing to deal with," another English teacher says. As they'd warned they'd do if negotiations didn't progress, the teachers have begun their slowdown, restricting themselves to six and a half hours of work each day. "I've got so much to catch up on . . ."

"I find work-to-rule a relief," says Kiko. "I got home at four o'clock the other day. It was the earliest I've ever been home as a teacher. There's only eight weeks of the school year left. My kids' stuff is gone. My stuff is gone. Even if I work my butt off I'll never catch up. So I'm giving myself a break."

"I've always felt that Berkeley High is such an extraordinary place," Susan says sadly. "This year for the first time I've heard kids say it's not a good school. It's hurtful to me. There's so much frustration among the students and the teachers. I can't help but think that if we'd done something about those frustrations, maybe the fire wouldn't have happened."

The math teacher nods. "It horrifies me that there's someone walking around who would *want* to do this. And to think that person is still here every day. Frustrated or not, what would make someone want to destroy life?"

"The kids are saying, 'Next time it'll be a shooting,' " Kiko reports.

"Now you're saying what we're all thinking," Susan responds. "Columbine."

The teachers sit together quietly for a moment. "Do you feel safe here?" the therapist asks then.

"I feel safe in my little world of ESL," says a Spanish teacher, a muscular man in his twenties. "Every one of my kids would be on my side. But I hate hall duty. I'm young, inexperienced. I feel pretty intimidated."

"Another thing that bugs me is the lack of support from the local merchants," says Kiko. "Theresa told us to go to Kinko's till we get some copiers on campus. I went yesterday, and they're charging us seven cents a copy! Last week there was a sign in the window at Top Dog that said 'Closed—school fire.' That place runs entirely on Berkeley High students. So do a lot of other businesses. And what are they doing to help when we need it? Nothing!"

"Why can't the local businesses chip in?" the therapist wonders aloud.

"The merchants were already mad at this school," the math teacher says. "Now they say, 'You just have a bad school. It's not our problem.'"

"Teachers are not the fad right now," Susan says. "We all know what the fad is: cell phones and your precious stocks. It's the indifference of this society, thinking it's all the schools' fault. There's no respect for teachers anymore. We're second-class citizens. It's like being a Vietnam vet."

On May 8, in the midst of the post-fire chaos and confusion, a delegation of Berkeley High teachers and students boards a bus for the state capital of Sacramento. There they demonstrate, along with 8,000 other California teachers, students, and parents, for increased teacher salaries. Berkeley High teachers carry signs: "Will Teach for Food" and "Fund Schools Now or Prisons Later."

"The driving force behind the demonstration," the May 12 issue of the *Jacket* reports, "was the fact that the state government has benefited from the booming economy with a $10 to $12 billion surplus. But Governor Gray Davis, while insisting he is going to make education his first priority, has been hesitant to commit discretionary funds to the schools."

The day after the rally, Governor Davis agrees to give California schools an additional $1.84 billion, or $328 more per pupil, in discretionary funding. This brings California's annual per-pupil budget up to $6,353—slightly lower than the 1997–1998 national average of $6,638, and significantly less than the $10,000 per pupil spent by other states, including New York and New Jersey.

"The important deal is more money for school districts to do their business," State Senate President Pro Tem John Burton tells the *San*

Francisco Chronicle. "It could mean new football jerseys, a kick in starting-teacher salaries, music programs. Whatever a district feels is important to their kids."

In mid-May, Theresa Saunders makes a rare guest appearance on the parent E-tree, submitting this response to rumors of an impending one-day school boycott:

> I have also heard this rumor. Apparently, this move is to be in support of teachers and their negotiation positions with the District. Please send out the message that school is in session on this day . . . When students miss days of instruction the District does not get paid the ADA (average daily attendance $ disbursed by the state) . . . We are already in a fiscal crisis . . . Parents who keep students out of school on this day should know that this means thousands of dollars lost to the District which clearly will have an impact. I am not suggesting that people not support the teachers if they want to do that . . . but I think that there might be more effective ways . . . such as meeting with Board members, writing letters, attending Board meetings, holding public meetings on the issues, etc.—Theresa Saunders

. . .

"I didn't know this place was so *big,*" Autumn's mother pants as she, Autumn, and RaShawn hike from the UC Berkeley football field down to the campus below. "Couldn't we have parked *closer?* This is too much exercise for me!" Autumn was pleased but not terribly surprised when her mother agreed to go check out Cal with her. "My mom is so funny. They announced it in our church when I got accepted. She tried to play it off like she's not excited. But she is *so* excited! She told me she was at work telling people, 'My daughter's going to Cal.' Then she thought to herself, 'That's *my* daughter going to Cal!'"

"My feet hurt," RaShawn chimes in.

"C'mon, you guys. Think of it as a free workout," Autumn says. She's a bit breathless herself, but it's not the walking that's making her head spin. *This is my school,* she thinks, looking around at the elaborate stone buildings, the lush, landscaped grounds, the fountains and the plazas, and the people: Cal students! *That's me,* Autumn tells herself. *Starting June 30 I'm gonna be a Cal student.* It still feels like a dream.

"I guess this is my dorm," Autumn says finally, matching the address on the tall, modern high-rise in front of her with the slip of paper in her hand. Along with their acceptance packets, both Autumn and Lillian were invited to join the Summer Bridge program, which starts right after graduation and offers "extra support in the transition between high school and college." They've already been to the first meeting. "It just happens everyone there was African-American," Autumn told Lauren sarcastically when they got back. "But it's cool," she added. "By joining Summer Bridge you automatically get a dorm room for the year on one of the African-American floors. And that's where we want to be."

Not so cool is the cost of the program: $2,900, just for two months. Since she found out she got into Cal, Autumn's been scrambling to raise the money for Summer Bridge *and* the $16,000, including dorm fees, it'll cost for her first year of school. She did get some help from the financial aid office—$720 for Summer Bridge, and a $3,000 Cal grant and $3,000 student loan for tuition. The financial aid packet came with an application for a $7,000 loan her mom could take out if she qualifies; they're going for that too. "My mom's credit history is kind of messed up. So we're not sure she'll get it." Autumn applied for a scholarship from her church, and Ms. Bled's been helping her apply for a few other scholarships: five hundred dollars here, a thousand dollars there. "I'm not stressing too hard about the money. I'm praying a lot—" she giggles "—but not stressing. It'll all come together somehow. It's *got* to."

Autumn, RaShawn, and their mom take the elevator up to the four-teenth floor, where there are some open rooms. When they filed their Cal applications, Autumn and Lillian put in a dorm request to be room-mates, but they still have to decide whether to go for a double—just the two of them—or the cheaper triple. Autumn peers into a couple of triples. She takes in the bunk beds, the desks crammed up against each other, and shakes her head emphatically. "Been there. Done that," she says. "It's gon' *have* to be a double. I been in a triple my whole life!"

As the end of the school year approaches, Mr. McKnight's determination to ready his seniors not only for graduation, but for lives lifted above their social legacy, takes on an intensified urgency. He starts holding lunchtime meetings in his classroom every Tuesday, preparing for the annual African-American Celebration of Excellence known to all at Berkeley High as "Black Graduation."

He has his students fitted for hats and scarves in their choice of African fabrics. ("The cost is $50. But some of us are living independent of our parents. If you have mitigating circumstances, see me and we'll try to make arrangements.") He solicits donations of time ("I need at least seven parents or older siblings to assist at the ceremony") and entertainment ("We want someone to sing for us—either a song of your choice *that is appropriate,* or the Negro National Anthem"). And he tells the students how many people they are allowed to thank when giving their speeches. ("It can be more than one person, but try to keep it to five.")

In these last moments before his students are released into a world that is likely to treat them far more harshly than he has, Mr. McKnight provokes discussions daily about the issues he most wants them to consider. He uses every vehicle at his disposal: *The Nubian* (which, despite his best intentions, the class has taken a whole semester to read); Malcolm X Day (a holiday for Berkeley schoolchildren, and he insists that his students will know why); local and international news headlines. He talks to his students about drinking and driving. Love and respect. Success, and what it takes to achieve it.

"What does the author of *The Nubian* mean," he asks today, "when he says that nothing is impossible when you're able to grip the spirit?"

"He means if you know yourself and you know God," Keith responds immediately, "you can do anything you want to."

Keith is feeling particularly powerful these days. For one thing, he just quit his job at Mel's Diner. "They were treating me like I couldn't just go and get another job. So I went and got one." He's at Starbucks now, a couple of doors down from Mel's. "The money's just as good, and the people are hella cool." Plus he just got a new tattoo: his nickname, "Black," above his sign—a scorpion that spirals down from his shoulder to his elbow, covering up the old Tasmanian Devil tattoo he got when he was too young to know better. And of course there's the biggest thing of all to be proud of. After all the changes school has put him through, Keith's about to walk the stage. Berkeley High, Class of 2000!

"That's good, Mr. Stephens. That's excellent. Examples?"

"This boy I know in Richmond got shot forty-two times," a girl offers, "and he still livin' 'cause he knew he wanted to live."

"It happened right by my house," says another girl. "I saw the whole thing. He said he could hear his mama cryin' and he told himself, 'Keep breathing.' "

"Yes," Mr. McKnight affirms. "He was shot in the bottoms of his feet. He smelled like a fireworks display, there was so much gunpowder in him. But he just kept breathing."

"I used to stay with him," a boy adds. "He playin' basketball now."

"You can't let someone hand you your destiny," a girl declares.

Keith nods vehemently. "You gotta *take* it."

"We've had basketball players at Berkeley High who can do more than Michael Jordan," Mr. McKnight says. "Why does Michael stand out, while others of equal talent don't even make the pros? For example, there's a young basketball player in West Oakland who can jump over cars . . ."

"That's Hops," Keith says. "He in jail now."

"Well, now we know why *he* didn't make the pros," Mr. McKnight says, shaking his head.

"Michael Jordan don't let no one tell him what to do," a girl says. "He went *beyond* Nike."

"He retired and he came back," Keith says passionately. "He's the only one who ever did that. He gripped his inner spirit 'cause he knew he had more work to do. And he was *still* the best player when he came back."

The period ends but the students—fully engaged, as every teacher longs for his or her students to be—don't move.

"You have unlimited potential," Mr. McKnight tells them. They look at him intently, eyes shining: sixteen sets brown, two sets blue. He tells it to them again. "You have unlimited potential. Most of us never fulfill our potential—perhaps because we never enter into the realm of gripping the spirit. But remember: your spirit is yours to grip. No one can take that from you. *No one*."

Jordan's spirit is sorely lagging when he drags himself back to school after his mom's return from Japan. The hole he's dug himself into is deep and dark; he's not sure he can climb out of it. He's not even sure he wants to. Each night he thinks about telling his mom how hopeless it's becoming, how bad he feels; each morning he gets in his car, drives to school, goes to one class, maybe two. Then he leaves—by himself, with a friend. He's losing the possibility of passing his classes the way a drowning person loses his senses. One day he realizes that he can't possibly pass Statistics; no point in showing up there anymore. The next day, it's CAS. Then Biology. His grandma and his favorite uncle, Rich, his mom's mom and disabled younger brother, are visiting from Michigan. That's the excuse Jordan gives himself for not telling his mom what's going on.

The day after Rich and his grandmother leave is Jordan's dad's birthday—the second one since he died. Jordan wakes up feeling exactly the way he did a year ago on this date: "depressed as hell." Determined not to sink as low as he did last year, Jordan has accepted a dinner invitation for tonight from Laurin, his mom's business partner and the man who introduced his mom to his dad thirty years ago. Now Jordan considers canceling. Sometimes being with Laurin just makes him feel worse that he can't be with his dad. This might be one of those times.

The phone rings as Jordan's getting ready to not go to school. He and his mom answer the phones in their bedrooms at the same time. It's his aunt, his mom's sister, and she's crying, hard. She's telling them that Rich died in his sleep last night from complications of surgery.

Jordan's mom collapses. Jordan holds her as she cries, feeling absolutely nothing. *I felt worse when the cat died,* he observes, as if from a great distance. "You should go to school," his mom sobs. "You really need to go to school." Jordan nods, disentangles himself from his mom, gets into his car. He drives toward school, as he does every day, but this time he turns around before he even gets there. He drives up into the hills. He pulls into a trailhead in Tilden Park. He walks for a while, then sits down on a rock. Jordan spends the next few hours sitting there, staring down at the bay, the Cal campus, the houses, the cars. His mind is blank. His chest is hollow. He gets in his car and goes home.

"You're not going to believe this," his mom says when he gets there. "I just got a call from Skidmore. You're in."

"Really," Jordan says flatly.

"Really! Isn't that great? The thing is, you have to tell them by tomorrow."

"I can tell them right now. I'm not going."

"Jordan. Promise me you'll think about it, at least. You can't make a decision in this state of mind. I'll call them in the morning, tell them your uncle just died. I'm sure they'll give you a few days . . ."

"Mom. I'm not going to Skidmore. And I don't want to hear about it any more. All right?" Jordan hardly ever yells at his mom, but he's yelling now.

He stomps downstairs, puts on his headphones, turns on some music—loud. He goes back upstairs. His mom is in the living room, talking on the phone.

"I need to talk to you," he says when she hangs up. Her face softens eagerly.

"I'm not doing well in school," he says.

"I know. You told me that. We agreed that you'd talk to your teachers—"

"No. You *don't* know. I'm flunking, Mom. I'm flunking CAS. I'm flunking Statistics. I'm probably flunking Biology." Jordan finally feels something: relief.

"Jordan! You told me you were having a hard time. You didn't tell me you were *failing*. How can you be flunking three classes?"

"It's amazingly easy, actually." Jordan chuckles mirthlessly. "You don't go to class. You don't take the tests. You don't turn in the homework. And just like that—" he snaps his fingers "—you flunk your classes."

"Honey. You're just upset. You can't be—"

"I'm not just upset, Mom. Don't you hear what I'm saying? *I'm flunking out of high school.*"

Natalie gets up. She sits back down. She takes several deep breaths. "There's still time, Jordan," she says calmly. "Let's figure out how we're going to get you through this. I'll call Mr. Jegers tonight. And I'm sure Ms. Crawford will understand—"

"There's nothing to understand," Jordan interrupts her. "Don't you get it? I don't *care*."

"Jordan. I know you're upset about Rich. And your dad. I know Rich's death would be a great excuse to stop doing your homework, stop going to school. But your uncle was a straight-A student. You know how he feels—felt—about education. If there's any way to honor him, it's to get in there and kick ass in school."

She's not going to hear me no matter what I say, Jordan thinks. He puts his head in his hands, tries to tune her out.

"I know you need me here right now, Jordan. But my mom needs me more," Natalie is saying. Jordan looks up at her, then down again. "I'm going to Michigan for a week. I'll do what I can for you before I leave, but I need you to promise me you'll handle school while I'm gone. I'm sorry, sweetie—" she touches Jordan's shoulder. He flinches at her touch. "If I could be in both places at once, believe me, I would be. I want you to stay at Ari's, okay? I don't want you to be alone right now."

Jordan says nothing.

"Okay?" Natalie asks.

"Whatever," Jordan mumbles.

"Promise me you'll get this under control while I'm gone," Natalie implores him. "I'll call you every night. And I can call your teachers from Michigan if you need me to . . ."

"I can't promise anything right now," Jordan says. He stands up, heads for the door. "I'm going out."

"No, you're not. Give me your car keys."

"What?"

"I don't want you driving when you're like this. Give me your car keys, Jordan."

Jordan glares at his mom from across the room, his face flushed with anger. Natalie looks back at him, her eyes still swollen from crying. For a long moment they stare at each other.

I'm eighteen, Jordan thinks. *She can't make me do anything anymore.*

He's eighteen, Natalie thinks. *But I'm still his mother.*

"Give me the keys," Natalie repeats. "I'll give them back to you when you're calmer."

"This is ridiculous," Jordan mutters. He takes the keys out of his pocket, tosses them onto the coffee table in front of his mother, and storms downstairs to his room.

June 2000: Class Dismissed

Jordan and his mom are walking across the Berkeley High courtyard, arguing as they go. Jordan is here to drop out of school. Natalie is here to keep him from doing that. Jordan's plan is to withdraw from his classes if they'll let him, take the Fs if they won't. "Whatever!" he says. This is something he says a lot lately. "As long as I don't have to spend another day at Berkeley High."

As they approach the administration portables, Natalie makes a final plea—the same one she's been making since she got back from burying her brother in Michigan two days ago. "I just think ten years from now you're going to wish you'd graduated with the Class of 2000. That's your group. Don't you want to walk the stage with them?"

Jordan stops in his tracks, his eyes flashing with anger. "Natalie!" he shouts. "Get this through your head! I don't *give* a shit!"

He stomps into the portable, asks the principal's secretary where he might find his counselor. "Mr. Barcenas is out on Operation Stay-in-School." The secretary looks past Jordan to Natalie. "He won't be back till lunchtime."

"Perfect," Jordan mutters.

"Let's try Rory Bled," Natalie suggests.

Jordan shrugs and follows her into the G building, past the line of students waiting for tardy passes at the folding table in the hallway, which now serves as the attendance office, the main school entrance, and an ID checkpoint. A few weeks after the fire, two weeks before the end of the school year, the stringent security has already slacked off. No one asks Jordan or Natalie for ID or a visitor's pass as they walk through the halls in the middle of third period.

Natalie pokes her head into Ms. Bled's office. "Rory—do you have a minute?"

"Hi, Natalie. Hey, Jordan." Ms. Bled knows Jordan and Natalie well. When she came back to Berkeley High in March, Jordan's Bard rejection was one of the many horror stories Ms. Bled was too late to fix. She points at the chairs facing her desk. "What's up?" she asks Jordan.

"I'm thinking about withdrawing from school," Jordan begins.

"Are you failing all your courses?" Ms. Bled asks calmly.

"Most."

"Are any of your classes redeemable?"

"Not PE. Not Statistics."

"You're going to UC Santa Cruz, right?"

"I was supposed to."

Ms. Bled glances at Natalie, back at Jordan. "Just so you know—you're not the first person to do this, Jordan. Another student got into Harvard and then failed his last semester of high school. The worst thing that'll happen is that Santa Cruz will send you a letter saying, 'We were happy to accept you but now you have to do something different.' Are you prepared to receive that letter?"

"Yes."

"Deep down? Because you did this to yourself." Ms. Bled's blue eyes are sympathetic but unwavering. "We all know the experience with Bard was very upsetting. But I also know your mom must be wondering why you did this to yourself."

"Can I talk to you alone?" Jordan asks Ms. Bled abruptly. Natalie hesitates, then stands up, kisses the top of her son's head, and leaves the room.

A half hour later Jordan joins her again. "Let's go," he says. He leads her out of the building and off the campus, past clusters of students bent over copies of the just-published yearbook, exclaiming over photos of themselves, writing messages in each other's books. When they get to the garage where Natalie's new Passat wagon is parked, she hands Jordan the keys. He turns on the upgraded sound system he talked her into buying, tunes the radio to his station, turns the volume up. As they cross Telegraph Avenue Jordan turns the radio off. "Ms. Bled said that with everything that's happened to me in the past two years and the past two weeks," he says, "it's a miracle I made it this far."

"What else did she say?" Natalie restrains herself from asking what she really wants to know: *Did she talk you into graduating, or at least trying to?*

"We went over my transcript. Turns out I might have enough credits to graduate after all." Jordan snickers. "How ironic. The same reason I want to get out of Berkeley High so bad is the same reason I might be able to graduate from Berkeley High. No one knowing what the hell's going on. Or caring."

Natalie shakes her head, taking in this information. "You'd better get that transcript checked twenty more times." She reaches over, briefly touches Jordan's cheek. "I just want you to wear that red gown that's hanging in your closet."

Jordan pulls into their driveway, turns off the engine, hands his mom the keys. "I'm on it, all right?" he says. "Now will you please get off my back?"

Every pew in the modest South Berkeley church is full, every inch of wall space is occupied. Hundreds of parents and grandparents, aunts and uncles, brothers and sisters and cousins and friends—all of them in their Sunday finery, all but a handful of them African-American— whisper and laugh, clutching bunches of flowers, disposable cameras, bobbing bouquets of "Congratulations Graduate!" balloons.

Suddenly the happy hum is pierced by a burst of drumbeats. Four dark-skinned men dressed in Kente cloth burst into the church and march down the center aisle, their hands flashing ebony against the pale skins of their drums. Right behind them—"Here they come!" the parents exclaim. "Look how beautiful they are!"—dressed in black, with scarves and caps in many different colors of African prints, their proud smiles flashing white against the many different brown tones of their skin, march the sixty graduating seniors of Berkeley High School's African-American Studies Department.

Keith's whole family is here—Mom, Dad, brother Kenneth, sisters Yolanda and Latisha, squirming four-year-old Alonzo, and Mama, Keith's grandmother, in a sparkling gold fez. A few rows away Autumn's mom, brothers, and stepfather sit beside Lillian's dad. Lauren and Emily are in the audience too. Lauren will be part of this ceremony two years from now; Emily, who's biracial like Autumn—only in Emily's case it's her dad who's black—decided not to participate. "I never went to African-American Studies classes, never went to BSU meetings. It wouldn't be right to suddenly show up now."

The pastor steps up to the lectern and leads the congregation in prayer. "We are here, Lord, to recognize these young academicians who have toiled so long and so hard. Please give them the courage to beat the odds. No matter what the media says, as long as they put their hands in Your hands, You'll be there with them every step of the way . . ."

"Yes!" "Thank you Jesus!" parents call out from the pews.

"We pray for the administration of Berkeley High school itself. In the days to come You will be the guiding force on the campus. Thank you for being a God of achievement. Amen!"

"Amen!" the congregation roars.

Mr. McKnight takes the pastor's place. He beams down at his students in their mudcloth scarves and Nefertiti print mortarboards—Keith in a borrowed-at-the-last-minute red-and-black scarf; one row behind him, Autumn in the black-and-white cap and scarf set she picked out and paid for weeks ago. "Don't you look wonderful," Mr. McKnight crows, reveling in this, his finest hour. "Isn't this wonderful!"

The audience calls out its assent. "Please put your cell phone or pager on vibrate," Mr. McKnight adds. "We are here for a secular activity but we are still in the house of God." He introduces the first student speaker, Keith's classmate, Ms. Calhoun.

"We are grateful to the ancestors," Ms. Calhoun says, "who took our beatings during slavery. We are grateful to our civil rights leaders: Dr. Booker T. Washington, Marcus Garvey, Dr. King, Malcolm X. To our teachers: Mr. McKnight, Ms. McKnight, Ms. Russ, and all the others, for being so unselfish to accept a job that pays so much less than you deserve . . ."

The students shout out and clap. "And most of all we are grateful to our parents—" Ms. Calhoun, crying now, is interrupted by her class-mates' applause. "Thank you," she chokes out. She wipes her eyes and returns to her seat.

Josh Gray—who was abandoned by his father, whose mother struggled with drug addiction, who was taken in a few months ago by his third-grade teacher and her husband, and who just received his acceptance letter from Howard University—speaks for the Black Student Union. "In this day, African-American youth are not expected to succeed. Prisons are the only public housing they're building for us."

"Preach!" the pastor cries out.

"We must strive to be the most well-educated young people the world has ever seen. We are going to be successful *by any means necessary.*"

"Awwight, Mr. President," Keith "hoorides" Josh from the pew. But as Josh slides past him after his speech, Keith gives him an affectionate pat on the back.

Dr. Michael Millben, an evangelist, activist, and husband of a California congressperson, delivers the keynote address. "This is the only African-American Studies Department in any high school, anywhere in America. After thirty-two years, Mr. Robert McKnight is still teaching, still nurturing. Stand and give him and his family a hand!"

The kids go wild, screaming their teacher's name. "I am confident that you can handle this cold, cold world," Dr. Millben tells the graduates. "Because you are the survivors of an organized conspiracy that has been put in place to destroy the black family, the black church, the power of black people. We have been living with a drug holocaust in our community, and you were born into the middle of it. The incarceration, the attorney fees, the bail bondsmen . . . The U.S. government sent fifty thousand troops to the Middle East in ninety days, but they can't stop fifty kilos from coming across the border? You are sitting here the survivors of an organized conspiracy."

On the dais, Theresa Saunders, dressed head to toe in African garb, jumps up out of her seat and dances in place, feet stomping, hands waving in the air, head nodding emphatically.

"One of you may supercede Oprah Winfrey," Millben continues. "Be the superintendent of schools. Find the cure for sickle-cell anemia. But even if I never see you again, I want you to promise me you'll always tell yourself, 'I think I can. *I think I can*!'"

"You accuse me of preaching in class." Mr. McKnight smiles at his students as their applause subsides. "*I* lecture. *That* was preaching. And now I'll introduce to you the principal of Berkeley High School, Ms. Theresa Saunders."

"Don't you just want to shout! It's God who keeps us going!" a fired-up Theresa Saunders cries into the microphone. "And I want to say thank you to this graduating class. You've been wonderful to me, as a principal and a person."

"Who—us?" Keith mutters, setting off a round of barely suppressed snickers from the students.

"Continue to press on," Saunders concludes her brief message. "I'll see you at the Greek!" The Greek Theater, an outdoor amphitheater on the UC Berkeley campus, is host to the Berkeley High graduation ceremony each year—but Saunders must know that she won't be seeing *all* of these students there in two weeks. "Our Celebration of Excellence is for everyone," Mr. McKnight has said. "That includes students who haven't earned the credits to graduate. I want these young people to have a sense of closure, of completion, so they can go on with their lives and know it's not the end of the world if they don't graduate. And I want to give the families a chance to celebrate their children."

Ms. Saunders takes her seat to scattered applause, and Lillian and Jamilah come to the podium. As they sing a Stevie Wonder song, their friend Jabris—who will join the Alvin Ailey dance troupe this summer—performs her own dance composition, "Olugbala (Love for the People)."

Autumn's AP English classmate Reggie comes up next, gives thanks to "the Heavenly Father and Mr. McKnight," then slams a poem about the civil rights movement.

The kids shout their approval. Then several of them call out, "What about Ms. Russ?"

"They say that," Mr. McKnight explains to the parents, "because they're here thanks to the tireless efforts of this teacher. And she deserves it all."

All sixty seniors are on their feet now, screaming her name. "Ms. Russ! Ms. Russ!"

The short, gray-haired white woman—normally seen in a worn cotton tank top, pull-on pants, and sensible shoes, speed-walking the halls with a Computer Academy student's schedule (or elbow) in her hand and a take-no-prisoners look on her face—steps out from behind the podium in a glittery black dress. She ducks her head, waves briefly at her students, and disappears again, but not before the glimmer of tears is visible on her face.

And then the main event begins. One by one, each student comes to the podium and says what he or she is here to say.

"My name is Joshua Gray. I will be attending Howard University in the fall of 2000. I stand on the shoulders of Ms. Russ, Mr. McKnight, my parents, and"—he points to the only white couple in the room—"my godparents."

"My name is Jamilah Bradshaw. I will be attending Spellman College, majoring in Psychology and African Studies. I stand on the shoulders of my parents, my teachers, and the ancestors . . ."

Coming off the stage, each of the sixty students receives a certificate of achievement from Mr. McKnight, a hug from Ms. Russ, and an impassioned ovation from every other student and from his or her family members—many of whom explode into ecstatic dances in the aisles. "That's my grandbaby!" "That's me he's talking about! I'm his mama!"

Always the eager comic, never the willing orator, Keith has to be shoved toward the podium when it's his turn to speak. His classmates shout, "Keith! Keith! Keith!" as he faces them. "My name is Keith Stephens. I stand on the shoulders of my parents." He waves at his family. "Stand up!" he says, and they do, Latisha waving Alonzo's tiny hand at his uncle. "I'll be attending San Francisco City College in the fall, majoring in Fire Science." Keith ducks his head shyly, then suddenly shoots his arms up above his head in a victory sign. He stands there for a moment, basking in the applause, before striding off the stage and into the waiting arms of Ms. Russ. "We did it," Patricia tells her husband as the audience cheers for their son. "This is our last kid. We raised four children—not one of them in jail or in trouble, and every one of them a high school graduate."

"My name is Lillian Burnett. I will be attending Xavier University in the fall . . ." Lillian changed her mind about going to Cal a few weeks ago, amidst promises to Autumn of calls and visits home. Autumn was disappointed but supportive when she heard Lillian's decision: "I want her to do what's best for her. And I know we'll always be friends no matter what." Anyway, Autumn has a more immediate problem to deal with right now. "My money's funny and my credit don't get it." Autumn's still short the $2,200 she owes for the Summer Bridge program. On top of that, the bill just came for her dorm fees—five hundred dollars, due *now*. "I flat out ain't got it."

"I've done all I can," her mom said when Autumn showed her the bill. "All I can do for you now is pray—and I hope that *you* come up with something." *Whatever it takes,* Autumn thought. The next day she asked Emily's mom if she could live in Emily's room next year—pay a little rent, chip in on utilities. Emily's mom said she'd love to have Autumn, but told her, "You really should have the dorm experience," and offered to lend her the five hundred dollars she needs. "That's heck of generous," Autumn said, hugging her, wondering how many thousands of dollars she'd owe to how many people by the time she graduated, and where she might turn for the rest.

"My name is Autumn Morris." Autumn stands tall behind the lectern. "I will be attending UC Berkeley in the fall. I haven't decided on my major yet. But I pray the Lord will give me the guidance to help me do something that's good for this world." Tears run down her cheeks. "I want to thank my family. And my best friend, Lillian Burnett, for everything she's done for me." As Autumn leaves the stage Lillian runs to meet her, grabs her best friend in a hug. The two girls bury their faces in each other's shoulders, crying, as their witnesses applaud.

"There's a ton of food in the kitchen," Mr. McKnight announces when the last student has spoken. "Please help yourselves. And now we will close with the Negro National Anthem."

> *"Sing a song full of the faith that the dark past has taught us*
> *Sing a song full of the hope that our present has brought us;*
> *Facing the rising sun of our new day begun*
> *Let us march on till victory is won . . ."*

· · ·

In the first week of June a long-overdue victory is won by the teachers of Berkeley.

"After a year of negotiations, two months of third-party mediations and three weeks of work-to-contract tactics, the BFT and the school board have come to a tentative agreement . . ." the *Jacket* reports. "Teachers will receive an average 2% raise this year and a 9.5% raise next year . . . there will be a big increase for new teachers from $29,000 to nearly $35,000 . . ."

The *San Francisco Chronicle* reports that Governor Davis's decision to double California's public-school funding "helped enormously." " 'It's going to be wonderful to have the teachers free to focus all their energies back on the classroom,' [School Superintendent] McLaughlin said."

But at beleaguered Berkeley High, where the WASC accreditation audit has left the school on probationary status, the teachers must still devote considerable energies to nonclassroom matters, chief among them producing a report that will convince the Western Association of Schools and Colleges to keep Berkeley High accredited.

As the students of Berkeley High prepare for their final exams, the shortcomings that have put the school's accreditation to the test make the front page of the widely read *East Bay Express*. "Can Berkeley High Be Saved?" the headline asks. "One Thing's for Sure: It Cannot Survive Another Year Like This One."

Enumerating the disasters that have befallen the school during the 1999–2000 school year and its mostly unsuccessful efforts to resolve them, the *Express* calls Berkeley High "the petri dish of educational theorists across the country" that "will give us telling details of the next educational trend, programmatic innovation, or structural disaster likely to visit the rest of the country soon."

Indeed, the topics of the workgroups into which the Berkeley High teachers divide themselves for the last WASC meetings of the year accurately mirror America's most pressing educational issues: Achievement Disparity. Safety and Discipline. Tracking. Technology. Schoolwide Standards. Schoolwide Staff Development.

By halfway through the final meeting of the Achievement Disparity workgroup, the eight teachers present have discussed neither achievement nor the disparity between white students and students of color—the ostensible subject of the meeting. Despite (or perhaps because of) the many years that Berkeley High, and the nation, has spent grappling with the achievement gap and the complex philosophical issues it raises, the issue is reduced here to a mere matter of logistics.

"I think students should automatically fail a class if they miss ten days in a semester," a history teacher asserts.

"I think it should be fifteen," says another.

"Denial of positive privileges wouldn't be as hard to implement," argues a Spanish teacher. "Plus it would provide an incentive. We'd tell the kids that if they flunk a class they wouldn't get to do dances, sports, field trips—all the reasons kids think Berkeley High is great."

"At the Prom they should have to check their name on a list and not get in if they're failing," an ESL teacher suggests.

Annie Johnston, Keith's former history teacher, raises her hand. "Everything you're talking about is totally disciplinary," she says wearily, as she has said many times before. "You're just asking how we can push kids into class and keep them there. I have kids who come every day and fail. What about them? We need to increase tutoring. And resources available to students. And training for teachers, so we can work more effectively with students who traditionally fail."

Across the hall in the Safety and Discipline workgroup the discussion is very much the same.

"I think we have to address the discipline problem from both directions," a Social Living teacher is saying. "With stricter rules *and* more support for students."

"At the beginning of the year we said we needed a hall policy for students who come to school and don't go to class," says an English teacher. "The point was so we could serve those students. We lost sight of that objective, and we created a hall policy that doesn't do much good."

"We wanted to make the school a place where kids have a connection. The classroom is one place where that connection occurs," a history teacher says. "The hall policy was supposed to be a means to an end. It turned into an end in itself."

Theresa Saunders slips into the room. "I'm glad you came," the English teacher tells her. "We're really frustrated. And we're not ready to write up our report. Do we really have to have it in to the WASC Commission on the sixth?"

Saunders nods. "All you have to say," she replies, "is what your group has done to move us from where we were in September to where we are now."

The teachers gaze silently at their principal. No one says what she alone seems unable or unwilling to grasp: from September through June the WASC meetings have been duly attended, the teachers' time spent, discussions held, proposals recorded. And yet most teachers believe that there has been no movement, no progress, nothing to show for those hours at all.

As the students' grades are being compiled and students huddle with teachers all over campus, frantically negotiating for passing grades, the *Jacket* gives Theresa Saunders a report card of her own.

Communication with Students	C−
Staff Relations	F
Dealing with Crises	C
Dedication	B
New Policies	D
Leadership	C

While acknowledging that "Saunders still works tirelessly for BHS. She is here in the early morning and stays often past midnight," the accompanying *Jacket* editorial does not show the principal much mercy. "Most of Saunders' policies are so destructive that it is lucky for the school if they fail."

A story in the same issue announces, "Record Number of Teachers to Depart Berkeley High." A *Jacket* survey of Berkeley High's 185 teachers found that "Two-thirds of BHS teachers are planning to stay next year. Half of the remaining ones (32 to 58 teachers) are leaving for sure, and the rest are undecided." Of those who have already decided to leave, 65 percent are going on to teach at other public high schools in California; 25 percent are going to public high schools in other states.

The *Jacket* quotes a few of the 101 teachers who completed the survey. "I can no longer martyr myself to this profession. I am expected to give blood every day out of the goodness of my heart, and I'm just not going to survive if this sacrifice continues."

"Let the students run the school; they're more competent than the majority of the adults presently making the key decisions. Maximum suggested age for a school board member: 19."

"The way in which this teaching staff is treated is like old bubble gum on the heel of a tennis shoe. It is amazing that everyone does not leave."

"Despite the multitude of problems at BHS this year, I find it an exciting, stimulating place to work . . . If I gave up hope for progress at this high school, I would feel as if I were giving up on the future of public education."

• • •

On the parent E-tree, a query from a private school parent—"Why should we send our children to BHS?"—elicits a flood of positive responses. One parent anonymously posts his "Top Ten Reasons":

10. Because most of us can't afford to send our kids to private schools.
9. There are more kids of color than in any private school, and kids from every socioeconomic background—in other words, diversity.
8. Tons of activities and clubs—from Hapa to Ice Cream Lovers.
7. There are many, many sports—60 teams, 32 sports.
6. There's a great music program that produces the pep band (going to Japan this summer), the jazz band (been to Japan and Europe over the years), and performing arts/drama groups.
5. There's CAS—Communication Arts and Sciences—a program lauded by UCSC admissions (28 CAS students applied to UCSC, with 15 accepted outright—four African-Americans, four Latinos, and seven white), which leads into the fact that Rick Ayers, the head of CAS, along with his students, produces a great newspaper. Two *Berkeley High Jacket* reporters were written up in *People Magazine* about a story they broke ahead of all the major papers.
4. Community service and political activism—there are BHS kids who have found their voices and want to be heard for causes they believe in.
3. Some excellent teachers (dedicated, stay after school for hours helping students).
2. The BHS Health Center—complete in its services and maintains confidentiality.

1. BHS has the greatest college counselor for a high school ever in Rory Bled—colleges really like BHS students.

It's dynamic, creative, often chaotic, but teaches kids more about life and success than a safe, cocoon-like environment you might find in a private school. If your child stays in private school, you may feel you have less to worry about, but don't let that lull you into a sense of security—private school students go out and drink and binge on weekends as much as, or more than, BHS kids . . . The real world will come to your child eventually, and Berkeley High provides a microcosm.

．　．　．

"Get back in the car!" the cop yells at Keith. Keith freezes, his hand on the open door of his mother's car, which he's just parked in front of his grandmother's West Berkeley house. The cop shoves him by the shoulders. *"I said get back in the car!"*

"What the fuck—" Keith sputters. He glances up at the porch, sees his grandma and his sister Latisha standing there, both of them looking mad—at the cop or at him, he can't tell. Latisha told him not to take the Intrepid, his mom's second car, because the registration was expired. But Keith's nephew Alonzo needed to be picked up from day care, and Keith was eager to use the driver's license he'd finally gotten yesterday, and the Intrepid was just sitting there. "Quit trippin'," Keith told Latisha, and drove off with his friend Dimitri in the passenger seat. "Ain't nothin' gonna go wrong," he muttered to Dimitri. And nothing did, until Keith pulled up in front of Mama's house and the unmarked Task Force cop car pulled up behind them.

The cop grabs Keith now, yanks his hands behind his back, presses a billy club against Keith's throat. Keith feels like he's about to pass out. "Leave him alone!" Latisha shouts. "He didn't do anything!"

Another cop, a big white guy, starts clubbing Keith on his back, his legs, his head. "Stop it!" Latisha screams and runs down to the sidewalk. The cop swings wildly, hitting her too. The neighbors hear their cries, gather around the scene. From her porch Mama calls out to her grandchildren, then pushes her way through the agitated crowd. She starts yelling at the cops to stop; she, too, is whacked with the club.

Police cars are coming from everywhere now. The cops jump out of their cars, shove the bystanders back. They put Keith, his grandmother, and his sister into three different cars. They take Keith and Latisha to the Berkeley City jail. They take Mama to Santa Rita Prison.

Latisha calls her mother at work. As soon as Patricia hears where Latisha's calling from, she starts to cry. "Mama's charged with inciting a riot," Latisha tells her. "They got me for interfering with an officer. And Mom—" Latisha's voice breaks. "Keith has two felonies on him. Including assault on a police officer. I know these po-lice are just probably talkin' shit, but they're saying he's gonna be in jail a long time."

"Oh, my God. Oh, my God," Patricia whispers. The room swirls around her. "Is Keith hurt real bad?" she gasps. "Do they know Mama has a heart condition? Does she have her medicine? How much is the bail?"

"I told them about Mama's heart. Keith's got a big knot on his head. I don't know about the bail."

"I'll be there as soon as I can," Patricia says. She clocks out, drives home, and gets on the phone. Latisha's bail is the cheapest—five thousand dollars. Mama's is eighteen thousand. Keith's is thirty-five. Patricia briefly considers calling her husband at work—she knows he's got a little something stashed away. But she also knows that she won't get the support she wants, financial or emotional. He'll blame the whole thing on Keith, tell her to let the boy take his knocks. She calls friends, church members, relatives instead.

By nine the next morning Patricia has paid the bail bondsman his ten percent fee—twenty-three hundred nonrefundable dollars—and Mama and Latisha are out of jail. She keeps making calls, trying to get enough for Keith, but it's no use. Today is Saturday; Keith's arraignment is Monday. She won't be able to get him out until he goes before the judge—

and even then, only if the judge lets him out without bail. Keith will have to spend the weekend—his Prom night—in jail.

Patricia can't stand to think any further ahead than that. All day Saturday, while she's taking pictures of the bruises on her mother's and daughter's bodies, and trying to find a lawyer who will take the case by Monday (preferably on spec, since she's now so deep in debt), Patricia struggles to keep her mind off Keith: what he must be going through in jail, what might happen to him in court, what happens to young black men once they're caught up in the prison system. At dinnertime, when Keith should have been getting dressed for his Prom, Patricia gives up trying. She goes to Keith's closet, finds the rented tux he hung in there just yesterday. She smooths the black satin lapels, straightens the stiff white shirt collar, rubs a scuff off the shiny black patent-leather shoes— just as she would have done if her baby were standing before her now, strong and proud and handsome. Then Patricia falls to her son's bedroom floor and cries as she's never cried before.

In a city of beauty, the Palace of Fine Arts is one of San Francisco's most breathtaking sights: ringed by Corinthian columns, reflected in a shimmering swan-filled pond, kissed night and day by the gentle breezes of the bay. Alongside it is the Exploratorium, the friendliest of kid-friendly museums, where parents bring children on weekends and teachers bring children on field trips so that they can learn to love science by twisting dials, blowing bubbles, measuring their own shadows.

Tonight the Exploratorium has been transformed into a night club for the delight of children who aren't really children any more: the Berkeley High School graduating Class of 2000. They arrive in twos and fours in rented cars and airport shuttles; in groups of eighteen in $950-a-night limos a city block long. The couples—about one-third of them interracial—emerge like royalty stepping down from their carriages. The boys are self-consciously chivalrous, the girls stiffly ladylike, in their custom-fitted tuxes and cutaway gowns, their white-on-black zoot suits and curry-colored saris. They are adorned with carnations pinned to their lapels and orchids circling their wrists; their hair is braided into dizzying concentric swirls, sprayed into elaborate sculptures, gelled into simple, startling spikes, flowing like spun silk down their lithe, naked backs.

They are greeted at the door by silver towers of "Class of 2000" balloons, by music seeping out from the dance floor, and by Billy Keys, Ms. Marantz, and Theresa Saunders, each armed with a metal detector and using it. Boys—or are they men, now?—are herded into one line; girls—women, now?—into another. Purses are searched, pockets are patted, bodies are swept. "No In And Out," one hand-lettered sign reads. "No Ticket, No In," reads another.

And then, with few exceptions—Keith's cousin Mimi, wearing one of the many bare-down-the-middle, wannabe Jennifer Lopez dresses on display here tonight, is deemed too nude for her own or someone else's good, and is frantically worked over by Ms. Marantz and Ms. Saunders, who finally give up trying to pin and tape Mimi's dress together and drape her instead in a teacher's borrowed sweater—their tickets are taken and the members of the Class of 2000 are admitted to the one, the only senior ball of their lives.

Graduating or not, Jordan is doing his Prom and doing it right. He and Kristen have broken up again—for good this time, he swears, since she told him she was seeing someone else on the very night that Jordan's uncle died. His date for the evening is Claire, a friend and nothing more, although she is the first girl he ever kissed, way back when they were in middle school together.

Jordan, Claire, and twenty or so of their friends—most of them private-school classmates before the Berkeley High years—kicked off the evening with an "informal dinner" at one girl's not-at-all-informal home. Way up a serpentine street in the North Berkeley hills, with panoramic bay views and manicured terraced gardens, the house—the whole scene—made Jordan feel what he feels so often: the paradox of his Berkeley High life. Wealthier by far than the vast majority of his fellow B-High students, he is poorer by far than most of the ones he hangs out with.

Indeed, it was a well-heeled group that gathered to see Jordan's entourage off to the ball. Parents in khaki shorts and designer T-shirts, sipping fine California wines, congratulating each other on their progeny's Ivy League admissions; Promgoers in traditional tuxes and long, flowing gowns, looking more like a finishing school class en route to a cotillion than a bunch of seniors on their way to the Berkeley High Prom. Mingling, chatting, posing graciously for the professional photographer who circulated through the crowd, adults and teens alike nibbled delicately from artfully arranged platters of sushi, asparagus spears, perfect long-stemmed strawberries. "So—where's Jordan off to in September?" someone's mom asked Jordan's. Looking conspicuously downtown in her trademark black clothes and hip, hennaed bob, Natalie answered smoothly "Santa Cruz," and took another bite of brie.

While the parents gossiped and lamented their children's ascent into adulthood, the teenagers clandestinely collected cash to fund the evening's main event: the booze-drinking, pot-smoking after-party at the home of a parent willing to provide the empty house but not the "refreshments." Older siblings were recruited to go and make the buy.

At 9:30 Jordan, Claire, and fourteen others piled into the buslike limo that pulled up outside the door. The limo they took to the Junior Prom last year had an indoor-outdoor hot tub; this one features a dance floor. At ten they arrive, disembark, join the line of seniors waiting to be frisked. Once they're inside, picture-taking is the first order of business. "Nine hundred kids, incompetent people," Jordan complains, an hour into his first wait on a photo line. He has his picture taken with Claire in a romantic pose utterly unrepresentative of their feelings for each other, then he waits an hour in another line to pose with a group of friends.

Jordan has accomplished all of that *and* danced himself into a drenching sweat by the time Autumn and her friends arrive. And what an entrance they make: statuesque Autumn in her three-hundred-dollar, pale green silk-and-velvet gown and matching chiffon shawl, a stick-on rhinestone "third eye" glittering on her forehead, a henna tattoo snaking down her bared back; Lillian in a body-hugging black knit dress, its revealing cutouts concealed from Ms. Marantz's scrutiny by the long coat she discards upon admittance; Emily wearing a short, clinging, silver silk dress and matching high-heeled mules from Bebe; Emily's childhood friend Nicole, pretty in pink satin. None of the girls is here with a boyfriend—including Autumn, who doesn't have one anymore. "Things just kind of came to a standstill" between her and Jareem after she went to his Prom a few weeks ago. "I still think he's hecka cool, but as far as being in a relationship, it's not happening. We weren't doing that much besides talking on the phone, so nobody's heartbroken or anything."

Instead, Autumn's Prom date is André, her ninth-grade boyfriend, whom she sees every week at church. "I thought it would be more fun going to the Prom with a friend instead of pumping it up into this big thing." Lillian's date is a popular boy named Ahmad; Nicole is with Dennis, a guy she met a week ago on the Prom ticket–buying line at school ($40 for one, $75 per couple). Emily is with Josh Gray, who worked at the movie theater on Shattuck for months to save up to buy his silver-gray suit and Italian leather shoes.

Autumn is in high spirits, standing on the picture line, although the evening got off to a rough start. According to the plan the four couples had agreed upon at their planning meeting a week ago (the written version of which was typed, copied, and distributed by Emily), their group was supposed to meet at Emily's house near Berkeley High at six. At 6:45 they were to drive in a caravan of borrowed cars to the Equinox restaurant at the San Francisco Hyatt. That's where Autumn's mother works; she'd arranged for them to have an eight o'clock dinner reservation and a 10 percent discount. But everyone was running late, and it was eight by the time everyone got to Emily's. "Come *on*, black people!" Emily fumed, sitting in her living room with her parents and Josh, eating cheese cubes and Wheat Thins, taking pictures with Josh's disposable camera. So Autumn had to call her mom, who had to call her boss, who squeezed them in at 9:30 and even brought them free cheese-cake for dessert.

"See? It's all good," Autumn told a slowly mellowing Emily as they were eating their cheesecake. Autumn called her mom on her new cell phone, which she held up at the table so that everyone could say "Thank you, Pam!" into it. Autumn's mom and stepfather were being hecka nice about the Prom: her mom had hooked up their dinner, and her stepfather had let Autumn take his Cadillac, even though she'd hardly even driven since she got her license a year ago. Plus, he gave her $70 to help with expenses. Tony could be generous like that, and Autumn appreciated it every time it happened.

"This is sooo beautiful," Autumn crooned as the waiter delivered her second glass of orange juice. "I've *got* to come back here some time." She looked around the lushly appointed room, dabbed at her lips with the thick linen napkin. "Yeah, *right,*" she grinned at her friends. At $55 a person, that wasn't likely to happen any time soon.

After dinner they'd driven across town to the Exploratorium, honking and waving along the way to classmates passing them in limos. Arriving, they'd parked and joined one line, then another.

As soon as their pictures are taken Autumn and the girls check their wraps and head for the dance floor. It looks beautiful, they agree, with disco lights flashing and puffs of artificial smoke wafting across the floor. But the music is wack—K.C. and the Sunshine Band, Michael *Jackson!*— which explains why mostly only white kids are dancing. So they fix themselves strawberry sundaes at the free ice cream bar, drink a few cups of orange soda, and spend a few happy, final hours with the Class of 00.

The Prom ends at two, and the four couples caravan back over the Bay Bridge to Berkeley. With Autumn in the lead they drive up into the hills and park at the fog-shrouded Lawrence Hall of Science, overlooking the glittering lights of their town. They hang out there for hours, reminiscing about the evening. "It wasn't a spectacular, submit-it-to-Oprah kind of Prom," Autumn says, "but it was hecka fun. All I wanted was to dress up and be with my friends at the end of our high school years together." She sighs contentedly. "And what I got was exactly what I wanted."

. . .

"Keith Stevens," the bailiff calls out.

"*Ste-fens!*" The fifteen friends and family members in the courtroom correct his pronunciation in one loud voice. The judge, the district attorney, and the lawyer who's here on Keith's behalf—who told them when he got here that the charges against Latisha and Mama have been dropped—all turn and scowl a warning in their direction.

A door opens. Keith emerges into the glassed-in witness box, accompanied by a beefy bailiff. There's a dark lump on his forehead; his hair is scruffy and matted; his black Playboy T-shirt—the one he was wearing when he was arrested three days ago—is ripped and limp with grime.

"Mr. Stephens has no prior charges, Your Honor," Keith's lawyer says. "We ask that he be released on his own recognizance."

"The people oppose this release," the DA snaps. "Mr. Stephens faces two misdemeanor counts: battery on a police officer and resisting arrest. We consider him a danger to the community."

"Do you understand the charges against you?" the judge asks Keith.

Keith nods, his face downcast.

"Mr. Stephens," the judge says, frowning again, "you must speak up when you're in a court of law."

"Yeah," Keith mutters.

"Two of his teachers are here, Your Honor," Keith's lawyer says quickly. He turns to Mr. McKnight and Ms. Russ, both of whom visited Keith in jail over the weekend, both of whom have found teachers to cover their classes this afternoon so they can attend Keith's arraignment. "You were not subpoenaed to be here, were you?" the lawyer asks them.

Both teachers stand. "No," says Ms. Russ. "No, sir," says Mr. McKnight.

"You know this young man?" the lawyer asks.

"I'm a teacher at Berkeley High School," Ms. Russ says. "I've known Keith for three years."

"Robert McKnight. Department chair, African-American Studies, Berkeley High School. I have been with Keith for three years as well."

"The defendant's attack on the police officer shows a lack of respect for the law," the DA interjects. "He mumbled his answers. He's smirking right now. And his friends are making noise in the courtroom. I object to letting him go on OR."

"What his friends are doing has nothing to do with him," Keith's lawyer says.

"Do you understand how serious this is?" the judge asks Keith. "Do you understand that you're facing up to one and a half years in county jail?"

"Yes, *ma'am*," Keith says loudly this time.

"I'm going to release you. You need to come back here on Friday at two o'clock with your lawyer. Do you understand?"

"Yes, ma'am," Keith says again. An hour later he appears in the court-house lobby, holding his baggy jeans up with his hand.

"You weren't supposed to take that car," his father greets him.

"They took your belt, huh?" his sisters tease him, threatening to pull down his pants.

"You awwight, little man?" his brother asks, clapping him on the back. Patricia pushes past her children and her husband, throws her arms around her son, and holds him close till he begs her to let him go.

"Officer Attacked After Traffic Stop," the front page of the *Berkeley Daily Planet* proclaimed the day after Keith's arrest. Outraged by the article's assertion that "a 21-year-old man allegedly hit a Berkeley police officer," Patricia saw to it that the *Planet* sent a reporter to the arraignment to get the family's side of the story.

"Family: Teen Was Victim in Police Confrontation," the *Planet*'s turn-about headline reads the day after the arraignment. "Keith Stephens just got his driver's license last Thursday, and the 18-year-old Berkeley High student was looking forward to Saturday night's Senior Ball. Instead, he spent the weekend in the Berkeley jail . . ."

"[BPD] Capt. Bobby Miller said Stephens 'jumped out of the car' and when the officers asked him to return to the car he refused and hit [BPD

Officer] Gardner in the head and body with his fist . . . Gardner used his baton to bring the suspect under control, said Miller . . .

"Stephens' mother, Patricia, said her son has held two jobs while in high school and he wants to be a firefighter . . . She said police pulled out the dashboard on her car, and she maintains they were looking for drugs.

" 'This is a case of driving while black,' she said. 'I feel he can have gold chains and a diamond earring. If he works he can have those things without dealing drugs.' "

Since the issue of racial profiling gained national prominence several months ago, there have been ACLU posters all over Berkeley High proclaiming that "Driving While Black (DWB) Is Not A Crime!" Even before Keith comes back to school on Tuesday, everyone at Berkeley High knows he's been DWBd—including Black Student Union president Josh Gray, who's been circulating a petition to that effect.

> DROP THE CHARGES AGAINST KEITH STEPHENS
> INVESTIGATE THE POLICE INVOLVED IN BRUTALIZING
> HIM AND HIS FAMILY

"Keith and I mess with each other," Josh explains, "but blood is thicker than water. We're good friends. We have deep talks sometimes about what we're doin' with our lives, about school, about being black men."

Josh shows Keith the petition as they're walking to Mr. McKnight's class, with Keith accepting high-fives and hugs from most of the black kids who pass him in the halls. "We should have a protest rally when you go to court on Friday," Josh says.

"I don't know if I deserve that, man," Keith says. "I did somethin' hella stupid. The lawyer says I signed a confession."

"What you mean, confession?" Josh asks. "You didn't do nothin'."

"The lawyer got the police report. It says I signed a confession when they arrested me."

"Well, did you?" Josh asks.

Keith shrugs. "I signed *somethin'*. When they first brung me in they was pushing papers at me, telling me to hurry up and sign 'em or else. The lawyer says we're gonna have to get Ms. Russ to testify that I'm . . . slow with my reading."

"That ain't no confession, Blood," Josh says. "That's *blackmail*." Within hours a flyer appears around campus, calling for a rally "in support of Keith Stephens and his family."

> We as a community must come together to express that racism and police brutality will not be tolerant.
> PLEASE COME WITH RESPECT!

The flyer is jointly signed by Josh and "Student Activist" Megan Parkinson, a white girl in Keith's Poetry class, who burst into tears when Ms. Theodore, their teacher, made Keith tell the class the whole story of his DWB. Ms. Theodore's is the only class Keith has ever had that has AP students like Megan in it—and, much to his surprise, Megan has got more petitions signed than anyone. The first signature she got was David Bye's, her AP English teacher. And then she got nearly the whole class to sign.

On Thursday night, Keith's lawyer tells him that his next court appearance has been postponed. Keith tells Josh, who says it's too late to call off the rally. "We already gave out two hundred flyers at school. We'll have the rally anyway."

Keith can hardly believe his eyes when his mom drives him and his family up to the courthouse on Friday. There must be fifty people here: A few of them are his cousins, a couple of friends, Ms. Johnston, and Josh of course, but the rest are kids and teachers he doesn't even know, and a whole bunch of them are white. They're waving banners and signs at the cars driving by on Martin Luther King Way; a lot of the drivers are honking back in support.

DROP THE CHARGES ON KEITH STEPHENS!

JUST BECAUSE I'M BEHIND THE WHEEL
DOESN'T MEAN THAT I WILL STEAL

THE ONLY COLORS THAT MATTER WHILE DRIVING ARE RED,
GREEN, AND YELLOW

DWB
ASSUME THE BEST INSTEAD OF THE WORST

"We're here to protest police brutality against Keith Stephens," Josh shouts into a bullhorn. "Berkeley is supposed to be so liberal. But even in Berkeley we have a system of racism. Now I'll introduce Keith Stephens."

Keith nudges his sister Latisha. "You talk," he tells her. Latisha frowns at Keith but takes the bullhorn anyway. "The police beat up an eighteen-year-old black man with gold teeth and an Afro," she says, "and his sixty-five-year-old grandmother, and his twenty-six-year-old sister, which is me. Now we're gonna walk around the corner to the Berkeley Police Department and tell them to put the officer on trial, not Keith."

As the protesters line up, and Keith's grandmother walks through the crowd kissing people's cheeks and thanking them for coming, Keith sidles up to Latisha and takes the bullhorn from her.

"I just want to thank you for showing up for me," he says, his voice reverberating through the open courthouse doors. "I'm kinda choked up to see all these people here for me. Thank you."

"ONE TWO THREE! STOP PO-LICE BRUTALITY!" the demonstrators shout, marching down Martin Luther King toward Berkeley High. They file into police headquarters, thunder up the stairs.

"JUSTICE FOR KEITH! JUSTICE FOR KEITH!" *This sure is a better way to come in here than the way I came in here before*, Keith thinks. Ten months ago he was carried up these stairs, hog-tied and bleeding, having been arrested for throwing dice in an alleyway. Last week he was locked up in jail here, battered by a billy club because the car he was driving had expired tags.

"DROP THE CHARGES ON KEITH! PUT THE COPS ON TRIAL!" The amplified chants boom through the silent halls. Uniformed policemen stare out from behind their desks; an internal affairs officer in a suit approaches the group and asks to speak to their spokesperson. Patricia steps forward. "We're here to file charges of police brutality," she says. He ushers her into his office and Latisha addresses the demonstrators. "Our job here is done for today. Thank you for coming," she says, "and we'll see you in court next time."

"Drop the charges on Keith! Put the cops on trial!" shout the Berkeley High students and three teachers—Annie Johnston, Amy Crawford, and Rick Ayers—as the crowd disperses. "Drop the charges on me!" Keith chants along, grinning his mischievous grin. "Put the cops on trial!"

But of course it's Keith, not the cops, who will be on trial next week, the Monday after graduation.

There is one event that always brings out every Berkeley High family, one event that brings the whole Berkeley High community together. That event is graduation. And as the first strains of "Pomp and Circumstance" waft through the Greek amphitheater on June 15, everyone there roars with one voice: the parents whose children are going to Yale, the parents whose children may be going to jail, the judges and the maids, the garbage collectors and computer consultants—the several thousand white, black, Latino, Asian, Native American, and multiracial families of the 730 graduating members of Berkeley High's Class of 2000.

As the procession of seniors emerges from the wings in a slow-moving blur of red and yellow, the roar erupts into cheers, and voices in the crowd become distinct. In Spanish, in Mandarin, in Farsi, in many dialects of English they scream their children's names, these parents who have carried their teenagers this far, only, now, to let them go. "Suquori!" "Xochitl!" "Ryan!" "Pranomphone!" "Ebonee!"

Determined to express their individuality right up to this very last of their Berkeley High moments, many seniors have decorated the tops of their caps, the one thing that's clearly visible from the rows of stone benches cut into the steep hillside. One boy's yellow cap sports a bright red hammer and sickle; another's, the Israeli flag. There are bouncing fuzzy yellow jackets, a Free Tibet bumper sticker, a glittering map of planet earth, a sign that says, "I'm Supposed To Be Naked."

From ground level other signs of distinction are visible: the red-white-and-green-striped scarves of the Chicano/Latino graduates; the varicolored mudcloth scarves of the African-American students; the white silk scarves of Asian Pride; the black-and-white CAS scarves whose motto—"Consciousness Through Creative Communications"—was coined, after much going-nowhere classroom debate, by the ever-on-task Autumn Morris. Many students wear more than one scarf. Lillian wears Asian Pride intertwined with her African Nefertiti print. Autumn wears mudcloth over CAS. And Keith wears a huge "Chevy's Fresh Mex" sombrero.

"Your diversity is your greatest asset," says the commencement speaker—not the traditional CEO or college dean, but popular teacher Wyn Skeels, named "honorary member of the Class of 2000" by his adoring students. "You are the most inspiring people I know. Now go out and create a world where the bottom line is, everybody wins." He quotes a Nelson Mandela poem, then concludes, "To the Class of 2000: I love you very much."

Ben Watson-Lamprey, the student speaker, greets the crowd, "Good afternoon students, teachers, parents, and arsonist," then offers a send-up of Mr. Wiggan that gives the kids—and many knowing parents—the opportunity to boo "Wiggins" one last time. The African-Haitian and Dance Production troupes perform a memorial to deceased dance teacher Marcia Singman; CAS student Christelle Lewis and Autumn's "other half" Daveed Diggs each slam a poem. Catherine from CAS and a girl named Jolie sing "Count on Me," Catherine's round, brown body swaying in sweet harmony with Jolie's tall, blue-eyed blondeness.

Theresa Saunders knows better than to address this group at length; she tells the seniors simply, "You are the class of the Millennium. You've been good, faithful, enduring." She turns to the superintendent of schools. "I present to you the Class of 2000. They have completed their graduation requirements and are thus ready to receive their diplomas."

"Wrong on both counts," Jordan whispers to the boy next to him, as the parents cheer. No one will actually receive a diploma today. At rehearsal this morning the seniors were advised that their black leather diploma folders would be empty—"In case anyone decides to do anything cute like take their clothes off or fill their water bottles with vodka. Those people will be doing community service tomorrow before they get their diplomas."

Furthermore, today's *San Francisco Chronicle* carried the headline "Berkeley High Grade Scandal" and claimed that ". . . at least 20 Berkeley High School seniors are under suspicion for allegedly paying a classmate to sneak into the school's administrative computer and raise their grades." No one knows better than Jordan how easily the vagaries of the Berkeley High computer can twist a student's fate. His presence on this stage, uncertain until an hour ago when he saw his name printed in the program with the others, is living proof of that.

"On behalf of the board of education," Superintendent McLaughlin replies, "we are ready to accept the Class of 2000."

And then the awarding of "diplomas" begins—moving in meaning, numbing by virtue of sheer numbers. For the next two hours a relay team of teachers, their years at "the most integrated high school in America" evidenced by their near-perfect pronunciation, reads each of the seven hundred and thirty names listed in the program. The seniors dance and shimmy and cartwheel and are pushed in a wheelchair across the stage; they hug each other and their teachers, glare at Mr. Wiggan in the wings, wave to their parents, take their seats, and wait for their 729 classmates to do the same.

Damn. I'm out, Jordan thinks, watching the others walk the stage. He waits for a surge of emotion; is not surprised when all that arises is a moment of relief—*I graduated after all*—followed by a heated rush of rage. *Don't make promises you can't keep,* Jordan silently tells his dead father. Even in his most deeply addicted moments, Jordan's dad always made one promise to his son. "No matter what," he must have told Jordan twenty times, "I'll be there to see you graduate from high school."

Jordan twists around in his folding metal chair and looks up to the far right side of the very top row, where his mom told him she'd be sitting. Above all the heads and waving arms and balloons and banners, incredibly, he sees her. He tips his cap in her direction; she waves back energetically. Even from here Jordan can see the ear-to-ear grin on her face. *At least I made her happy,* he thinks. *That's gotta be worth something.*

Autumn and Lillian have been separated throughout the two-hour ceremony by the several hundred students between the Bs (Lillian) and the Ms (Autumn). Freed, finally, from the tyranny of the alphabet, they find each other after they've both walked the stage. "We just made a big-ass memory," Autumn tells Lillian. "You don't make a memory like that every day. It's right up there with freaking *marriage!* Being *born!*"

The two girls lean their heads as close together as their caps will allow. "I'm gonna miss you, Lil," Autumn says, thinking, *If you really go through with that Xavier thing.* Lately Lil's been talking like she just might change her mind and go to Cal with Autumn after all. Despite her vow to support Lil whatever she does, Autumn has secretly added that to her list of prayers, right below finding the money for Summer Bridge, which starts in two weeks, and for college. *After all I've been through to get into Cal, God's just got to find me a way to go there,* Autumn tells herself every day. Just in case her prayers don't come through, Emily's mom has promised to help with the first payment.

"Can you spend the night tonight?" Autumn asks Lil.

"Fo' sho," Lil says.

"We can take pictures with your family, then you can get a ride home with us," Autumn says. *At least we'll have the next two weeks together,* she thinks.

Keith knows exactly where his family is sitting: right behind Mama, easy to spot in her red sequined baseball cap. He waves to his mom; his eyes are glued to her the whole time he's walking across the stage. Patricia jumps up and down, her arms flying around her head. *Dang,* Keith realizes, *she's crying again.* With newfound maturity befitting a high school graduate, he decides to consider this from *her* point of view. *I guess that's something to her, to see her last child walk the stage.* He hopes she's not crying because she's worrying about his court case. *Ain't no way I'm goin' to jail,* he tells himself for maybe the hundredth time. *I can't be a fireman with that kinda thing on my record.*

Keith takes his seat, pulls his sombrero onto his head. He feels sad for a minute, thinking of all the people he started with at Berkeley High who aren't here today. *Four years flew by hella fast.*

He glances up at the stage, sees Ms. Russ hugging his friend Dimitri. He remembers all the times Ms. Russ warned him that if he didn't finish this paper, didn't take that class, he wouldn't get to graduate. *I knew I'd make it,* he thinks. *I'm glad Ms. Russ had my back. But I never doubted it for a minute.*

Afterword

Everything We Need to Know We Can Learn
from Our High Schools

As I write this it's June 16, the day after graduation. My one year, Autumn, Jordan, and Keith's four years at Berkeley High are over. My editor waits for the manuscript; the printer waits for the disk. Impossible as it seems, this book will be in stores twelve weeks from today. The project is concluding; it's time to draw conclusions.

But conclusions invite predictions. And one of many lessons I've learned during this, my last year of high school, is the danger of making predictions—especially where the lives of teenagers are concerned. In September I thought Autumn was likely to end up at a junior or state college, Jordan would glide effortlessly into Bard, Keith would fail too many classes to graduate. Those were the odds. For better and for worse, all three kids beat them.

This morning I asked Autumn, Jordan, and Keith where they thought they'd be ten years from now. For the first time ever, all three of them answered a question of mine in exactly the same way: they laughed. And then each of them said, in his or her own language and inflection, that they have no idea what they'll be doing next month, let alone when they're twenty-eight years old. And how could they? Autumn is scheduled to start at UC Berkeley in two weeks, and she doesn't know how she's going to pay for it. Jordan still hasn't figured out whether he's eligible to go to UC Santa Cruz in September, or if he wants to go, or what he might do once he gets there. Keith plans to go to junior college, try out for the team, give his NFL dream one last try, with Fire Science as a backup plan—but the criminal "justice" system has other plans for Keith.

And Berkeley High itself? "You picked a hell of a year to write about," teachers kept telling me: when the college adviser bungled the seniors' college applications; when four hundred students walked out of their classes in protest; when teachers boycotted staff meetings and held demonstrations and work slow-downs; and the local media's favorite story seemed to be "What's Wrong with Berkeley High."

"Every year's an amazing year at Berkeley High," I kept answering, until an arsonist—believed to be a staff member, and to this day on the loose—nearly burned down the school. Even on graduation day, Berkeley High captured headlines with a grade-tampering scandal that has caused the school to withhold the diplomas of the entire graduating class. The school will open in September (another prediction!) with its campus still fire-ravaged, its accreditation still uncertain, its teachers—including Greg Giglio, who has taken a job at the mostly white high school in mostly white Pleasanton, where he lives—quitting in record numbers, and its entire administration, it has just been announced, replaced. Theresa Saunders has been assigned to a district post, overseeing the district's music program and its efforts to close the achievement gap. Vice Principal Doris Wallace-Tanner is taking a medical leave of absence. Guillermo Barcenas is being demoted from his temporary assignment as Vice Principal back to counselor.

Berkeley High is a behemoth of flaws and contradictions. And if I had it to do all over again, I wouldn't send my kids anywhere else.

In "Why I Love Berkeley High," his response to an exposé of the school in a local newspaper, Class of 2000 senior Noam Biale wrote, "There is a vitality at Berkeley High that I believe is unparalleled . . . The impossible task that Berkeley High has before it is to make the school work for everyone. However, the complexity of this duty is so deeply rooted in society that the school has little hope for accomplishing it . . ."

Noam is right. As a nation we have tough questions to answer, tough decisions to make, dramatically different priorities to manifest if our schools are to change for the better. This one prediction I willingly risk: if we continue to turn our heads from these questions, continue to delay these decisions, we will never have the teenagers, the schools, or the society we claim to want.

We must first ask ourselves, and answer honestly, what we want our schools to *do*. If the purpose of educating our children is to prepare a tiny number of them to own and run the country, a slightly larger number of them to ensure the profitability of our corporations, and the vast majority to flip our burgers, clean our hotel rooms, and fill our prisons—in short, to maintain our greed-driven, stratified society as it now exists—then we are doing an excellent job, and we should change nothing.

If, on the other hand, we want our schools to mend, not perpetuate, the sharpening division between Americans of different races and classes; to produce the kind of brilliant, compassionate human beings we all want to work with and drive alongside of and live next door to; to recognize and nurture the miracle that is every child's mind, heart, and potential—then we must radically restructure the American system of education.

I cast my vote for the latter. Toward that end—derived from what I saw, heard, and felt during my years as a parent, volunteer, and journalist at "the most integrated high school in America"—I offer this five-point plan.

1. Abolish private schools

Private schools are a prime instrument for maintaining inequities in education and in society. If we are to fulfill America's yet-unkept promise of democracy, we must first close the hatches through which those with money and privilege escape the common fate. "To the extent change is possible," Berkeley High parent and UC Berkeley professor Pedro Noguera writes in the June 2, 2000, issue of *The Nation,* "it is more likely to occur in education than in any other sector."

Such change cannot occur as long as wealthy children are taught in small, well-equipped classes by highly skilled professionals, and poor children founder in overcrowded, decaying classrooms with untrained "emergency credential" teachers. We must close the escape hatch—because until public schools have to be good enough for everyone, they won't be good enough for anyone.

In the interim we must immediately abolish private-school vouchers, an insidiously seductive scheme to siphon much-needed public funds from desperately underfunded public schools.

2. Make public schools more like private schools

Everything parents pay for when they write checks to private schools can be replicated in public schools—if we as a nation are willing to write the check. (Wondering where the money will come from? Hint to legislators: check the federal budget. In fiscal year 2000 the government is spending $291 billion on the military and $35 billion on education.) We should exponentially increase per-pupil spending in *every* school. In the process we should bring to a long-overdue end the disparity between the funding of affluent suburban schools and the funding of schools in poor neighborhoods—and put to rest the dangerous notion of decreasing funds to schools whose students perform poorly on standardized tests. Then we will be able to offer *every* child:

- A modern, well equipped, and—dare I suggest it?—beautiful, safe, student-friendly campus of 1,000 students or less. (Small schools have been proven to be safer and more effective. Their students have higher grade point averages, higher attendance and graduation rates, and lower rates of failed classes, retention, and violence);
- The choice to attend magnet schools that nurture particular interests and talents: in the arts, or in medicine, computer technology, religion, ecology, etc.
- Classes of twenty students or less;
- An engaging, rigorous curriculum taught by motivated, talented teachers;
- Challenging but attainable academic standards, measured

not by distracting, discriminatory, mass-administered standardized testing (which leads to "ram, remember, re-gurgitate" teaching) but by the achievement of individual goals (see below);

- A personalized education plan, modeled on the Individual Education Plan currently used for special ed students and the Individual Learning Plan implemented by many charter schools, which brings together teacher, family, and student to set and monitor goals and milestones for each child's academic, vocational, and personal development;

- *Real* guidance counselors with the time, training, and dedication it takes to be the mentors, role models, and allies all young people need—on site, at school, where students spend most of their waking hours.

3. Abolish segregated schools and segregated classes

As long as our neighborhoods are separate and unequal, so will our neighborhood public schools be. As long as our neighborhood public schools are separate and unequal, so will our neighborhoods be. We cannot level the economic and social playing field, we cannot offer equal opportunity to all, without providing all with an equal education. We cannot offer all an equal education as long as our school districts and schools are segregated. By combining busing with school choice (as the Berkeley Unified School District does), or by any means possible, we must ensure that the population of every American school—its administrators and teachers as well as its students—mirrors the population of the city or region that it serves.

In the interim, we must end the practice of tracking. Aptly named, the practice sends wealthy children down the road to greater wealth and entitlement, while it slams poor children into the dead end of deepening demoralization and poverty. Let's make school a sanctuary from, not an enforcer of, inequity, division, and "me-first" individualism. Let's give all of our children the benefit of each other—by educating them in heterogeneous classes where rich kids and poor kids, "challenged" and "advanced" kids, native Spanish speakers and fourth-year Latin students learn together and learn from one another. Let's include in our definition of "higher standards" the expectation that our children will learn to respect, admire, and share their gifts and needs with others. Let's put all our children in the same boat, then work together to raise the level of the river.

4. Pay teachers what they're worth

What is the value of a good teacher to a child, a community, a nation? Should a teacher earn the same salary as a sales clerk? (Many do, in a calculation of their hourly wage.) A prison guard? (In California, starting teachers earn around two-thirds as much.) A software developer? An advertising executive? A senator? (Not even close.)

Should teachers be paid for half of the hours they work? For most of the hours? For all of them?

Should teachers be able to afford to live in the communities where they teach?

Should teachers be trained thoroughly before they enter a classroom, and continuously as long as they're there?

Should we be able to keep and reward excellent teachers and promptly rescue our children from the others?

As every adult who's been influenced by a teacher knows, there is no more significant determinant of a child's success or a school's ability to educate its students than its teachers. Whether we do it because we value our children, or we do it to sharpen America's competitive edge in the global marketplace, the important thing is that we just do it: retrain or fire bad teachers; pay good teachers fairly for what they do.

5. Get families into the schools

Endless studies have been conducted and analyzed, countless programs devised, many hands wrung over the lack of parental involvement—particularly that of minority parents—in the schools. The problem is serious: in order to succeed, kids need their parents, and so do the schools. Solving the problem will be difficult, but it is not hard to understand.

Parents must invest their time and money wisely. Most of the parents who attend teacher conferences, back-to-school nights, and PTA meetings are those who have reason to believe that participating in their children's education is a worthwhile investment. That is, they believe that the school is willing and able to educate their children, and that a good education will improve their children's chances of success in life. Not coincidentally, these tend to be the same parents who have the most flexible work schedules (so they can volunteer at school during the day), the most help at home (so they can attend nighttime meetings), the most disposable income (so they can sponsor field trips and donate computers). They also tend to be the parents who have reaped the benefits of education in their own lives, whose circumstances are better than their parents' because of it.

On the other hand, parents (and grandparents and other guardians) who don't believe that the school is willing and/or able to provide their child with an education, or who believe that whatever education their child gets will not ensure a better life—for example, if they believe that their child is likely to be arrested for Driving While Black, no matter how well he does in school—might consider a PTA meeting to be a waste of time. Not coincidentally, these are often the same parents who speak little or no English, have inflexible working hours, younger children and no babysitter at home, no extra money or computers to give away. For many of them, even those who spent more years in school than *their* parents did, school didn't help: life is harder for them than it was for their forebears.

While we're progressing down the long, winding road to equity and excellence in education, with the final goal of equal opportunity for all, we can take baby steps in the right direction.

- Require employers to give parents and guardians an hour off each week to work in their children's schools. Sound like a radical idea? The U.S. military currently does exactly that.

- Make full-family participation possible and popular: provide child care, food, and translation for all evening events; use only universally accessible communication channels (no vital information transmitted via E-mail until *all* families are online); invite and value the contributions of families from *all* segments of the school community (hold tamale sales *and* bake sales; sell sweet potato pie *and* brownies).

- Turn high schools into community centers, where families can get the help they need to maximize their children's success in school: information about school programs and resources; referrals for employment, medical care, counseling, legal representation; training in computers, literacy, language, etc.

- Encourage community use of school facilities for recreation, entertainment, adult education, and community service. Many high schools have the best theater, the best track, the best library in town—and many of them lock their gates at night. Local artists can perform in the school auditorium. Cooking classrooms can be used to feed the homeless with food harvested from student gardens. Students can teach their parents to use computers in their own classrooms. Parents can shoot hoops together on weekends in the gym.

• • •

As soon as the graduation ceremony was over, I did what I've done nearly every day this past year, and probably won't have cause to do again: I ran around looking for Jordan, Autumn, and Keith. As usual I found them in different places, scattered about as far from each other as they could possibly be.

I found Jordan on top of the hill overlooking the Greek amphitheater with his mom, his aunt, uncle and cousins, and an old friend of his parents', a TV producer who'd flown in from New York. Natalie wouldn't let Jordan take off his cap and gown; she was taking pictures with her digital camera and couldn't seem to get enough of the sight.

I found Autumn on the street outside the theater with Lillian, Emily, and Jamilah. Autumn was "cuttin' up," as she would say, hollering at her now ex-classmates as they drove by, throwing herself into boys' arms, being silly and wild and exuberant—as I only got to see her, this past year, when she didn't know I was watching.

I found Keith in the near-abandoned amphitheater pit, standing alone among the empty folding chairs and trampled red and yellow carnations. He had his sombrero on; he seemed dazed but happy. As I watched he looked up, away from me, then a grin spread across his face. Following his eyes I saw his mother pushing her way through the tide of several thousand parents and graduates streaming out of the Greek. Finally Patricia reached her boy, grabbed him up in what Keith would call "a fat-ass hug." But unlike the many other times I saw Keith and his mom embracing, this time he wasn't the first to pull away.

As I left the Greek I watched all the Berkeley High seniors, now Berkeley High graduates, hugging each other good-bye. While their parents looked on curiously, Latino boys hugged Laotian girls; short blonde girls hugged tall black boys; nearly everyone who passed her bent down to hug Anna, the one special ed graduate, in her wheelchair. Most of the kids' parents didn't speak to each other; they didn't seem to have met before. "Congratulations," one African-American mother said to one white dad as their children laughed and hugged. Eagerly, he smiled and said the same thing back to her.

And then the Latino kids got into their parents' cars with their Latino families, and the Laotian kids got into their parents' cars with their Laotian families, and Anna was lifted into her van, and all the members of the Berkeley High Class of 2000 went off to live their futures; went off their separate ways.

and multi-textured sights, sounds, smells, and emotions I was experiencing daily at Berkeley High. I included the students' college essays and poems in the book; I quoted from their conversations, faithfully recounted their reactions. And yet I wondered: how would I bring forth their voices, their vitality, after the book was published? It couldn't just be me at the bookstore podium, at the radio microphone, in the TV studio. Somehow, it had to be the teenagers themselves.

Walking into a poetry slam at Berkeley High one night in May, I read the slogan the kids had scribbled on the blackboard: "Welcome Slammers! Because the next generation can speak for itself!" Suddenly, I envisioned a book tour that would manifest the medium *and* the message of *Class Dismissed*, a book tour that would give teenagers a way to speak, literally, for themselves.

And that's exactly what has happened. Autumn, Keith, and many of the poets whose work appears in *Class Dismissed*, along with several up-and-coming Berkeley High slammers, and one gospel singing senior, and teacher Rick Ayers—a.k.a. "The *Class Dismissed* Poetry Posse"—have appeared with me at dozens of bookstores, schools, churches, PTA meetings, and educators' conferences all over northern California. (Jordan, ninety miles away in Santa Cruz and in a new place in his life, was present in my heart and on the page but not in the flesh.) When the CAS program needed money to take seventy-five students on an educational trip to Cuba, we did a benefit performance at the Little Theater on campus, bringing our road show "home" and raising several thousand dollars in the process. (One of the evening's highlights was the auctioning off of a "Dinner With Keith," which yielded the princely sum of $500.)

Throughout the past year, the *Class Dismissed* Poetry Posse has transfixed, challenged, and brought together all kinds of people in all kinds of places, provoking spirited debate about education, race, teenage life, and opportunity among mixed groups of young and old, black and white, rich and poor, high school drop-outs and MBAs. "I'm shocked," a middle-aged white woman told Autumn after a typically breathtaking Posse performance in a suburban bookstore at the epicenter of then-booming Silicon Valley. Autumn looked up from the book she was autographing and met the woman's eyes. "That's a start," she said calmly.

As Autumn, Jordan, and Keith inspired me to do, I dreamed big for *Class Dismissed*. The book hit Bay Area bestseller lists quickly and stayed there for months, urging me on to bring this kind of discussion to a national level. To a great extent this goal, too, has been reached. Since constraints of money and school schedules keep the Posse from coming along when I travel out of state, the Berkeley High videography class (thank you, Dharini Rasiah, and your students!) made a "Poetry Posse To Go" video that travels with me whenever the Posse can't. I've played that video for high school students in Chicago and school superintendents in Monterey, for gay youth in Seattle and activist teachers in New York, for newspaper reporters in Phoenix and bookstore customers in Santa Cruz. Always, the power of the young people's passions causes jaws to drop, discussions to flow, hearts to open.

Autumn, Jordan, Keith and I have received hundreds of letters and E-mails from readers everywhere (including a former Berkeley High teacher whose new students wrote us from Senegal). Teachers and students in high schools (including Berkeley High), junior colleges, universities, and teaching colleges tell us they're studying the book in their classes. (Education students in Tacoma E-mailed me a list of questions about the book and the kids; a few days later, courtesy of their professor, I stood before them, answering those questions in person.) Administrators write to say they're using the book to critique and set direction for their districts. Berkeley High grads, from the class of '47 to the class of '02, write letters comparing the Berkeley High they knew to the one I wrote about, weaving a digital-oral history of the school.

And then there are the letters from the parents. "My daughter had life education at BHS," wrote the mother of a Class of 2000 grad who is now away at college. This mom and her longshoreman husband sacrificed much so their daughter could be "driven to school and met after school every day of her life." "Because of her time at BHS I worry about her very little, miss her terribly," the mom wrote. "She's capable of handling most anything. She speaks up for herself, and any other cause she has a passion for. She's clear that she is part of a larger community and has responsibilities associated with that."

"For the past three years my career goal has been to come back to BHS as a Latin teacher," that daughter wrote to me, after she received a copy of *Class Dismissed* as a Christmas gift from her mom. "I appreciate the fact that you see how special Berkeley High really is, and that you decided to tell the world."

Every week, still, we get letters from moms and dads who have searched the pages of *Class Dismissed* for answers to their most wrenching questions: what's going right and wrong in their teenagers' lives, where to send their kids to school, how to best support them there. Imagine a world in which hearing teenagers' voices, understanding and meeting teenagers' needs, and nurturing teenagers' gifts becomes a priority for schools, for teachers, for families! That this book has contributed to that process is more gratifying than I can say.

Nearly every letter we receive begins with the same question: "What ever happened to Autumn, Jordan, and Keith?" People ask, "Did Autumn get enough money to go to UC Berkeley? Did Jordan get into UC Santa Cruz? Did Keith go to jail?" And, "What ever happened to Berkeley High? Did they ever catch the arsonist?" Happily, the news is (nearly) all good.

AUTUMN'S STORY

No, Autumn didn't get enough money to go to UC Berkeley—but she went there anyway. When the UC financial aid office offered only a fraction of what her first year there would cost, Autumn and her mom both took out loans that have made their already precarious finances even more uncertain. "My money's funny and my credit don't get it," Autumn jokes, then adds intently, "But there was no way I was going to get into one of the best universities in the world and not go because of money!" A reader who remains anonymous agreed: having read of Autumn's predicament in *Class Dismissed*, she sent Autumn a money order for $500.

While taking a full course load, continuing to work at Youth Radio, and doing interviews and appearances on behalf of *Class Dismissed*, Autumn also served as an active member of the Black Recruitment and Retention Center on the UC Berkeley campus. Wearing the black T-shirt that says "Represent" on the front and "Less than 4.8%"—the percentage of African-American students at UCB since the elimination of affirmative action—on the back, Autumn traveled to local inner-city high schools with the BRRC, encouraging kids of color to apply to the university. She lived on the African-American dorm floor, where the students flow into and out of each other's tiny rooms, sharing computers (Autumn still doesn't have one of her own), microwave popcorn, CDs, and stories of life as members of an endangered minority at a prestigious American university.

At the end of first semester Autumn left California for the first time in her life. She rode a Greyhound bus to New Orleans to visit her best friend Lillian at Xavier College, arriving right in the middle of Mardi Gras. Everything about the South seemed new and strange and wonderful to Autumn: the trees, the food, the architecture, the air. She came home resolved to make the change she'd been contemplating: to move to Atlanta and apply to Spelman College, a historically black college in Atlanta. While acknowledging some weariness with the struggle for parity at UC Berkeley, Autumn says her main motivation for moving is to "see something new, be somewhere new. I'm tired of being at college, looking down the street, and seeing my high school!" Tired of dorm life, too, she's talking to her friend Jamilah from Berkeley High, who's now at Spelman, about the two of them renting an apartment in Atlanta together.

Asked often what it was like to have a book written about her, Autumn wrote her answer in an essay she called "A Year In The Life," which was published on the Youth Radio Web site, www.YouthInControl.org.

"In July 1999, a woman called asking me if I was interested in being in a book she wanted to write. After the first meeting I agreed to let this woman whom I just met into my school and into my life. . . .

"There were times when I wished I did not have to be responsible for having an opinion on everything that was going on. I knew as soon as something big happened Meredith would be around to ask me how I felt about it. But wasn't this what I wanted? To have someone care about what I was thinking and how I felt? I thought about what Meredith was trying to accomplish and how much my cooperation impacted the outcome of her project. In a small significant way I was helping Meredith to change the way other people would look at public education. . . .

"When I first opened the book and saw my name on the pages I lost my breath! I just hope that through the lives of Jordan, Keith, and myself, people will see that although we shared the same high school we did not share the same experience there . . . and it is important to allow everyone a chance at the same opportunities."

JORDAN'S STORY

Yes, Jordan did get into UC Santa Cruz, and that's where he is today: taking courses in astronomy and psychology, living in an apartment-style dorm with a bunch of guys, including a close friend from Berkeley High, and loving the college life. Since he moved to Santa Cruz, Jordan has maintained emotional as well as geographic distance from *Class Dismissed*. Of the three students I wrote about, Jordan is the only one who has experienced negative feedback as a result of his participation in the book. The criticism he's heard, most of it from friends' parents, echoes the dissenting voice in an otherwise unanimous chorus of support the book has enjoyed throughout the Berkeley High and Berkeley communities: that *Class Dismissed* stereotypes "the rich white hills people," and that the book's characterization of Jordan, his friends, and his friends' parents suffers from that bias. "It's not our fault that other people don't volunteer at the school," one white mother told me angrily. "It's not our fault that other kids don't do as well at Berkeley High as our kids do. You made it sound like there's something bad about us putting so much energy into the school!"

"It's great that you have the time and the resources to give," I told that mother. "It's great that your children are succeeding at Berkeley

High. The question is, how can we work together to make it possible for *all* parents to participate in their kids' education? How can we work together to make it possible for *all* kids to succeed at Berkeley High?"

As is true of most of the issues I wrote about in *Class Dismissed*, this one extends far beyond the bounds of Berkeley High, of Berkeley, of education, even. At its sharpest edge, this question cuts to the heart of race relations in America. What is the culpability, the complicity, the responsibility of those who have much (in this case, the affluent white parents) in relation to those who have little (in this case, the lower-income parents and children of color)?

Do we truly believe that each community, each school is a village, and that it takes our common effort to raise the children in it? If so, how do we go about allocating to each of them the same amount of care and hope and resources? When there isn't enough to go around—and it's a rare public school that truly has enough for any student: enough counselors, enough supplies, enough motivated teachers, enough love— do we fight each other for the crumbs, or work together to provide more for every child?

Some of the adults in Jordan's life were concerned, too, by the book's exposure of the turmoil he experienced during his senior year. "I thought that the book would be interesting to look back on when I got older," Jordan wrote in response to E-mailed questions from the Tacoma college students. "I didn't care at the time if my life was published. I don't regret it, but I don't know if I would do it again."

When asked if he felt his portrayal was an accurate one, Jordan replied that he takes the book with "a grain of salt per page," characteristically empathizing with the challenges faced by his biographer. "Imagine being a photographer and trying to capture an image on film as you see it with your eye, then imagine trying to take the same picture using a person's words as your lens and you have to infer what they feel and think as they talk to you. This is next to impossible."

Jordan also shared his reflections on Berkeley High, one year later, with the Tacoma teachers-in-training. While calling his Berkeley High teachers "some of the most interested and interesting teachers that I have ever met," he also blamed the burn-out that's epidemic at Berkeley High, and at most public high schools, on student and administration disrespect. "I believe strongly," he concluded, "that environment influences teacher mood."

KEITH'S STORY

No, Keith didn't go to jail. But he did spend six months of his life—his first semester at San Francisco City College, his first semester on a college football team—fighting to keep from ending up there. From the day before the Prom in June 2000, when he was beaten and arrested by Berkeley police, through December of that year, Keith and his mother, sisters, brother, and grandmother spent nearly every weekday in court. It took weeks to pick a jury for the first trial: "The D.A.'s trying to find fifteen people in Oakland who don't hate the police. There *ain't* fifteen people in Oakland who don't hate the police!" Keith commented at the time. Then, when an Oakland police scandal captured local headlines, the judge declared a mistrial.

The D.A. offered Keith one deal, then another and another. Initially charging him with resisting arrest and battery on a police officer, the D.A. offered to reduce the charges to obstructing a police officer in the commission of duty, then to disturbing the peace. "They the ones who disturbed the peace, not me!" Keith protested. Facing a year of jail time, being offered reduced sentences of five months, then three months, then probation, Keith and his family held their ground. "I didn't do anything wrong," Keith kept saying, and so his case went to trial again.

Again, a jury was painstakingly selected. Witnesses were called. Finally, the jury reported that they were hopelessly deadlocked. The judge declared a hung jury. The second trial, too, had come to nothing.

A very expensive nothing. Keith's legal fees were mounting. His family had already borrowed from everyone they knew. At *Class Dismissed* events we started taking up collections, but they were tiny drops in a big, empty bucket. Keith's lawyer supported Keith's position, but he knew the family couldn't afford to pay his fees through another trial. As a last resort, he suggested that Keith retain a public defender instead. That was a tough moment in the halls of the Alameda County Courthouse. I'd seen the Stephens family through some painful times, but I've never seen them as disheartened as they were right then. "Please," Keith's mom begged the lawyer, "ask the judge to drop the charges. Just try one more time."

The D.A. made a final offer: deferred prosecution. If Keith didn't get arrested for the next year, the charges would be dropped. If he did, the original charges would be added to the new offense. Keith knew he was taking a big chance, accepting this offer. "If the Berkeley Police want to find a reason to arrest me, they gon' do that. And this gives 'em a whole year to do it." Still, Keith wouldn't have to plead guilty when he knew he was innocent. He took the deal.

Within weeks, the police officer who beat and arrested Keith—and several other young African-American men, as it turns out—left his post, taking an extended "disability leave" from the Berkeley Police Department.

Not long after that Keith called me, upset. "The cops drove by my grandma's house," he told me. "My brother was outside. They thought he was me. They yelled something at him about knowing who he was."

A month later, Keith was fired from his job as a security guard because of his police record, he says—a record he's not supposed to have.

Keith's lawyer plans to sue the City of Berkeley, the Berkeley Police Department, and the officer who beat and arrested Keith. In the meantime, Keith is going on with his life: doing his homework, training with the football team, dyeing his hair bright orange, taking care of his nephews. "I missed all those classes 'cause of court, but I still got B's," he told me proudly when he got his first report card. Now he's hoping to transfer to a four-year college. "I'm thinking USC or UCLA," he says, grinning. (His gold teeth are buried in his dresser drawer now; he "retired" them after his arrest.) "I want to get out of Berkeley, but I don't want to go too far."

BERKELEY HIGH'S STORY; AMERICA'S STORY

"The news is all too familiar," I wrote in "Deadly Ambivalence," a cover story published in the on-line magazine Salon.com on March 6, 2001. The story appeared the day after that fateful Monday when a fifteen-year-old boy did what he'd spent the previous weekend telling his friends—and their parents—what he was going to do: shoot up his San Diego high school. "Another school shooting, two teenagers dead, 13 injured, thousands traumatized. The heart aches, although we've seen it all before."

I wrote the story as this latest tragedy unfolded, typing with my eyes glued to the TV, horrorstruck by the now-predictable visuals: the SWAT teams running in formation into yet another sun-bleached suburban high school; the blond teenagers running, sobbing, out of it; the frantic parents; the blood-spattered gurneys; the helicopters hovering over-head—and this time, the inane yet destructive commentary of President George W. Bush, labeling the shooting spree by a fifteen-year-old child "an act of cowardice."

"Our teenagers need to know that they matter," I wrote. "Whether their parents can afford private school or not, they need to see that in their classrooms, in their school libraries, in their teachers' eyes. They need to know that those who are entrusted with giving them what they need—their parents, yes, but their country, too—will give them the best we have to offer.

"The burning question raised by San Diego—and by the children we have lost at Columbine, the children we have lost to violence in inner-city schools, the students we are losing far less mediagenically in public school classrooms every day—is not why this is happening, but what we are willing to do about it. As long as American public schools are monuments to our ambivalence about what, exactly, our children de-serve, our teenagers will rightfully conclude that nothing they feel, or learn, or do, really matters. We have seen the consequences of that conclusion, and it is deadly."

Anna Quindlen weighed in, with an essay in *Newsweek* calling for smaller schools. "The experts say that the megaschool is a big mistake. . . . In the wake of the Columbine shootings James Garbarino of Cornell, an expert on adolescent crime, said that if he could do one thing to stop violence, it would be to ensure that teenagers are not in high schools bigger than 400 to 500 students. Yet nearly three out of four teenagers today go to a high school with an enrollment of more than 1,000."

And in "School Shootings and White Denial," a passionate polemic published by the on-line news service AlterNet and circulated widely (the author received more than 7,500 E-mails in response; I myself received the article from nearly twenty people), white journalist Tim Wise wrote:

> If any black child in America—especially in the mostly white suburbs of Littleton, or Santee—were to openly discuss their plans to murder fellow students, as happened both at Columbine and now Santana High, you can bet your ass that somebody would have turned them in, and the cops would have beat a path to their doorstep. But when whites discuss their murderous intentions, our stereotypes of what danger looks like cause us to ignore it—they're just "talking" and won't really do anything. . . .
>
> White Americans decided to ignore dysfunction and violence when it only affected other communities . . . unless you address the emptiness, pain, isolation and lack of hope felt by children of color and the poor, then don't be shocked when the support systems aren't there for your kids either.

Against the backdrop of the continuing crisis in the nation's schools, and the continuing campaigning of our new "education President" for school vouchers and other programs that would gut the public schools and widen the gaping chasm of educational inequity, Berkeley High struggles forward.

No, the arsonist has not yet been caught, and the wounds he or she left behind are even more evident now. The school is undergoing another major renovation to replace the burned classrooms and offices, and to add a new gym and cafeteria. With the few trees that once bordered the campus now plowed under by the bulldozers' blades, the singed, boarded-up B building is readily visible from the streets of downtown Berkeley: a hulking, ominous reminder of the traumatic year suffered by the town's only high school.

Still, shining through the rubble there are bright signs of hope. The success and popularity of CAS, the Computer Academy, and a new environmental studies "academy," Common Ground, have inspired discussion of creating more "schools-within-a-school" at Berkeley High— reflecting the growing national awareness among administrators, teachers, parents, and students of the need for more personal connection between school and student. Although this new round of construction— and the state of urban blight to which it has condemned the campus—is difficult to endure, there is widespread anticipation of the new, improved facilities; guarded optimism that Berkeley High will rise from the ashes.

"Berkeley High is like a TV evangelist," Poetry Posse slammer Niles X'ian Lichtenstein wrote in a poem he performs often at *Class Dismissed* events, "because we're born again every year." If the school is truly to be reborn—ready, willing, and finally able to educate all of its students—that will be with thanks in large part to a new group called PCAD: Parents of Children of African Descent. Near the end of last year's first semester, those parents discovered that half of Berkeley High's African-American ninth-graders—one-third of the 875-student freshman class—were already failing their core courses. Determined to keep what has happened to previous generations of Berkeley High kids of color—and kids of color nationwide—from happening to theirs, the parents brought that information, and their outrage, to the new principal, who invited the parents to come up with a plan.

The resulting "PCAD Intervention Plan" spawned the creation and funding of "Rebound," an "alternative learning community" within Berkeley High designed to give failing ninth-graders what they need to get on track for graduation: classes of no more than twelve students; one-on-one tutoring and mentoring by Berkeley High seniors; adult "learning partners" recruited from each student's family or community; culturally sensitive teachers who stay on their students, as the kids say, "like white on rice."

The $140,000 initially allocated to the program by the city and the school board is far less than what's needed to serve all the kids who want to join Rebound. And there are powerful people in Berkeley trying to shut Rebound down, citing remedial programs already in place, and questioning the allocation of funds to students at the bottom of the academic heap rather than those at the top. But community leaders from the mayor to the local NAACP, as well as the principal, many teachers, and parents of all races and economic backgrounds continue to be active, vocal advocates for the program—which has been quick to demonstrate impressive improvements in the students' grades and attendance.

Rebound won't solve all of its students' problems, or Berkeley High's problems, or America's. But in the proud tradition of the Berkeley schools, the first district to desegregate back in 1968, Rebound is carving a path, showing that another way is possible.

As Autumn says, It's a start.

Acknowledgments

My heartfelt thanks to the everyday heroes of the Berkeley High community, especially:

Rick Ayers, Amy Crawford, Greg Giglio, Robert McKnight, Alan Miller, Dana Richards, Flora Russ, Madalyn Theodore, and the many other Berkeley High teachers who invited me into their classrooms, their conversations, and their thoughts, informing and energizing me with countless midnight phone calls and 5:00 a.m. E-mails;

Susan Groves, for sending me to all the right people with all the right questions;

Rory Bled, for sharing stats and reflections;

Theresa Saunders, for providing access to the school;

Rebecca Weissman (Class of 2000), for vital contributions both photographic and strategic;

Ian Buchanan (Class of 2001), and the staff of the *Berkeley High Jacket*, for making me their journalistic exchange student;

David Manson (Yellowjackets coach, 1997–'99), for coaching me through thorny manuscript questions (and others);

My son Peter Harper Graham (Class of '97) for helping to frame the book at its conception, for giving me the wisest three words of advice a writer—or a mother—could hope to hear, and for his unwavering, enlightening love;

My son Jesse Drew Graham (Class of '98) for devoting his time, talent, and heart to drawing the map for this book (page ix), for sharing a multitude of insights drawn from his Berkeley High years and his extraordinary life, and for having the courage, always, to draw, to live, and to love outside the lines.

I am also grateful to:

Gary Orfield, Professor of Education and Social Policy at Harvard, for engaging with this project from the start, and for offering provocative, profoundly helpful critiques throughout;

April Sinclair, for writing books that teenagers (including my own) love to read, and for enriching this one with her pointed questions and full-bodied laughter;

Peter Barnes and Leyna Bernstein, for the gift of time, space, and poached salmon at Mesa Refuge;

Stephanie Hamilton, editor, writer, and friend extraordinaire, for the last-minute manuscript critique and for having my back on this and many other matters;

Toni Burbank and Barb Burg of Bantam Books, and Bob Bender and Johanna Li of Simon & Schuster, for their ongoing support, counsel, and friendship;

The folks at St. Martin's Press: my editor, Diane Higgins, her remarkably able assistant, Nichole Argyres, publicist Joan Higgins, and attorney Surie Rudoff for legal assistance beyond the call of duty;

My wildly brilliant, wildly energetic, and wildly human literary agent, Amy Rennert, for her boundless faith, determination, acumen, and honesty.

My "own" publicists, Leslie Rossman and Darcy Cohan of Open Books Publicity, for giving the phrase, "Go for it!" new meaning.

I offer special thanks to the three women who were with me (often literally) as I walked the halls of Berkeley High, pawed through piles of educational and sociological treatises, and talked and talked and talked and talked, struggling to make sense of it all:

Sara Momii Roberts (Class of '96) for her diligent research assistance, expert translation from Adultspeak to Youthspeak, and nonstop dedication to the project, to truth and justice, and to our friendship. "You da *bomb*, Sar!"

My friend, racquetball partner, and fellow ex–Berkeley High mom Julie Whitten, for sharing the wisdom of her twenty-five teaching years; for greeting each new chapter with eager enthusiasm; for bringing to the manuscript a proofreader's eye for detail, an English teacher's love of language, an activist's abhorrence of prejudice, and a mother's passion for children's rights.

Merci, aussi, to the love of my life, Katrine Andrée Simone Thomas: for reading every word (in her third language, no less) with avid attention and unbridled outrage; for adding a much-needed non-American perspective to this most American of projects, and most of all, for making my life a living heaven—sunrise to sunset, 24-7.

Finally, I would like to thank those people who gave to this project the greatest gift of all.

To Natalie Van Osdol, Pamela Smith, and Patricia and Kenneth Stephens: thank you for trusting me with your children.

To Jordan Etra, Autumn Morris, and Keith Stephens: thank you for trusting me—and the world—with your dreams.

About the Author

© Joe Pugliese

Meredith Maran is the author of the memoirs *What It's Like to Live Now* and *Notes from an Incomplete Revolution,* and co-author of *Ben and Jerry's Double Dip.* Maran writes for *O–The Oprah Magazine, Vibe, Mademoiselle,* Salon.com, *The San Francisco Chronicle, Parenting, Utne Reader,* and *Tikkun,* among other magazines and newspapers. Since the first publication of *Class Dismissed,* Meredith has been consulting and speaking frequently to those who advocate for and make policy affecting young people: school administrators, educators, social service professionals, churches, and parent groups. She lives seven minutes by bicycle from Berkeley High, where her two sons recently attended high school.

To contact Meredith—and Jordan, Autumn, and Keith—please go to
www.meredithmaran.com or write to them c/o
Meredith Maran
St. Martin's Press
175 Fifth Avenue, New York, NY 10010.